# ¡Que vivan los tamales!

*A series of course-adoption books on Latin America*

SERIES ADVISORY EDITOR: *Lyman L. Johnson,*
*University of North Carolina at Charlotte*

For a complete list of Diálogos series titles,
please visit unmpress.com

# ¡QUE VIVAN LOS TAMALES!

Food and the Making of Mexican Identity

Jeffrey M. Pilcher

University of New Mexico Press
Albuquerque

© *1998 University of New Mexico Press*
*All rights reserved.*

*Library of Congress Cataloging-in Publication Data*
Pilcher, Jeffrey M. 1965–
Que vivan los tamales! : food and the making of Mexican identity /
Jeffrey M. Pilcher.
p.    cm. — (Diálogos)
Includes bibliographical references and index.
ISBN 0-8263-1873-8 (paper)
1. Cookery, Mexican—Social life and customs.
2. Food habits—Mexico—History.
3. Mexico—Social life and customs.
I. Title.  II. Series:
Diálogos (Albuquerque, New Mexico)
TX716.M4P54    1998
394.1'0972—dc21    97-46508
CIP

ISBN-13: 978-0-8263-1873-2

*Visit the University of New Mexico Press website at*
*unmpress.com*

*For Sean, Nikki, and Dianna*

# Contents

# Preface

"Tell me what you eat, and I'll tell you who you are," offered the French gastronome Jean Anthelme Brillat-Savarin. I wrote this book with a similar goal, to interpret the Mexican national identity — as embodied by the mestizo, the mixed-race offspring of Native American and Spanish parents — through the history of Mexico's cuisines. Such an undertaking would not have been possible without the generosity of many people, who not only told me what they ate, but shared it as well. A few of those meals were so memorable that I want to thank the cooks. María Dolores Torres Yzábal always welcomed me with a splendid table. María Hernández taught me to make my first tamales and will always be remembered for her delicious treats. Pano López brought tears to my eyes in his rustic kitchen, while Norma González made my mouth water for her *barbacoa*. Abigail Mendoza instructed me in the spiritual art of *metate* maintenance. Marilyn Tausend and Carmen Barnard made every bite an adventure. Diana Kennedy, the foremost authority on Mexico's cuisines, kindly shared her encyclopedic knowledge and profoundly influenced my work.

However delightful the field work, I relied primarily on the assistance of archivists and librarians. I thank first the helpful staffs of Centro de Estudios de la Historia Mexicana, Condumex, the Archivo Histórico de la Secretaría de Educación Pública, the Archivo Histórico de la Secretaría de Salud, the Archivo Histórico de la Ciudad de México, the Archivo General de la Nación, the Hemeroteca and Biblioteca Nacional, and the Fondo Reservado de la Biblioteca de México. Adolfo Chávez, Pedro Daniel Martínez, and the staff of the Instituto Nacional de Nutrición cheerfully answered questions and provided information from their nutritional surveys.

Brigitte Boehm and Gail Mummert of El Colegio de Michoacán kindly
assisted me in gaining access to the papers of Ramón Fernández y Fernández despite construction work at the library. Erwin Levold and his
colleagues at the Rockefeller Archives dug up fascinating materials on solar
cookers and nutrition programs. Debbe Causey's interlibrary loans allowed
this book to be finished in the twentieth century. David Holtby's editorial
assistance likewise speeded it to completion. The Citadel Development
Foundation, the Rockefeller Archives, Paul Boller, and especially Marjorie
Smith generously funded my research.

I also want to thank the many historians who guided me on the improbable, enchanting path into their profession. William Beezley constantly
encouraged me through words and deeds to write more interesting history.
John Hart, Don Worcester, and Don Coerver offered valuable advice, as did
Paul Vanderwood, who read the entire manuscript not once but twice.
Charles Harris and Ray Sadler started me on the road to Mexican history in
the first place. Donna Gabaccia sharpened my sociological understanding of
food and shared many wonderful meals. Wendy Waters gave me countless
sources and suggestions. Linda Curcio and Chris von Nagy aided and
abetted in a delicious summer of research. Mary Kay Vaughan, Anne Staples,
and Rod Camp introduced me to many intriguing people in Mexico. Fritz
Schwaller and Barry Sell escorted me through the nuances of Náhuatl. Anne
Rubenstein and Glen Kuecker challenged me to take postmodern detours
that turned out to be paved with gold. Lyman Johnson assisted me in a
difficult job market and accepted this book for the Diálogos series. My
colleagues in North and South Carolina offered warm and deeply appre-
ciated welcomes. Ida Altman, Ty Cashion, Matt Esposito, Judy Ewell,
Don Frazier, Jorge Hernández, José Luis Juárez, Dave LaFrance, Sonya
Lipsett-Rivera, Rosalva Loreto López, Colin MacLachlan, Michael Meyer,
Pedro Santoni, Carlos Schaeffer, and John Super also encouraged me in
important ways.

While I hope this interpretation will encourage further research into
Mexico's rich culinary history, I must warn scholars about the difficulties
involved. Sitting in the handsome leather chairs of the Condumex reading
room, I could never maintain any semblance of concentration. I paged for
hours through well-worn cookbooks in search of the original recipe for
*mole poblano*, but was always distracted by my grumbling stomach. In this
book I hope to convey some of the expectation I felt each day, waiting
anxiously for two o'clock, when the neighborhood *fondas* fired up their
grills.

# Introduction

The first thing Aztec women did when preparing a festival, according to the
Spanish priest Bernardino de Sahagún, was to make lots of tamales. They
also relished chile pepper stews and seed-dough breads, but the cornhusk-
wrapped dumplings known as tamales held pride of place in pre-Columbian
banquets. For the festival of the jaguar god Tezcatlipoca they stuffed tamales with beans and chiles, while celebrations of the fire god Huehueteotl
featured shrimp and chile sauce tamales.[1] These same recipes reappeared,
with some modifications, five centuries later in 1992 at the First Annual
Week of the Tamal, sponsored by the National Museum of Popular Culture. The speakers at this event, including authors Laura Esquivel and Paco
Ignacio Taibo, hailed tamales as icons of the Mexican nation. One might
imagine that this has always been true, that shouts of *"¡Que vivan los tamales!"* (Long live tamales) have echoed through the ages. But to do so would
be to ignore the treacherous course of Mexican history and the apocalyptic
battles of the Spanish Conquest, the Wars of Independence, and the Revolution of 1910. These wars were violent outbreaks of a profound and ongoing struggle to define Mexico's cultural identity. The dinner table also
became a battlefield as the wheat bread of Spanish bakers challenged the
corn tamales of native women for inclusion in the Mexican national cuisine.

The final outcome of this struggle was not victory for one but, rather, a
fusion of both; wheat and corn came to be seen as a complementary pair,
each an authentic representation of a mestizo national cuisine. Eating such
a mixed cuisine of foods from both Europe and America may provide Mexicans with little national distinction in the postmodern restaurant world.
Nor is this global culinary exchange new; cooks since antiquity have spiced

their dishes with exotic ingredients from distant lands. Yet Mexican intellectuals of the twentieth century assigned a unique importance to their
mestizo heritage, which unified Old and New World civilizations to form,
in the words of José Vasconcelos, a cosmic race. This book examines the
importance of a mestizo cuisine — and of the women who created it — in
forging the Mexican identity.

While people have long recognized the connections between cuisine and
identity, the aphorisim that you are what you eat has seldom been applied to
the study of modern nationalism. Nevertheless, cuisine and other seemingly mundane aspects of daily life compose an important part of the cultures that bind people into national communities. Witness the numerous
culinary stereotypes of foreigners — "Krauts," "Frogs," "Limeys," and
"Macaronis" — as well as the deep emotional attachment to childhood
foods such as hot dogs and apple pie. Benedict Anderson, in his book
*Imagined Communities*, insightfully described the process of cultural formation that gave birth to nations. He showed that these political communities
developed not from folk cultures of the distant past, but rather as a product
of the Enlightenment in the eighteenth century. The standardization of
vernacular languages through the spread of print and literature allowed
people from different ethnic groups to imagine "national" communities
that had not previously existed.[2]

Culinary literature has great potential for contributing to the creation of
these national cultures. Cookbook authors help unify a country by encouraging the interchange of foods between different regions, classes, and ethnic groups, and thereby building a sense of community within the kitchen.
But these same works also have the power to exclude ethnic minorities or
the lower classes by designating their foods as unfit for civilized tables.
Government officials often try to dictate national cuisines by encouraging
the consumption of particular foods for economic or nutritional purposes.
At the same time, urban women may construct a national cuisine out of
simple curiosity by exchanging recipes with neighbors from diverse back-
grounds. The conflicting motivations for writing cookbooks as well as the
arbitrary selection of recipes ensures that national cuisines are diverse and
constantly evolving repertoires rather than immutable recipe collections
preserved from the distant past, regardless of the claims of authenticity
made by their authors. Uniting these multiple visions of the national cuisine is the common goal of making the abstract ideology of nationalism
meaningful through the familiar domestic culture of the kitchen.

The making of a Mexican national cuisine was a long and contentious
process, as was the forging of the Mexican nation itself. The Spanish con-

quest of America brought together two vastly different cultures with equally distinct culinary traditions. While the conquistadors spoke with awe of Moctezuma's splendid banquets, European settlers tried to transplant their cuisine of wheat to the New World and to eradicate the existing culture of corn. In the former task they succeeded, but only in part, for the new environment required adaptations of Old World cuisine. In the latter goal they failed completely as large parts of New Spain remained stubbornly Indian. The result of this process was a pronounced regionalism, with Spanish culture predominating around Mexico City and to the north while Indian ways prevailed in the south. Following independence in 1821, Mexican elites attempted to bridge the differences of region and class by formulating a national culture, including a national cuisine. Their efforts largely failed in the nineteenth century because they defined the Mexican nation and its cuisine in European terms and excluded the lower classes, particularly Native Americans. Only in the mid-twentieth century did an inclusive national cuisine emerge that combined Indian corn tortillas with European wheat bread.

Yet the acceptance of a mestizo cuisine was far from inevitable. At the turn of the twentieth century, Mexican elites launched a full-scale attack on maize, which they blamed for the failure of national development campaigns. Using spurious applications of the newly developed science of nutrition, intellectuals claimed that corn was inherently inferior to wheat and that progress would only be possible if the government could wean Indians of corn and teach them to eat wheat. This "tortilla discourse" was articulated during the dictatorship of Porfirio Díaz (1876–1911) and implemented by the educational missions of revolutionary governments (1911–1940). Mexican elites ultimately achieved their goal, but not in the manner they had originally envisioned. Agricultural and industrial modernization served not to replace the tortilla but, rather, to commodify it, transforming corn from a subsistence crop to a market commodity. Finally in the 1940s, after peasant radicalism had been tamed, a growing urban middle class, self-confident in its mestizo identity, appropriated the popular foods of the streets and the countryside, and proclaimed them to be the Mexican national cuisine.

The study of national cuisines, in Mexico and elsewhere, offers new perspectives on the roles of gender, class, and geography in forging nations. Cuisine illuminates the complex interplay between regional and national identities, as well as providing a view from below of how women and the lower classes have influenced nationalist ideology.

The process of unifying regional cooking styles into a national cuisine illustrates the new spatial conceptions implicit in the formation of national identities. Arjun Appadurai, in a study of cookbooks in contemporary India, described how middle-class women have combined the diverse regional and ethnic foods of the subcontinent into a unified national cuisine. Cookbook authors established standardized Indian menus, then suggested a variety of local specialties for soups, vegetables, cereals, and sauces. The mixing of dishes from different regions in cookbooks and restaurants tempted people to explore the culinary "other," and in this way helped to dissolve regional, ethnic, and caste boundaries and to foster Indian nationalism.[3] Mexican culinary literature documents the historical transformation of regional dishes into components of a national cuisine. Cookbooks of the early republic recognized only a handful of regional variants, primarily those of heavy Spanish settlement. At the end of the nineteenth century, women started to publish community cookbooks, expanding the collection of regional recipes available to cooks throughout the country. Finally, in the 1940s authors made a standard practice of including what they considered the most representative recipes of each state in the republic. This cultural and economic integration resulted in a more inclusive nation, but the franchise was often purchased at the expense of local traditions.

The class origins of Mexico's national cuisine raise other important questions. Just as Benedict Anderson attributed modern nationalism to bourgeois consumer culture, Jack Goody has shown the importance of social divisions and unequal access to food in the development of cuisine. Egyptian pharaohs, for example, ate more animal protein than their subjects and as a result towered over them by as much as ten centimeters. Elites also sought to garnish their food with rare ingredients and practiced elaborate rituals to distinguish court cuisine from common fare.[4] But one should beware of distinctions between high and low, for the term *haute cuisine* conveys two quite different meanings: a social hierarchy maintained through the use of costly ingredients and elaborate presentations, and a gastronomic "high" usually associated with sublime pleasures of the table.

Historian Michael Freeman argued that the latter meaning, a gustatory approach to foods, did not develop from court foods alone. He dated the appearance of Chinese cuisine in its modern form to the Song dynasty (960–1279), when four factors converged to produce a culture of gastronomy. First, China possessed diverse regional ingredients allowing cooks to experiment and create a broad range of possible menus. Next, the rise of a middle class yielded a large body of critical eaters beyond the ritual-bound environs of the royal court. These two elements derived from a third, an agricultural revolution that made diverse ingredients available to a sizable public. Finally, the Chinese people held cultural attitudes emphasizing genuine pleasure in consuming tasty food.[5]

Freeman's definition, a sort of critical mass approach to cuisine, assumed cities to be the centers of gastronomic innovation. Jean-François Revel drew even more explicit distinctions between peasant and cosmopolitan cuisines. The former he described as parochial products of seasons and soil, transmitted by sturdy oral traditions and tied to the countryside from which they arose. Cosmopolitan cuisines, by contrast, were elegant and effervescent, an international artistry of individual chefs. Revel, like Freeman, conceded that peasant traditions served as indispensable raw materials for the creation of haute cuisine, but he believed that chefs had to transcend everyday methods to realize great art. Revel's history of haute cuisine thus followed an evolutionary, almost positivist, trajectory that began with Stone Age barbecues and culminated in the genius of nineteenth-century French chef Antonin Carême.[6]

A hundred years of anthropology have nevertheless shown that many paths lead to civilization. Diana Kennedy, the foremost author of Mexican cookbooks, and Craig Claiborne, *The New York Times* food critic, described Mexican cuisine as "peasant food raised to the level of high and sophisticated art."[7] The recipes in Kennedy's classic volume, *The Cuisines of Mexico*, consisted not of regional ingredients refined by Mexico City chefs, as Revel's theory would suggest. Instead, it was the peasant women themselves who made their cooking a "high and sophisticated art." Nevertheless, the association with peasant food, however sophisticated, repelled many fashionable Mexicans, who preferred to import European haute cuisine rather than share tamales with the masses. The popular origins of the national cuisine inspired within the elite an ambivalent mixture of nostalgic love and aristocratic scorn, which, in turn, influenced their national self-perceptions and development policies.

Finally, the study of cuisine illustrates the significance of women and domestic culture in the formation of national identities. Explicit nationalist rhetoric appeared in some of the first community cookbooks published by women in the late-nineteenth century and became increasingly common in the twentieth century. How these domestic visions of the Mexican nation differed from government ideology will be a continuing theme of this work. But that it differed from official propaganda does not imply that cookbook authors attempted to subvert the patriarchal order. Middle-class women from the 1890s to the 1950s articulated a conservative, religious nationalism that favored social cohesion over radical reforms. They were, at least, more honest about their interests than the Institutional Revolutionary

Party (PRI), which mouthed the rhetoric of class conflict while pursuing trickle-down economic growth. And by proclaiming their culinary patriotism, women have established their claim to citizenship and thereby gained a basis for political participation. Laura Esquivel's best-selling novel *Like Water for Chocolate* is so persuasive because it cloaks a controversial feminist viewpoint in an unmistakable patriotic love for Mexican food.[8] Lower-class women have also shaped the Mexican nation by preserving and refining the pre-Columbian cuisine of tortillas and tamales. After all, despite centuries of efforts to change them, Mexicans remain a people of corn.[9]

*ONE*

# The People of Corn

*Native American Cuisine*

❧

Canoes by the thousands blanketed Lake Texcoco, swimming like insects toward their nest. Torches danced over the dark waters to the rhythmic hum of churning paddles. Narrow five-meter skiffs darted nimbly along, carrying fresh fish and game from countless small villages along the shore. Bulky twenty-meter boats rode low in the water, weighted down by piles of maize from agricultural centers in the south. A few of these dugouts had originated at port cities such as Texcoco and Tacubaya with freight on the final leg of voyages from provinces as distant as the Yucatán peninsula. The pilots guided their canoes through a network of five shallow lakes that zigzagged between shadowy mountain ridges and dark pine forests within the Valley of Mexico, converging in the central and largest lake around the glowing beacons of Tenochtitlán. This island city, home of the Mexica people and capital of the Aztec empire, lit up the night with thousands of hearth and temple fires; its population of more than two hundred thousand people attracted goods in trade and tribute from throughout Mesoamerica.[1]

As the sun rose over Popocatépetl (Smoking Mountain) and its volcanic spouse Iztaccíhuatl (White Woman), a steady stream of canoes entered the city. Poling through shallow channels, the boatmen passed neat rows of white-walled, flat-roofed homes, occasionally interrupted by parks, markets, and temples. Canoe traffic grew heavier near the city center, where passenger boats conducted visitors to the main plaza, water carriers floated door to door with ceramic jugs, and waste haulers collected sewage to fertilize corn fields. Finally the canals reached the central square, seat of the imperial government. Dominating this plaza was a massive pyramid large enough to serve as a platform for two huge temples dedicated to the rain god Tlaloc and the war god Huitzilopochtli. Clustered around its base stood a host of government palaces including warehouses to which the canoes brought interminable loads of tribute.[2]

Merchant cargoes, meanwhile, converged on the great market of Tlatelolco at the island's northern end. Countless canoes waited in the adjacent channel for longshoremen to unload their provisions. The boat handlers then departed in search of return loads while customs agents descended on the newly arrived merchandise. These officials sorted through mountains of corn, beans, cotton, and cacti, collecting the government's percentage and sending it to nearby huts. Next, porters heaved the bulky baskets over their shoulders and weaved through crowds to the appropriate stands. Depositing their burdens, they returned to the waterfront, leaving merchants to display the products to hordes of housewives and servants. Every morning sixty thousand shoppers and shopkeepers, dayworkers and dignitaries gathered at this monument to commerce.[3]

Entering the market at the vegetable street, customers plunged immediately into a bewildering maze of colors, shapes, smells, and sounds. Vendors spread gardens of greens over white cotton blankets on the ground. They offered piles of red plump tomatoes, purple sweet potatoes, brown jicama roots, and green cactus paddles. Squashes and chiles varied in color from bright red and yellow to deep green and black, while countless red, yellow, orange, and green mushrooms added further splashes of color. Most gorgeous of all were the edible flowers of cacao, squash, and maguey plants waiting for some shopper to carry them home for soups or tamales. The merchants, not content with their colorful displays, sliced open samples and shoved them under the noses of passing shoppers. Aromatic roots resembling onions and leeks competed with bundles of pungent oregano, purslane, sorrel, and watercress. No European counterparts at all existed for many pre-Columbian herbs such as *hoja santa*, with its distinctive anise taste, and *epazote*, used to flavor bean stews. Other plants bore a coincidental resemblance to European plants, as in the case of *guaje* seeds, which tasted like garlic. Eager vendors attracted greater attention to their produce by chanting repetitive Náhuatl syllables, and these market calls, cries, barters, and curses resounded across the city.[4]

Where the vegetables finally ended, meatsellers and fishmongers took up their trades. Stalls ran for blocks along the market's boundary, with meats displayed both by the cut and on the paw, for unlike Old World shops featuring beef and pork, in Tlatelolco rabbits, dogs, gophers, and possums composed the bulk of butchers' sales. Specialty meats included the *axolotl*, a larval salamander found in nearby lagoons; armadillos, highly prized for their flesh; and iguanas, lizards described by Christopher Columbus as having white meat that "tastes like chicken."[5] The Indians likewise delighted in venison from both the Chichimeca wilderness and the Yucatán peninsula. The Gulf Coast also provided many exotic delicacies to the fish traders who arranged their catches in rows parallel to the meat market. Dried shrimp ranging in size from minute specks to huge spirals lay in piles next to crabs, clams, snails, and oysters. The vendors also offered countless species of fish, salt-cured herring carried from distant coasts and clear-eyed trout pulled from nearby streams. White fish from western lakes brought the highest prices for its tender flesh. Other luxuries included lobsters, frogs, turtles, snakes, eel, and octopi as well as caviar from fish and insect eggs.[6]

Continuing toward the market center, shoppers entered the colorful fruit section. Some of these products had Old World counterparts such as apples, plums, and cherries. Others were unique to the Western Hemisphere, especially avocados and cactus fruits. The Spanish priest Toribio de Benavente Motolinía later likened the former to large pears with the taste of pine nuts. Of the many varieties of cactus fruit, he preferred the white-skinned ones, which he described as "very refreshing" with the taste of pears and grapes. The Indians also enjoyed black-skinned zapotes, salmon-colored mameys, firm green chayotes, yellow pulpy guavas, and countless other tropical delights.[7]

After this tour of Mesoamerican foods, the weary yet satisfied visitor had only penetrated the market center. Farther east, merchants sold ceramic cooking wares and other household goods; southward, multicolored textiles continued into the distance; and to the north, together with additional bundles of cloth and fur, lay streets filled with dried grains, pulses, and chiles. Just beyond the rabbit-skin salesmen were seemingly endless rows of corn in a multitude of colors—white, yellow, blue, red, and speckled combinations—in addition to piles of amaranth, nuts, and squash seeds. Legumes provided equal variety including tiny black beans from the Gulf Coast, plump brown specimens from nearby fields, and small white ones carried from distant provinces. Nearby rose mountains of salt as well as myriad dried chiles. Fortunately, by this point the exit had also come into view beyond a street of squawking birds.[8]

In culinary matters, a person could travel the breadth of Mesoamerica without leaving this vast square. But to gain historical perspective on the market of Tlatelolco, and to trace its influences on Mexico's national cuisine, one must consider three basic themes: the material culture that unified

Native American cuisines while preserving rich regional variations; the social relationships that depended on the feeding of gods and people; and the cultural significance of taste for pre-Columbian cooking and eating.

### *"Dura pero segura"*

"Hard but sure," traditional Mesoamerican cooking required enormous effort.[9] For thousands of years Indian women performed penance each morning, kneeling for hours to grind up corn and pat out tortillas. This ordeal nevertheless had a purpose, for Mesoamerican cooking evolved to provide dependable sustenance in an unforgiving environment. The riches of Tlatelolco belied the everyday fare of common *campesinos*, who ate an essentially vegetarian diet based on maize. Frost or hail could destroy a crop, plunging whole villages over the brink of starvation. The material culture of pre-Columbian cuisine therefore reflected the imperative of fail-safe cooking. In contrast to modern French chefs, with their lavish ingredients and intricate techniques, Mesoamerican women devised ingenious ways of cooking frugal yet tasteful meals. And these peasant cooks created a cuisine every bit as rich and diverse as any in the Old World.

Material scarcity had not always cursed the people of the Americas. Humans first arrived in the Western Hemisphere some fifty thousand years ago, after crossing a land bridge from Asia in pursuit of migrating mastodon herds. These wooly beasts nevertheless added little to the primitive diet, according to archaeologist Richard MacNeish, who observed that the hunters "probably found one mammoth in a lifetime and never got over talking about it."[10] Meat did compose a large proportion of the diet, but it came in the form of less dangerous game such as antelope, sloth, horses, and very large rabbits. Even these species had become extinct by 7200 B.C. because of climatic changes that left North America a vast desert. With no large mammals subject to domestication, work was done exclusively by human power until the introduction of European horse and cattle. And save for a limited supply of deer and smaller game, the people of Mesoamerica had to depend on an essentially vegetarian diet.[11]

Agriculture developed slowly in the Americas, as did sedentary life and hierarchical civilizations. Even before the extinction of large mammals, women in primitive bands had begun the process of plant domestication, by gathering seeds, pods, fruits, and leaves. Their work of sowing and gathering, weeding and winnowing caused genetic mutations that increased the productivity of these plants so that chiles, tomatoes, avocados, and squash, the principal condiments of pre-Columbian cuisine, had reached their modern form by 5000 B.C. Nevertheless, wild maize still grew to a length of just a few centimeters, and gathering remained a more important food source than cultivation. Not until 1500 B.C. was corn fully domesticated to produce a large, hard kernel that could be stored for long periods and support sedentary populations. By this time, also, the bean had yielded a softened seed coat that made it edible after cooking. The Olmecs, the first people to grow this improved maize, built impressive monuments around the southern Gulf Coast (c. 1200–400 B.C.). While they have been described as the base culture for Mesoamerica, because their pyramids, plazas, and ball courts set architectural standards for succeeding civilizations, they cooked their corn by the relatively primitive methods of boiling or popping.[12]

It was probably in the central highlands that some unknown woman conceived the culinary soul of Mesoamerica, the tortilla. These corn griddle cakes, marvels of simplicity and economy, demonstrated the genius of the New World *campesino* kitchen. Cooks prepared them with just three simple utensils: a *cazuela* (earthenware pot), a *metate* (grinding stone), and a *comal* (griddle). The corn was first simmered briefly in the *cazuela* with mineral lime (CaO), which helped loosen the indigestible husks and also added valuable nutrients including calcium, riboflavin, and niacin. The cook then knelt down and laboriously ground the wet corn on a *metate*, a three-legged grinding stone, which has not appeared in Olmec archaeological sites. The smooth dough was then patted into thin disks and cooked briefly over the *comal*. The shape of the tortilla assured that it cooked in just over a minute, an important consideration given the scarcity of firewood. Moreover, it could be rolled tightly around meat or vegetable fillings to form a taco, which kept foods hot for the longest possible time. This technique allowed tortillas to be used as eating utensils and even plates, reducing material requirements to an absolute minimum. And although economical, tortillas also possessed an artistic aspect, for hot off the griddle they melted in the mouth, leaving a lingering taste of corn.[13]

While tortillas served as the staple of everyday meals, tamales provided the hallmark of festive banquets. Archaeologists have yet to locate the origins of these confections, but fossil corn husks indicate they may have been consumed around the pyramids of the Sun and the Moon at Teotihuacán in the central valley of Mexico (c. 250 B.C.–A.D. 750). Cooks made them by spreading corn dough inside a husk, adding chile sauce and perhaps some bits of meat or beans, folding the packages up, carefully sealing them to prevent water from seeping in, and steaming them in an *olla*. For exclusive banquets in Tenochtitlán, wealthy hostesses passed around baskets of tamales along with handsome basalt *molcajetes* (mortars) full of chile sauce. But in the hectic market of Tlatelolco, as in simple village squares, women pulled tamales hot from the *olla* and sold them to eager customers.[14]

The Mesoamerican combination of maize, beans, squash, and chiles formed a balanced diet, notwithstanding the shortage of animal protein. The staple grain maize accounted for as much as 80 percent of calorie intake, and provided an excellent source of complex carbohydrates. Proteins essential for regenerating body tissue came largely from beans, which are more than one-fifth protein by weight. Modern scientists have shown that even a small portion of beans can assure adequate nutrition in a maize-based diet, because of a synergistic effect that multiplied the nutritional value provided by either food separately.[15] Squash added trace minerals and water, important benefits in the arid climate. Rounding out the basic diet were the remarkably nutritious chile peppers. They supplied vitamins A and C as well as various forms of B, aided digestion, inhibited intestinal disease, and even helped lower body temperature by causing sweating, which cools by evaporation. Pre-Columbian peoples also recognized the chile's pharmacological uses; healers prescribed them for a wide range of ailments and lovers favored them as aphrodisiacs. Recent research indicates that chile eating stimulates the release of endorphins, the brain's natural opiates.[16]

A wide variety of regional produce supplemented these four basics of the Mesoamerican diet. Coastal dwellers ate large quantities of fish, while tropical areas yielded nuts and seeds. People in the arid highlands harvested the maguey cactus and fermented its sap to make *pulque*, a mildly alcoholic and highly nutritious drink. Within the central valley, an algae called *tecuitlatl* grew abundantly in the waters of Lake Texcoco. The Indians collected and dried it into cakes, then cooked it with tomatoes and chiles. This algae provided an invaluable source of protein, but in an ironic parallel with modern Mexico, it thrived on human wastes from the city of Tenochtitlán. Consequently, Moctezuma's subjects suffered from gastrointestinal diseases, which they might have called Quetzalcóatl's Revenge, after the Toltec god exiled for trying to end the practice of human sacrifice.[17]

Although tortillas and tamales were consumed throughout Middle America, from the arid central highlands to the tropical rain forests of the coasts, climatic variation gave rise to diverse cooking styles. Within the mountainous terrain, frequent changes of altitude, climate, and soil gave rise to countless individual microclimates, so that *campesinos* living in any given valley harvested foods that were distinct from those of their neighbors on the slopes. Chiles exemplified this diversity, for even modern botanists have not agreed on the classification of perhaps ninety different varieties. Sophie Coe, in her fascinating book *America's First Cuisines*, showed how distinct the Maya cuisine of the Yucatán peninsula was from that of central Mexico.[18] Within the Aztec empire itself, along the Gulf Coast in the Huasteca (the land of plenty), Totonac Indians specialized in creating tamales, while to the south, around Oaxaca, the Mixtecs were known for the diversity of their dishes. The cuisines of both regions earned the Mexica's admiration.[19]

Aztec imperial policy ensured the availability of ample and diverse foods for the residents of Tenochtitlán. First, the construction of *chinampas* achieved a virtual agricultural revolution that assured ample supplies of staple foods. Although often referred to as "floating gardens," *chinampa* fields actually consisted of mounds of soil reclaimed from the freshwater swamps of Lake Chalco-Xochimilco. The builders alternated narrow strips of farmland with irrigation canals to water them. Large-scale drainage work began at the command of Itzcóatl (1426–1440) and culminated in the reign of Moctezuma the Elder (1440–1467), when almost one hundred square kilometers lay under intense cultivation. The use of aquatic plants for fertilizer and a complex rotation of maize, beans, and vegetables yielded high productivity with virtually no fallow.[20] In addition, Aztec tribute demands assembled an incredible range of regional produce in the capital. The Totonac town of Papantla, for example, sent bundles of chile peppers and vanilla pods.[21]

The subsistence diet of Mesoamerican *campesinos* would not have satisfied carnivorous European appetites. The diverse game available at the market of Tlatelolco was beyond the reach of commoners except on rare festive occasions. As a result, well-fed nobles often stood ten centimeters taller than the rest of the population.[22] But height is not the sole measure of a meaningful existence. Scientists have shown that people can function normally even with dramatically reduced diets.[23] Relics of pre-Columbian pottery and weaving certainly testify to the artistic genius of the supposedly undernourished common folk. In some ways the vegetarian masses may have been more healthy than meat-loving European nobles with their recurring bouts of constipation and gout. To state the obvious, other patterns of life, not consistent with European expectations, can be equally valid for the people who follow them.

## Reading the Aztec Menu

Tlaloc, the Lord of Rain and Thunder, gazed down through the clouds from his mountain home overlooking the Valley of Mexico. This serpent-faced god ruled humans capriciously; he sent both gentle showers to water their fields and ruthless hail to demolish their crops. Mortals climbed the slopes to his temple each spring to beg Tlaloc for mercy on their tender sprouts of corn. On the day of the Great Vigil, Uey Tezoztli (May 3), the lords of Tenochtitlán, Texcoco, Tlacopán, and other cities gathered at the summit to feed Tlaloc. They clothed the rain god with golden rings, jeweled necklaces, and feathered crowns, and offered him the blood of a sacrificial victim as well as tamales, stews, and chocolate. When the rites had ended, a guard of one hundred warriors stood watch until the food had rotted so that Tlaloc could eat his meal in peace. If the sentinels neglected their duty, the Mexica's sworn enemies from Tlaxcala could steal the offerings, with terrible consequences for farmers in the valley below. The Tlaxcalans reportedly slipped past the sleeping guard on one occasion to despoil the offerings, but once inside the temple they found themselves trapped. Mexica warriors sprang out from hiding places and slaughtered the intruders to the last man.[24]

The Great Vigil of Uey Tezoztli illustrated the vital importance of food in pre-Columbian societies. Offerings of tamales, chocolate, and human blood provided the foundations for amicable relations with the gods. If not properly fed, these supernatural powers would destroy the offending mortals, ravaging their crops or devastating them with plagues. Gifts of food also served as the basis for human interrelations at all levels of society, ranging from the domestic to the imperial. Mothers preserved family bonds by feeding their husbands and children, neighbors reaffirmed communal ties when they gathered for banquets, and subject towns acknowledged Aztec supremacy by satisfying Tenochtitlán's appetite for staple grains and luxury goods. Festivals even became social battlegrounds, both covert, as when rival nobles competed to sponsor the most lavish banquets, and overt, such as the struggles over sacred foods fought by Mexica and Tlaxcalans. The close connection between cuisine and class survived long after the conquest and even influenced the development of Mexico's national cuisine.

The cultivation and preparation of food largely defined pre-Columbian domestic spaces. Anthropologist Guillermo Bonfil Batalla has observed that maize fields and kitchen gardens determined the layout of household enclosures, while the dwellings themselves centered around spaces for storing, shucking, and cooking corn.[25] Women derived much of their self-worth from skill at the *metate*, the ability to grind maize so they could feed tortillas and tamales to their husbands and children. A Mexica proverb defined a good housewife as one who fed her family well. Midwives warned newborn girls of their future burdens: "Thou wilt become fatigued, thou wilt become tired; thou art to provide water, to grind maize, to drudge."[26] Wedding ceremonies likewise emphasized the woman's role in feeding her family; the mother-in-law fed four mouthfuls of tamales to the bride who, in turn, fed tamales to her new husband.[27]

Ritualized feeding also served to define a person's communal affiliations and social rank. The Mexica calendar abounded with religious and civic festivals, each having its own special foods and functions. For a summer feast of Tlaloc, neighbors exchanged pots of *etzalli*, a stew of corn and beans seasoned with chile sauce. Young warriors took advantage of this communal hospitality by playing a form of trick-or-treat, extorting bowls of stew with threats of housewrecking. Competitive banqueting rose to a high art among Mexica nobles, who achieved status by holding lavish feasts. These events proved enormously expensive, for an ambitious host presented feathers, cloaks, and jewels to each of his guests. He also had to provide an elaborate menu with several stews, delicate tortillas, and costly chocolate. The rewards for a successful feast included "recognition, fame, and distinction"; while failure left a person "shamed [and] belittled."[28]

Cuisine gave the Mexica a ready way of asserting their ethnic identity and of distinguishing themselves from other societies. The Otomí, a northern tribe considered barbaric by the Mexica, supposedly picked their corn before it ripened, while the Toluca, a similarly marginalized group on the western slopes, did not eat chiles. The Tarascans, a people living farther to the west, reportedly cooked with neither skill nor sanitation. These imperial rivals, who regularly defeated Mexica warriors in battle, received the ultimate snub: in a land where fresh tortillas were the height of culinary excellence, the Tarascans ate leftovers. These chauvinistic descriptions resembled the ancient Chinese definition of a barbarian as someone who drank milk and the classical Greek scorn for people who cooked with animal fat instead of olive oil. The Mexica stereotypes did not account for the rich variety of regional cuisines. Modern travelers can find delicious tamales made of green corn, and day-old tortillas are essential for making *chilaquiles*. But the Mexica reports did demonstrate the importance of food as an identifying social trait. People who ate tortillas freshly made of golden corn and spiced with chile peppers could claim the Toltec mantle of civilization; all others still wandered the Chichimec wilderness of savagery.[29]

Culinary rules reinforced class as well as ethnic divisions and helped assure the legitimacy of the Mexica elite. Fernando Cortés noticed a rigid system of manners, which bolstered social distinctions in Tenochtitlán. Many of these rules might seem appropriate in a modern guide to proper behavior, including exhortations to "swallow at intervals, keep chewing, and don't stuff your mouths." Mexica mothers also admonished their children against slurping ("are you dogs?") and "making angry faces." These guidelines not only laid down correct procedures for everyday activities such as eating tortillas (using three fingers of the right hand); they also demanded that commoners show self-restraint in their behavior and respect for their social superiors.[30] Moreover, the Aztec state derived much of its legitimacy by feeding Tenochtitlán through the control of tribute and the maintenance of *chinampa* "floating" gardens. Ideally, Mexica nobles acted as patrons as well, supporting their clients with food.[31] They played out this paternalistic role during the Great Feast of the Lords, an ostensible charity event held during summer months when corn bins lay empty. Poor recipients waited meekly in line for hours to collect a handful of tamales and a gourd of gruel dipped out of a canoe. Any hungry person who asked for seconds received, instead, a slap in the face. This bizarre and humiliating procession served as a symbolic reenactment of the great famine of One Rabbit (1454), when Moctezuma the Elder used canoes to distribute tamales and gruel to save his starving people.[32]

The ritual feeding of gods demanded the most valuable sacrifices, for human blood alone could placate their supernatural appetites. And not just any human would suffice — only the blood of the strongest warriors would do. The gods rejected barbarians as unworthy, "like old and stale tortillas."[33] When nobles made their offerings during the Great Vigil, they knew that if they displeased Tlaloc, he would withhold life-giving rains. For the festival of the jaguar god Tezcatlipoca, priests took a handsome youth, opened his chest with an obsidian knife, and extracted the still-beating heart. The festival of the fertility god Xipe Totec featured gladiatorial sacrifices in which tethered warriors fought to the death. The bloodshed culminated every fifty-two years in the New Fire Ceremony, when priests fed the sun with human hearts.[34]

Human sacrifice and the ritual cannibalism that accompanied it have been the most sensational aspects of Mexica culture both for Spanish conquistadors and modern readers. Explanations for these practices have been no less sensational, ranging from sixteenth-century claims of Satanic visitation to twentieth-century invocations of Thomas Malthus. The latter theory — that protein hunger caused by vegetarian diets forced the Mexica into large-scale human sacrifice and cannibalism — was most recently advanced by Michael Harner and Marvin Harris. It represented an extreme example of the cultural ecology school popular among anthropologists in the 1970s, although their claim actually dates back more than a century to the conservative intellectual Lucas Alamán.[35] Virtually all scholars now reject this theory because only a small elite of priests and warriors actually ate human flesh. Moreover, as anthropologist Marshall Sahlins observed, if the efficient production of (human) protein was the ultimate goal of Mexica civilization, the costly and elaborate rituals surrounding the sacrifices defeated the purpose.[36]

A more plausible explanation for these practices lies in the mutual obligations imposed by eating. The Mexica believed that women had the basic responsibility of feeding men, and men, in turn, took up the duty of feeding the gods.[37] Nothing was free in this world; before farmers could cultivate maize, priests had to fertilize the soil with sacrificial victims. The flesh of young warriors revitalized the fields and their free-flowing blood assured steady rains. The Mexica did not see this relationship in scientific terms of decomposing bodies providing nutrients to the soil, which, in turn, assured ample harvests. As Inga Clendinnen observed, their perception was much more direct: corn really was "our sustenance, our flesh." They called babies "maize blossoms," young girls were "tender green ears," and a warrior in his prime represented "Lord Corn Cob."

Pre-Columbian people respected maize and treated it with elaborate etiquette. Women carefully blew on kernels before placing them in the cooking pot to give them courage for confronting the fire. Once every eight years they "rested" the corn, cooking it plainly, "for we brought much torment to it — we ate it, we put chilli on it, we salted it . . . we added lime. And we tired it to death, so we revived it." They neglected maize at their peril; a person who saw a kernel lying on the ground and failed to pick it up might be stricken with hunger for the insult. Such beliefs continue to the present among Mexico City women, many of whom believe that burning a tortilla on the *comal* will cause bad luck. The reciprocity between humans and corn likewise survives in the words of a Náhuatl folk song: "We eat the earth then the earth eats us."[38]

Cuisine clearly fulfilled an important role in the construction of Mesoamerican social hierarchies. Women naturally defined much of their identity around the foods they cooked, and even male warriors and priests showed a deep concern for feeding the gods as a means of maintaining the cosmic balance. Nevertheless, the place of food in such ritual situations offers little indication of the pre-Columbian conception of taste. While the simple pleasure of eating is often overlooked, it constitutes an important aspect of human culture.

## "Worse than the Epicureans"

Moctezuma dined with a grandeur befitting the *tlatoani*, "he who spoke" for the Mexica people. Each day servants prepared some three hundred dishes for his personal satisfaction, plus a thousand more for the royal household. The entrées, kept warm over small braziers, included spicy stews of turkey, duck, partridge, pheasant, quail, squab, fish, rabbit, and venison. The dining service likewise left no doubt about the prestige of Aztec royalty. Seated on a leather cushion, with a few select nobles in attendance, Moctezuma reviewed a seemingly endless parade of food. He took freshly made tortillas from female servants, deftly folded them into the shape of a spoon, and selected delicate morsels from the richly spiced stews. At times he honored the nobles by feeding them a few bites. Finally, to culminate this display of conspicuous consumption, the *tlatoani* literally drank money. Cacao beans circulated as currency among merchants, and when ground to a powder, steeped in boiling water, sweetened with honey, and whipped to a frothy head, chocolate became the drink of lords.[39]

Tenochtitlán's banquet halls provided a level of pageantry unsurpassed by any Old World imperial capital, but that alone was no guarantee the Mexica assigned importance to taste. Court cooks of medieval Europe often sacrificed taste for grandeur, for example, sewing birds back into their plumage and plating foods with gold and silver.[40] Moreover, a powerful current in Mesoamerican philosophy urged moderation and simplicity in food and drink. Parents fed their children Spartan diets and cautioned them about the dangers of gluttony. A fable related that Moctezuma the Elder had once sent messengers to consult the goddess Coatlicue atop the sacred mountain of Coatepec, but the Mexica nobles had grown so fat that they sank in the sandy slopes. The moral was clear: Wealth had corrupted the warriors who once ate snakes from the marshes of Lake Texcoco.[41]

The ideal of simplicity was nevertheless compatible with the pleasures of the table. Pre-Columbian Indians found nothing wrong with the gratification of appetites, such as those for food or sex, so long as they were indulged in moderation.[42] The Mexica drew a distinction between voracious gluttony and sublime satisfaction; they described a bad cook as "gluttonous, stuffed, distended with food," while a good cook was "one who likes good food — an epicure, a taster [of food]."[43] Even Moctezuma's cooks followed the ideals of simplicity and moderation when preparing royal banquet foods. Although the Mexica left no cookbooks, the Spanish priest Bernardino de Sahagún compiled a vast list of foods along with their appropriate condiments. Indians made turkey with several different sauces, including yellow, green, and red chiles. Yellow chiles and tomatoes were used to flavor white fish and fowl, while dark fish went better with red *bermejo* chiles and ground squash seeds. Another red chile, the *chiltécpitl*, formed the proper sauce for shrimp, and green chiles provided the natural spice for frogs.[44]

The Mayan dish *papadzules* (food of the nobles) likewise illustrated the skillful simplicity of pre-Columbian cuisine. This variation of enchiladas, which can still be found in Yucatecan restaurants, combined two separate sauces. A woman began by grinding squash seeds on the *metate*, moistening them with *epazote* tea to make a thick sauce, and using it to coat freshly made tortillas. Over this went a tomato puree simmered with *habanero* peppers, kept whole to add flavor but not piquancy. In place of the cheese unavailable in pre-Columbian times, cooks added hard-boiled and diced bird eggs, while the use of freshly made tortillas obviated the need for frying in fat. The secret to the dish lay in the dark green oil, laboriously extracted by kneading the moistened seeds. Both Mayan and Aztec gourmets took great care in matching meats and vegetables with complementary sauces, an unpretentious approach reminiscent of the fresh simplicity of Italian peasant food rather than of the heavy sauces of classical French cuisine.

Pre-Columbian cooks also dedicated themselves to the artful presentation of food. Because of its supple nature, corn dough yielded a remarkable range of foods that in modern Mexico are known collectively as *antojitos* (little whimsies). The Mexica prepared tortillas in the shapes of butterflies and leaves as well as tamales imprinted with sea-shell designs or garnished with seeds and beans. Other common maize treats included oval-shaped *tlacoyos*, snake-headed *polkanes*, and canoelike *chalupas*. Religious rituals inspired some of the finest confectionery, including maize and amaranth breads resembling gods, animals, people, and mountains. Astrologers predicted that girls born on the most favorable day, Xochitl (flower), would become fine weavers of cloth and skilled at decorating tamales — female counterparts of painters and sculptors.[45] This may seem hard to believe for people who have only eaten Mexican food in the United States, where the plate is scarcely visible through sloppy piles of lettuce, cheese, rice, and beans. But clearly native civilizations placed a premium on artistic design that unfortunately is seen only rarely in Mexican restaurants north of the Rio Grande.

These two characteristics of Aztec tamales, elaborate design and simple ingredients, challenge established theories of cuisine. Comparative studies based on European and Asian societies invariably attribute haute cuisine to an exclusive aristocracy or an urban bourgeoisie. Mesoamerican nobles likewise considered delicate food and drink to be their exclusive birthright. They warned their daughters to prepare such dishes only for lords, and they stereotyped a bad cook as "very much a commoner."[46] The Aztec state even enacted sumptuary laws, but their enforcement was problematical. Officials might prevent commoners from buying exotic fish and game, but the genius of pre-Columbian cooking lay in the artistic manipulation of corn dough, the twisting and pleating of tamales into delicate forms, and the spicing with herbs and chiles.[47]

The centers of Mesoamerica's popular cuisine were village markets and public festivals. Tlatelolco, with sixty thousand daily visitors and whole streets devoted to prepared foods, provided a fertile environment for gastronomic innovation. And the Aztec capital was merely the central point in an elaborate network of markets operating throughout Mesoamerica. Although virtually any item could be found at Tlatelolco, many towns specialized in particular commodities. Connoisseurs of dog meat went to Acolman for the tastiest breeds, while the finest dinner wares were sold in the markets of Texcoco.[48] Smaller markets rotated on regular schedules, every five, nine, or twenty days, to allow traders time to reach the most remote villages. Many people visited markets simply for the spectacle, the delicious stews and the latest gossip. Indians enjoyed these fairs so much that after the conquest Spanish priests often berated them for visiting markets instead of attending Mass. Diego Durán described one such woman, who despite her advanced age attended every market in the region. She dropped dead one afternoon while carrying home a small bundle of corn, and was buried in the marketplace.[49] With this constant coming and going, even distant villages were exposed to diverse traditions that stimulated a popular cuisine.

Public festivals also provided opportunities for common people to enjoy elaborate food. The Mexica counterpart of Easter, Tlacaxipehualiztli, featured twisted chains of tortillas called *cocolli*, made from special bundles of maize that were hung from the ceiling. Even the poorest families joined in the celebration, although they might be unable to afford more than a few shriveled ears. Sahagún's elite informants ridiculed the attempts of common folk to participate: "perhaps only leftover, bitter sauces, and stale tamales and tortillas were offered."[50] But we should be wary of such contemptuous phrases; these same nobles feasted each spring on the corn and bean *etzalli* stew cooked by commoners. Specially chosen lower-class cooks had the honor of preparing amaranth cake figures dedicated to Tlaloc in the wintertime Festival of Falling Water. And with the arrival of summer, *campesinos* flocked to Tenochtitlán to decorate the capital with flowers and to make tamales of turkey and dog. These people ate simply on a daily basis, mere gruel for breakfast and tortillas for dinner, but for festivals they splurged, and in the words of Diego Durán, behaved "worse than the Epicureans."[51]

An innovative popular cuisine developed in Mesoamerica on the modest foundations of corn and chiles. The versatility of maize helped make cooking an art among women who lacked access to more elaborate produce. Tamales assumed a great variety of forms and flavors with no ingredients beyond maize, herbs, and chiles. A cook could shape corn confections into ovals, canoes, animals, or stellar constellations; her fancy was limited only by her imagination and dexterity. Moreover, tortilla making constituted an art unto itself. Although often considered by modern nutritionists as merely a mass of carbohydrates, these maize griddle cakes possessed unquestionable aesthetic qualities. In a Michelin-rated restaurant one would expect the culinary delights of freshly cooked tortillas, the tantalizing, soft texture and incomparable, savory taste, but unexpectedly finding them in a humble village seems miraculous.

The spicy taste of chiles, like the deadening mass of maize, has often led to misinterpretations of pre-Columbian cuisine. Many authors, including some Mexicans, have drawn a connection between fiery chiles and dreary diets; impoverished peoples supposedly gnawed peppers to numb themselves to their hunger. This idea may seem reasonable in a country such as the United States, where biting into excruciatingly hot jalapeños fulfills a bizarre rite of passage. By contrast, people in Mexico and Thailand generally eat chiles for the taste, not the heat. Because the body develops a tolerance to acids in the capsicums, more potent chiles become necessary to attain the same flavors. And the flavors of various peppers blend in subtle ways to create some of the most remarkable dishes in any cuisine. The innovative California vintner Robert Mondavi compared the complexities of Cabernet Sauvignon wine to *ancho* and *mulato* chiles.[52] If peppers merely deadened the taste buds, one would expect to find them consumed only by the most impoverished segments of society. Chiles, in fact, crowned the banquets of Mexica nobles and satisfied the tribute requirements of distant provinces.

Cooking techniques likewise helped heighten the flavor of common dishes. Rather than simply leaving the foods to stew, women toasted their ingredients first on the *comal*. They used this method not just for tortillas, but also to cook chiles, tomatoes, nuts, and seeds, and on the streets of Mexico City, descendants of the Mexica still sell pumpkin seeds roasted on tiny braziers. Modern chemists have found this to be a highly sophisticated technique. A complex transformation known as the Maillard reaction takes place in foods at about 155°C, which can only be achieved with dry ingredients since water boils at 100°C. This browning process breaks down molecules and recombines them to form "sweet and bitter derivatives" as well as "fragrant volatile molecules," in the words of scientist Harold McGee. More than a hundred different chemical reactions enhanced the flavor of pre-Columbian foods.[53]

The cooks of Mesoamerica developed a remarkable popular cuisine that could be shared by even the most humble *campesinos*. Difficult material conditions and animal protein shortages actually encouraged culinary experimentation by making the search for diverse ingredients an everyday necessity. This resulted in a variety of regional cuisines united by corn and chile peppers. The malleability of maize allowed women to indulge their gastronomic imaginations, creating superlative dishes from the everyday tortilla to the festive tamal. And the spicy chile made even the most mundane foods interesting, which is perhaps what makes a society interested in food. The existence of diverse regional cuisines, highlighted by elaborate festival dishes and seasoned by zesty chiles, ultimately became features of Mexico's national cuisine. But before this happened, pre-Columbian foods underwent profound changes as a result of the Spanish conquest.


## A Market in Ruins


In the year One Reed (1519), the market of Tlatelolco clamored with gossip of strangers who had appeared from the eastern sea. Inside the royal palace, messengers told the *tlatoani* incredible stories of the Spanish conquistadors. Moctezuma listened in terror as they described the deafening roar of cannons, the metallic gleam of arms and armor, the towering figures of horses, and the enormous fangs of dogs. He was equally amazed to hear of their food, which was "like fasting food, very large, white, not heavy, like chaff, like dried maize stalks." Supernatural invasion seemed imminent; perhaps the exiled Toltec god Quetzalcóatl had returned to claim the Aztec throne. This news so tortured Moctezuma that his "heart seemed as though it had been washed in chile water."[54]

The *tlatoani* tried vainly to ward off the Spanish invasion. He employed wizards and magicians, sent bribes and threats, but the conquistadors continued their relentless advance. In November, as *campesinos* brought in the corn harvest, Moctezuma came face to face with Fernando Cortés. The Mexica lords offered the newcomers gifts of gold and silver, while Tlatelolca cooks fed them turkey-hen stews and delicate white tortillas.[55] The unwashed foreigners, made doubly repulsive by their company of Tlaxcalan warriors, responded to the hospitality with a series of demands that the Mexica renounce their gods and bow down before the distant Spanish king. Eventually the Europeans seized Moctezuma as a hostage and massacred hundreds of unarmed nobles while they celebrated the feast of Huitzilopochtli. The enraged Mexica killed their former *tlatoani* and expelled the invaders from Tenochtitlán, inflicting heavy casualties, but failing to destroy them.

The Spaniards recovered from this setback and returned a year later with implacable force. By March 1521, when they laid siege to Tenochtitlán, they had recruited great numbers of Indian allies from disaffected subjects of the Aztec empire. The Mexica, meanwhile, had been weakened by exposure to European diseases, particularly smallpox, against which they had no immunities. Under the leadership of a new *tlatoani*, Cuauhtémoc (Descending Eagle), they fought desperately to defend their capital. The close-quarters battle for Tenochtitlán nullified the advantages of horse and cannon, and the Europeans set about systematically demolishing every temple, house, and wall. They took control of the lake with brigantines and cut off the Mexica's supply of food, reducing the island's defenders to starvation. The people of Tlatelolco captured the impact of this struggle in an epic poem lamenting the destruction of their city and its great market.

> Broken spears lie in the roads;
> we have torn our hair in our grief.
> The houses are roofless now, and their walls
> are red with blood.
>
> Worms are swarming in the streets and plazas,
> and the walls are splattered with gore.
> The water has turned red, as if it were dyed,
> and when we drink it,
> it has the taste of brine.
>
> We have pounded our hands in despair
> against the adobe walls,

for our inheritance, our city, is lost and dead.
The shields of our warriors were its defense,
but they could not save it.

We have chewed dry twigs and salt grasses;
we have filled our mouths with dust and bits of adobe;
we have eaten lizards, rats and worms.[56]

Weakened by starvation, the defenders could hold out no longer. On August 13, 1521, they succumbed to the European conquerors and their Indian confederates. Cuauhtémoc slipped away in a canoe, hoping to continue the struggle from the mainland, but he was captured and ultimately tortured and killed. The Aztec empire had fallen, leaving only songs of sorrow.

Weep, my people:
know that with these disasters
we have lost the Mexican nation.
The water has turned bitter,
our food is bitter![57]

The Spaniards leveled what remained of Tenochtitlán, and over the ruins they built a new capital in the image of Europe. Christian cathedrals rose from the foundations of ancient pyramids, and Old World crops sprang from fields that once nourished maize. The native empires were reduced to villages in which the people struggled to adapt to the new conditions. The old gods were denied the blood of human sacrifices, but their festivals continued with the trappings of the new religion. Never again would a Mexica *tlatoani* feast on tamales in the banquet halls of Tenochtitlán, but the cuisine of corn survived in markets and villages.

*T W O*

# The Conquests of Wheat

## *Culinary Encounters in the Colonial Period*

Sor Andrea de la Asunción gathered up the white sleeves and black habit of the order of St. Dominic and set out to fulfill her holy calling. Beneath the vaulted ceiling of a convent kitchen in Puebla de los Angeles, she began by choosing red and black chiles and toasting them on the *comal*. A beatific glow suffused her brow as she ground the peppers to a smooth paste on the *metate*. From the Native American grinding stone she turned to the Old World spice rack, selecting cloves, cinnamon, peppercorns, and coriander and sesame seeds, which she fried in a skillet. After grinding them into the chiles, along with boiled tomatoes, she simmered the mixture over a low flame in an earthenware *cazuela*, occasionally anointing it with turkey broth. Divine aromas bubbled from the deep brown sauce, but when she spooned a bit on her palm to taste, something was still missing. Andrea cast about the ceramic-tiled kitchen for inspiration, then alighted upon chocolate, the ancient drink of Aztec lords. The moment the bittersweet tablet melted into the sauce, she had created *mole poblano*, the Mexican national dish.[1]

Or so goes the legend. Modern authors have used this colonial dish, combining spices from the Old World with chiles from the New, as a symbol of the mestizo Mexican nation. Alfonso Reyes, Carlos de Gante, Artemio del Valle Arizpe, Salvador Novo, Amando Farga, Paco Ignacio Taibo, Mayo Antonio Sánchez, and Alfredo Ramos Espinosa have produced a literary genre exploring the mysterious origins of this dish. About 1680 the nuns of Puebla supposedly created *mole* in honor of Viceroy Tomás Antonio de la Cerda y Aragón. Another version of the *mole* legend — with a satirical rather than divine view of the national identity — attributed the mixture to a certain Fray Pascual, who accidentally spilled the spice tray into the dinner pot.[2] The authors of these tales, although relying on vivid imagination rather than historical research, correctly perceived the importance of *mole*, and of cuisine, in the blending of cultures that forged modern Mexico.

Unfortunately, little documentary evidence exists describing the evolution of Mexican cuisine. John Super conducted an exhaustive search and found not a single cookbook published in Latin America during the colonial period.[3] The first printed recipes for *mole* appeared in the nineteenth century shortly after Mexican independence. José Luis Juárez and Rosalva Loreto López have uncovered manuscript cookbooks from the mid-eighteenth century, but before that the trail goes cold.[4]

Nevertheless, *mole poblano* has inspired a historiography of several competing interpretations. Judith Friedlander made an innovative attempt to trace the origins of *mole* through its ingredients. In her excellent anthropological study of Indian identity in a Morelos village, she pointed out that the majority of the components came from the Old World. Native products included only chiles, chocolate, the turkey, and the name, which derived from the Náhuatl word *molli* (sauce). The dish was traditionally served for religious celebrations when priests made their greatest efforts to convert the natives to European practices. Friedlander therefore concluded that Spanish missionaries introduced *mole* to Indian communities. This approach, while important to understanding colonial cuisine, assumed that Spanish conquistadors annihilated the local culture and did not give sufficient credit to native traditions.[5]

The search must therefore turn to the Indian influence on *mole*. Margaret Park Redfield, in an earlier anthropological study of another Morelos village, described the dish as an essentially pre-Columbian artifact. Indian women made their most obvious contribution through the expert blending of chiles to create subtle flavors, a skill that Spanish nuns obviously learned from their American sisters. Moreover, the *metate* remained the *mole*-making utensil of choice until the twentieth-century invention of electric blenders. These contributions notwithstanding, the indigenous cuisine placed primary emphasis on simplicity. Sahagún's descriptions revealed that Indian cooks selected a few chiles and condiments that complemented a particular dish, as opposed to the colonial habit of dumping the whole kitchen cabinet into the *cazuela*.[6]

The complexity of *mole* has inspired another interpretation, the baroque. Its proponents, including most modern Mexican commentators, have attempted to place cooking within the artistic milieu of seventeenth-century New Spain. Architects, musicians, painters, and poets of the age lavished their work with ostentatious ornamentation. *Mole poblano*, with its elaborate ingredients, supposedly represented the gastronomic counterpart of the celestial ceiling fresco or the recursive musical fugue. Modern descriptions of *mole* resonate with the baroque aesthetic: a palate in constant motion between effervescent tastes of spices, each playing chords within a symphony of flavors. But while this image holds a certain poetic charm, it lacks heuristic value.[7]

In reality, all of these interpretations contain an element of the truth. The cooks of New Spain created an elaborate new cuisine combining ingredients and cooking techniques from both sides of the Atlantic. But the process of *mestizaje* began at the margins of culinary systems, with the mixing of condiments such as chiles and meats. The staple grains corn and wheat remained for the most part mutually exclusive, with bread feeding a wealthy Creole society and tortillas becoming the province of poor and Indian communities. The hierarchical associations of food within New Spain helped delay the emergence of a self-conscious national cuisine, just as colonial social divisions slowed the unification of the Mexican nation itself.

## The Spanish Grocer

"The grocer, not the conquistador, is the real Spanish father of Mexican society."[8] These words of Justo Sierra, the great Porfirian educator and intellectual, aptly summarized the Spanish presence in the New World. Emperor Charles V, fearing that Cortés and his men would establish independent kingdoms, sent trusted administrators to rule the newly conquered territories. Henceforth government remained largely in the hands of peninsular bureaucrats, who had little attachment to their colonial subjects. These officials dreamed primarily of returning home to Spain as rich men and were discouraged from marrying provincial women. Shopkeepers and other settlers thus bore much of the responsibility for creating a European society on American soil. Grocers, in particular, contributed to New Spain's development by satisfying the colonists' hunger for familiar Iberian foods.

The introduction of European crops was a natural step in the conquest of America, for Spanish cuisine itself had resulted from a long series of invasions. A millennium before Christ, Iberian people had cultivated wheat and herded sheep using methods developed in Syria and Egypt. The first challenges to Iberian domination came from Celtic invaders who occupied the peninsula's northern areas between the ninth and sixth centuries. These blond, blue-eyed immigrants added physical variety to the rather dark-

skinned inhabitants, particularly in the central plateau where the two
groups intermarried, and they may also have been the first to ferment
grapes in the peninsula. Spain's wine industry nevertheless owed its origins
to Phoenicians who settled along the Mediterranean coast at about the
same time. Successive Greek and Carthaginian colonists also introduced
olives and chickpeas.[9]

Spaniards thus acquired a culinary trilogy they valued as highly as the
Indians esteemed corn, beans, and squash. The Mediterranean staples of
wheat bread, olive oil, and vinifera wine were firmly established in the
peninsula when Roman armies expelled the Carthaginians. Indeed, Hispania's olive oil soon commanded high prices within the empire, and its
wines flooded Italian markets. Iberian fishermen, meanwhile, supplied the
classical world with *garum*, a highly valued and highly pungent sauce made
from decomposed anchovy intestines.[10] Finally, Hispania shared the Roman preference for wheat over breads made of other grains, such as rye and
barley. Diphilus of Siphonos described wheat as "more nourishing, more
digestible, and in every way superior."[11] The Romans prized white bread so
highly they reportedly added chalk to achieve "purity."[12]

The next great advance in Iberian agriculture following the collapse of
the Roman empire came not with the fifth-century Visigothic invasions
from the north; instead, medieval Spain drew its culinary inspiration from
Muslims who overran the peninsula between 711 and 722. For a century
after the Prophet Muhammad's death in 632, the soldiers of Islam had
swept across Africa and Asia, conquering or converting all in their path.
They also accumulated considerable scientific knowledge in their travels.
The Moors revolutionized agriculture in Al-Andalus, as they called Spain,
through the use of sophisticated fertilizers and irrigation works. In addition, they carried a wide range of crops from India to Europe. Heat-
resistant grains such as rice and sorghum increased Iberian productivity by
adding a summer growing season to the traditional winter wheat. The
Arabs also introduced spinach, eggplant, artichokes, and watermelons, as
well as sugar and saffron. Asian citrus fruits, especially limes, lemons, and
bitter oranges, likewise found fertile soil in Spain. The Moors loved fruit so
much that they continued to cultivate Iberian vineyards despite the
Qur'an's prohibition on alcoholic beverages.[13]

Islamic agricultural interests reflected a sensual delight in food that differed sharply from the Christian ideal of abstinence. Muhammad promised
endless pleasure gardens to the faithful, and many considered earthly gratification a legitimate prelude to Paradise. Moreover, with their access to the
spices of the Indies, Muslims could satisfy their desires for heavenly foods.

Banquets from Baghdad to Granada featured dishes perfumed with pepper, ginger, cinnamon, clove, cardamom, mace, nutmeg, saffron, and sugar. A thirteenth-century Hispanic-Moorish cookbook explained that "the knowledgeable use of spices is the principal base of prepared dishes, because it is the cement of cooking, and upon it cooking is built."[14] Muslim cooks were also skilled in using sugar to create pastries, nougats, syrups, and custards. These confections, often based on almonds, dates, honey, and cream, were likewise fragrant with cinnamon, citrus, and rosewater. But not all of the smells of Moorish cooking were sweet, as the Christians observed when they dubbed the Arabic stews *olla podrida* (rotten pottage).[15]

Muslim foods nevertheless became common in royal courts throughout medieval Christendom. The Normans brought Arabic cuisine to France and England from Sicily, which they conquered in the eleventh century, while Frederick Barbarosa spread it to Germany two hundred years later. But Islamic culture had its greatest influence among the Christian kingdoms of Spain. The Reconquest of the Iberian peninsula from the Moors extended over nearly eight centuries, culminating with the fall of Granada to Ferdinand and Isabella in 1492. During this lengthy period of fighting, countless Christian knights were seduced by the sensual pleasures of Muslim cuisine.[16]

Yet the highly spiced dishes of classical Arabic cooking became accessible to only a small elite. Jaime Vicens Vives, the great Spanish economic historian, observed that the medieval Iberian economy depended "on two elements — wheat and sheep."[17] Popular cuisine consisted largely of preservation techniques such as cheese making, which was a vital part of the shepherd's life. Old sheep eventually made it into the stewing pot, but on a daily basis peasants started their *ollas* with stale bread soaked in water. To this they added chickpeas for a steamy *puchero*, onions and cucumber for a cold *gazpacho*, or, if nothing else, garlic and olive oil for a simple *sopa de pan* (bread soup). Wheat bread held such a central place in Europeans' lives that it took on popular religious significance, particularly for women. An altarpiece from fifteenth-century Portinari, for example, showed Christ disguised as a sheaf of wheat ready to be milled for the Eucharist wafer. A shepherd living in the Pyrenees Mountains even risked heresy by suggesting that "the soul of man is bread."[18]

Wheat bread held particular importance for those Spaniards who migrated to the Americas. A series of disastrous grain harvests had struck the peninsula beginning in 1504, as a consequence of the agrarian policies of Ferdinand and Isabella. In an attempt to foment Iberian wool production, the Catholic monarchs had allowed shepherds to run their animals through farmers' fields and to cut down whole forests to provide pasture. The resulting famines ravaged the Spanish countryside, and memories of hunger drove the conquistadors on their New World exploits. Moreover, the impoverished southwestern crescent of Extremadura and Andalucía provided the vast majority of colonists. Their voracious appetites for wheat and meat transformed the Americas.[19]

## Creoles and the Columbian Exchange

New Spain's first recorded banquet took place in 1538, when Viceroy Antonio de Mendoza and Conquistador Fernando Cortés joined to celebrate a peace signed by Emperor Charles V and his French adversary King Francis I. Mendoza and Cortés put aside their own rivalry — a prelude to conflicts between peninsular-born Spaniards and their Creole cousins — to stage a lavish spectacle. The entertainment depicted a wide range of people, including Indians, Africans, and Turks, but the food was strictly European. Bernal Díaz del Castillo recalled tables loaded with salads, hams, roasted kid, marinated partridge, stuffed chickens, quail pies, *torta real*, and for the servants, a whole roasted oxen stuffed with chicken, quail, and doves.[20] For such an extravagant feast, the cooks had access to imported Spanish wines, olive oil, vinegar, and spices. On a daily basis, however, colonists had to cultivate their own foods. Recipe changes became inevitable when Old World crops failed to grow in New World fields. Nevertheless, Creoles maintained a European cuisine whenever possible and incorporated native ingredients only at the periphery of their diets.

The introduction of livestock proved to be the greatest success story in the culinary conquest of America. As early as 1493 Columbus had brought horses, cattle, goats, sheep, chickens, and pigs to the New World. Within a decade after the conquest of New Spain, swine had become so numerous that stockmen lost interest, and the Mexico City council began enacting regulations to clear them off the streets. Sheep, which had fared poorly in the tropical lowlands, multiplied rapidly in the arid plains of central and northern New Spain. Horses, goats, and chickens likewise became established in the colony, but the most phenomenal growth in livestock was from cattle. Herds literally overran the countryside, driving Indians from their fields. Urban meat prices fell so low in the sixteenth century that ranchers slaughtered the animals for their hides and often left the carcasses to rot.[21]

Spanish immigrants ate more meat than ever before, but obtaining bread was difficult at first. Although cattle could be turned loose to graze, then rounded up when needed, wheat required substantial investments, both agricultural and industrial. Iron plows were needed to till the soil properly, which, in turn, required expensive draft animals. The grain also demanded ample irrigation both for the December planting and March maturation. After harvest the crop had to be ground into flour, a costly process that gave rise to European stereotypes of millers as "shrewd, thieving, cheating, destined by definition for the fires of hell."[22] The final step, baking, required brick ovens and abundant fuel. In the colony's early years, before Spaniards established sufficient mills and bakeries, native women prepared wheat in the only manner they knew — as tortillas.[23] Wheat tortillas, one of the first examples of Mexico's hybrid cuisine, persisted in remote northern areas, but Europeans living in cities demanded familiar crusty bread.

Wine and olive oil, two other essentials of Mediterranean cuisine, never became affordable in New Spain. Grapevines and olive trees simply refused to grow in the colony, although they flourished in the valleys of Peru. Mexico City's council heard constant complaints about shortages of these products, yet it could do little to lower the prices charged by Spanish grocers.[24] Economic reality thus forced Creole cooks to fry with pork fat instead of olive oil. Lard held an ambivalent status in the cuisines of early modern Europe; it was scorned by Spaniards and Italians, but was indispensable for most of the French.[25] The colonists of New Spain came to depend so heavily on pork fat that, in 1562, they received special Papal dispensation from fasting requirements.[26]

For wine the Creoles developed no universally accepted substitute. The elite, who could afford the steep prices, continued to drink imported wines and sherries. Less fortunate settlers adopted the fermented native drink, *pulque*, or the distilled sugarcane liquor, *aguardiente*.[27] Perhaps the most popular beverage of New Spain was not alcohol at all, but rather chocolate. The once-bitter drink of pre-Columbian lords acquired a devoted following among Creoles, who added sugar and spices. Thomas Gage, an English priest who visited New Spain in the seventeenth century, described the women of Chiapas as being so addicted to chocolate that they drank it during Mass. When threats failed to stop this practice, the bishop excommunicated the offenders; to which the women responded ironically by poisoning his cup of chocolate.[28] Churchmen themselves were not immune to the frothy drink's lure. Fray Francisco Ortiz went before the Holy Office of the Inquisition, in 1650, on charges of consuming chocolate before Mass. He might have escaped detection except on one occasion, when he deserted the altar to drink with women for half an hour before returning to complete the Mass.[29]

In most cases of American ingredients incorporated into Creole cuisine, European counterparts already existed. Turkey and other American game fit readily into Spanish recipes for stewed chickens or roasted partridges. Mexican rice likewise followed peninsular cooking techniques except for the use of tomatoes instead of saffron. And indigenous beans often replaced the traditional Iberian chickpeas, known because of their tough skin as "musket balls."[30] Learning to use chile peppers required more creativity, but the search for spices had motivated Columbus in the first place, and colonists experimented eagerly with these novel condiments. Red *ancho* peppers imparted a delicious new piquancy to *chorizo*, an already spicy smoked sausage from Extremadura. Unsmoked Creole *chorizo*, made with New Spain's "very sweet and savory" pork, particularly from the valley of Toluca west of Mexico City, rivaled the Old World's finest sausages.[31]

The European cuisines from which Creoles took much of their inspiration were likewise undergoing changes during the colonial period. About the turn of the eighteenth century, French chefs revolutionized continental kitchens by replacing the sugar and spices of medieval foods with the salt and herbs characteristic of modern cooking. This *nouvelle cuisine* gained enormous popularity in royal courts and in noble houses from England to Russia. French influences became particularly evident in Spain after 1700, when the Bourbon prince Philip V succeeded the last Habsburg monarch Charles II.[32] Gallic cooking nevertheless proceeded slowly to the Americas, despite the efforts of viceroys such as Teodoro de la Croix and visitors including Jean Chappe D'auteroche. Historian José Luis Juárez has demonstrated that eighteenth-century colonial manuscript cookbooks held only a superficial resemblance to the new French style. A typical recipe for *sopa francesa* insisted on French bread, but also included many spices that had disappeared from continental cooking.[33]

Italians had a much greater influence than the French on Hispanic cuisine. Northern Italian princes had dictated Renaissance fashions two centuries before Gallic chefs asserted their gastronomic hegemony over Europe. Diego Granado's *Libro del arte de cocina* (Book of the Art of Cooking), published in Madrid in 1599, included few French recipes but many Italian ones such as a Lombard vegetable torte, Venetian grilled chops, Milanese stuffed cabbage, and Roman macaroni and cheese.[34] Personal ties likewise bound the Castilian court to Italian cuisine. Guilio Alberoni exemplified this connection; a humble cook from Parma, he rose to become *de facto* prime minister of Spain. He entered the service of the Duke of Vendôme, and accompanied the French general to Madrid during the War of Spanish Succession (1700–1713). Through the judicious use of Parmesan cheese and prosciutto, Alberoni ingratiated himself with the royal court of Philip V. By 1717 he had become a Catholic cardinal and government minister, but he proved a less successful statesman than chef, and two years later was exiled.[35]

Italian dishes appeared prominently in the cuisine of New Spain. Spaghetti with tomato sauce became a common dry soup, *fideos*, which seems appropriate given that the tomatoes now ubiquitous in southern Italian cooking originated in America. Perhaps the most interesting twist given by Creole cooks to Italian cuisine was the creation of *chiles en nogada*, a green chile pepper stuffed with minced meat, covered with a pure white walnut sauce, and garnished with bright red pomegranate seeds. The green, white, and red of the Mexican flag have made this a modern national icon, but historical texts demonstrate its Italian roots. Mexico's first published cookbooks, dated 1831, contained recognizable versions of *chiles en nogada*. The stuffing added only mutton, eggs, and capers to modern recipes of shredded pork fried with garlic, onion, tomato, parsley, cinnamon, cloves, and candied fruit.[36] The primary difference lay in the walnut sauce, which, unlike cream-enriched modern versions, was originally an oil-based salad dressing. Cooks used it to season many New World vegetables such as squash, avocados, and of course stuffed chiles.[37] Diego Granado gave a comparable European recipe in 1599 for stuffed cabbage in "*una composicion llamada nogada*," but he had copied it from the cookbooks of Renaissance Italy.[38]

*Chiles en nogada* exemplified the triumphs of New Spain's Creole cuisine. Colonial cooks, in attempting to re-create European foods, actually developed a highly innovative culinary repertoire. Forced to use native ingredients such as chiles and low-status European ones like pork fat, they improvised dishes that were both delicious and distinct from those eaten in the peninsula. Yet they tried valiantly to maintain ties to the homeland and, in particular, demanded the European staff of life, wheat bread. Native Americans reacted in a similar manner to the gastronomic encounter by incorporating Old World plants and animals into their diet whenever convenient, but clinging tenaciously to the foundation of their traditional cuisine, corn.

## Culinary Blending in the Countryside

The people of Mesoamerica had been eating tortillas for two thousand years before Fernando Cortés stepped off the ship from Cuba. Their lives centered around maize; it provided the essence of their identity. The vast majority of men, save for a few warriors and merchants, raised corn for subsistence, while women were cooks who derived much of their self-worth from skill at the *metate*. The efforts of Cortés and his followers to transform New Spain into a replica of the old therefore met with stubborn resistance from Native Americans reluctant to abandon their traditional cuisine. European settlers eventually satisfied their own demand for wheat through forced Indian labor, but the natives largely refused to eat this foreign grain. Like the Creoles, they adopted primarily those new foods that fit into their already established cuisine.

Spanish attempts to indoctrinate Native Americans to European culture and religion began with the *encomienda*, which assigned Indian communities to individual conquistadors. Although justified as a means for converting the pagans to Catholicism, these grants became a means for Spaniards to extort as much labor as possible, regardless of the suffering of those commended to their care.[39] The system rapidly proved self-defeating, and in 1549 labor tribute was abolished, because of the large numbers of natives who died from Spanish disease and abuse. Sherburne F. Cook and Woodrow Borah have estimated that in the century following the conquest, the pre-Columbian population of perhaps twenty-five million had fallen to less than one million.[40]

Spanish officials sought to protect the natives by formally segregating the colony into two distinct societies, the *república de los españoles* and the *república de los indios*. Native Americans generally lived in agrarian villages and raised subsistence crops on lands held communally according to pre-Columbian customs. Although Mexico City contained several Indian neighborhoods, most indigenous communities lay south of the capital, a legacy of the nomadic Chichimec warriors who had limited the Aztec empire's northward expansion. Spanish society, meanwhile, concentrated in urban areas in the central highlands and in silver-mining communities in the north.

Supplying wheat to Creole markets placed onerous burdens on the Native American population. Even after the abolition of *encomienda* tribute labor, rotating *repartimiento* drafts assigned Indians to public works including flood control, silver mines, and wheat farms. Moreover, historian Charles Gibson has shown that wheat farms served as the foundation for Spanish usurpation of Indian lands in central Mexico. About the end of the sixteenth century, large haciendas came to dominate wheat production around Mexico City, drawing *repartimiento* workers from nearby villages such as Tacuba and Tacubaya. Other major wheat zones developed to the east, around Atlixco in the province of Puebla, and to the west, at Zamora

and Valladolid in Michoacán.[41] A few entrepreneurial Indians also grew
for European markets, to the irritation of Spanish competitors. The natives
of Oaxaca, for example, supplied the limited urban wheat demand from
their own lands and often ground flour in mills owned by *caciques* (native
nobles) and *cofradías* (religious brotherhoods).[42] These cases notwithstanding, commercial agriculture often provided a means of subjugating Indians.
But Europeans did not propagate wheat only for pecuniary motives.

Spanish missionaries preached the goodness of wheat as part of their
evangelical message to pagan Indians. Father Sahagún instructed them to
eat "that which the Castilian people eat, because it is good food, that with
which they are raised, they are strong and pure and wise. . . . You will become
the same way if you eat their food."[43] Although Sahagún later questioned the
wisdom of acculturating Indians, wheat remained a religious necessity because it was the only grain recognized by the Roman Catholic Church for
the Holy Eucharist. Since the eleventh century, priests could substitute no
other bread for the body of Christ. The unreliability of colonial pack trains,
which often delivered spoiled flour, made wheat production essential to
religious missions, and priests stationed in the desolate north frequently
complained of their inability to say Mass for lack of altar breads.[44]

The friars also launched campaigns against native festival foods that were
identified with pagan practices. To facilitate the extirpation of idolatry,
Diego Durán compiled a lengthy list of suspect pre-Columbian feasts and
their associated dishes.[45] Amaranth stood out as anathema because the Indians shaped it into idols and ate it for communion. The friars issued a ban
against its cultivation, but with little effect because this nutritious grain
grew prolifically in the wild.[46] They could scarcely outlaw maize without
precipitating widespread starvation, so instead they taught women to make
the sign of the cross over the dough before forming it into tortillas.[47] Priests
concentrated on introducing European foods at religious feasts; for example, in the pueblo of Tepoztlán, south of Mexico City, lentils were consumed only during Holy Week. This campaign succeeded in persuading
even isolated communities to purchase wheat bread for the altars of patron
saints. But these loaves often sat beside tamales, indicating the continued
veneration of Young Lord Maize Cob.[48]

Native Americans, when left to their own devices, almost invariably
planted corn instead of wheat, in part because they disliked the taste of the
foreign grain. The *Florentine Codex* records their initial reaction to bread as
being "like famine food . . . like dried maize stalks."[49] Spaniards, accustomed to presenting bread as alms in their homeland, were shocked to find
that they could not even give it away to beggars. Juan Suárez de Peralta

explained that "destitute natives would not think of accepting bread, and I don't mean crumbs, but a good pound-and-a-half loaf, they shove it back in your face."[50]

Economic considerations also contributed to Indian rejection, for they found the foreign grain to be a poor subsistence crop. Unlike corn, which yielded well from the forests of Yucatán to the mountains of Toluca, wheat grew only under favorable conditions and was highly susceptible to disease. The summer showers that nurtured maize rusted wheat, making it generally suitable only for the arid winter season, which required ample irrigation. Additional capital outlays for producing wheat bread included plows, oxen, mills, and ovens. Moreover, the European grain proved disappointing at harvest time. In the words of Fernand Braudel, "Wheat's unpardonable fault was its low yield."[51] Modern authorities have estimated wheat's yield to be only 80 percent of corn's when measured by seed, and 70 percent by area planted. Even after the expansion of European wheat farms, the grain sold for as much as ten times the price of maize.[52] As a result, within the boundaries of Mexico City, common people cultivated corn in small *milpa* gardens to supplement their miserable wages. And fields planted in wheat often reverted to corn when Spanish attention lapsed. The villagers of Apasco in the Mixtec Alta, for example, abandoned the foreign grain immediately after the death of their *encomendero*. In the New Mexico revolt of 1680, Pueblo insurgents expelled the Spaniards from Santa Fe and, for good measure, destroyed their wheat fields.[53]

European livestock met with mixed reactions from the indigenous people. Franciscan friars observed that the first appearance of cattle often sent astonished villagers fleeing into the mountains. Indians complained bitterly throughout the colonial period about the damage to corn fields caused by grazing herds. While eventually acquiring a taste for beef, they often preferred to buy it from Spaniards rather than raise the troublesome animals themselves.[54] Moreover, according to Spanish chroniclers, the natives' initial reaction to pork fat was absolute disgust.[55] Nevertheless, they later discovered that blending pork fat into the batter for tamales made them fluffier and more delicate. The Indians displayed greater enthusiasm for sheep, which were valued for both meat and wool. Their favorite animals, however, were chickens, smaller versions of the native turkey. Certainly, they had more affection for these birds than for the conquistadors; the Náhuatl word *Caxtillan* meant "land of chickens."[56]

Male farmers and herdsmen did not alone determine which European plants and animals would enter the native cuisine. Women often mediated cultural change through their control of the domestic sphere. Vegetable gardens were perhaps the most important place for incorporating new culinary influences. Such plots, fertilized by kitchen scraps and household pets, had long served as places for experimentation. In pre-Columbian times, these apparently haphazard gardens yielded a wide variety of herbs, fruits, and vegetables. After the conquest, women added cabbages, cucumbers, artichokes, lettuce, radishes, and European beans. The prestige attached to Spanish vegetables in some cases led to the neglect of native varieties such as *quelites*. Yet despite the constant encouragement by priests to consume wheat bread, the sight of women bent over *metates* remained a ubiquitous feature of the Mexican landscape well into the twentieth century.[57]

The general preference for corn is confirmed by those exceptional Native Americans who adopted wheat bread, for they stood outside traditional village society. Mexico City market women sold wheat bread to Spaniards as early as 1550, and this proximity marked the first step toward acculturation. Likewise, when Oaxaca's growing capital, Antequera, engulfed the community of Jalatlaco, the village men, deprived of their corn fields, went to work as city bakers.[58] But Indians typically entered the baking trade only by force, and the "public service" industries supplied by *repartimiento* labor drafts included bakeries. Moreover, criminals commonly served eight-to-ten-year sentences kneading dough. Unfree labor was essential because of the slavelike conditions and frequent beatings in these establishments. Despite the harsh conditions, Indian workers did begin to eat bread because their meager pay often included a few loaves.[59]

Colonial bakers acquired a reputation for deviant behavior that continues to the present day. Their antics provided material for an entire genre of lewd songs and dances composed by eighteenth-century street musicians. One of these bawdy tunes, "The Dance of the Bakers," began as a duet:

> He is really a baker
> who doesn't indulge himself;
> and if you give him a tiny
> kiss, he'll start to work.
>
> She is really a baker
> who doesn't indulge herself;
> take off your underpants
> because I want to party.[60]

Bakers often named their creations "kisses" and "underpants," and engaged in flirtatious wordplay with maids who came to buy bread. Even when freed from forced labor after independence, Mexican bakers retained unusual habits — working nights to have bread ready in the morning — and also kept the picaresque stereotype of being humorous but drunken flirts.[61]

The grain map that ultimately emerged in New Spain corresponded to settlement patterns. Spaniards made their greatest impact in the northern half of the colony. Silver mines and cattle ranches developed in this arid country formerly inhabited only by nomadic Chichimec Indians. The dry climate also proved most suitable to wheat growing, at least in irrigated fields along rivers. Native Americans, meanwhile, retained their cultural and political autonomy best in the area south of Mexico City. The lack of mineral wealth and the difficulty of transporting agricultural goods to markets kept European settlers to a minimum. Those who came planted wheat in areas around Antequera, Chilpancingo, and the Mixtec Alta, but the slight demand for European crops enabled Indians to retain their ancestral lands and eating habits.[62]

At the village level, a comprehensive model for wheat acculturation remains elusive. Climate and markets determined the large outline of the grain map, but a detailed examination reveals an unsystematic patchwork of wheat and corn fields. The residents of one community in Oaxaca rejected European agricultural techniques because the metal plow "injured the land," while a neighboring town had its own forge to make such implements.[63] The sixteenth-century *Relaciones geográficas* listed villagers who refused to grow any European crops at all, others who raised fruits and vegetables, and a few who planted wheat fields. Perhaps the people of Teotitlán del Valle and Macuilxóchitl who grew wheat simply had a more persuasive Dominican friar than nearby towns that continued with the traditional corn. Social relationships, rather than purely economic ones, hold the key to understanding the historical development of Mexican cuisine.[64]

## They Were What They Ate

Thomas Gage observed an unusual ritual in seventeenth-century Chiapas, where gentlemen would drape themselves casually in their doorways each afternoon "to see and to be seen, and there for half an hour will they stand shaking off the crumbs of bread from their clothes."[65] The Englishman ridiculed these "presumptuous and arrogant" Creoles who claimed to pick partridge bones from their teeth when they could only afford to eat beans. Yet his preening dandies, like the impoverished but proud hidalgos of the novel *Lazarillo de Tormes*, said much about early modern Hispanic society.

Proper appearances were essential to maintaining status within this hierarchical world. Processions held on holy days, for example, gave rise to
arguments over the marching order of various guilds and confraternities.
The relation between parade position and social rank was so intimate that
these disputes often degenerated into fist fights. Creole gentlemen likewise
paraded their status within New Spain's racial hierarchy by wearing ruffled
collars and eating wheat bread.[66]

European colonists throughout the New World concerned themselves
greatly with outward displays of status. English sugar planters in the Caribbean, for example, spent enormous amounts of money importing food,
clothes, and furniture to maintain a lifestyle appropriate to their social
position. They followed European standards regardless of the discomforts
involved in eating meat-laden banquets on humid afternoons or in wearing
woolen coats and trousers under the tropical sun. Historian Richard Dunn
attributed this rather unhealthy esteem for European customs to the hierarchical connotations of food and dress in early modern society: "Each rank
in the social order, from aristocrats at the top to beggars at the bottom, had
its own distinct style of dress, diet, and habitation. . . . So the masters
dressed and ate like the gentry in England, while the slaves . . . went semi-
naked and ate tropical produce."[67]

Status symbols assumed even greater significance in New Spain because
of the complexity of racial boundaries. Unlike the European–African di-
chotomy of the sugar islands, the people of colonial Mexico filled an entire
spectrum. Every major race of humanity was represented, including Native
Americans, European settlers, African slaves, and even a few Asian immigrants from the Spanish-dominated Philippine Islands. Africans made important contributions to the colony; for example, Juan Garrido or Handsome John, a former slave who fought with Cortés during the conquest, was
the first wheat farmer in New Spain. Nevertheless, Africans were con-
signed to the bottom of the social hierarchy. Spaniards occupied the summit and attached great importance to racial purity. Their concern dated
back to the Reconquest and the medieval concept of honor, for purity of
Spanish blood indicated both a family's trustworthiness as loyal Christians
and its control over the chastity of its women.[68]

This ideal notwithstanding, a scarcity of European women in the colony
made race mixture inevitable, which led in turn to the development of the
system of castes. Peninsular Spaniards claimed a racial superiority over
Creoles, in addition to their political advantages arising from the crown's
distrust of colonial loyalty. The Creole population indeed included substantial numbers of mestizo children who adopted the racial identity of

their European parent. Other mestizos, scorned by Spanish fathers, were raised as Indians in their mothers' native community. But not all people of mixed blood gained acceptance in either of the two societies. An urban underclass appeared of mestizos who had adopted European culture, but lacking a Spanish patron, had little hope of economic advancement. They, along with Africans and mulattoes, could find only menial labor, and were referred to contemptuously by elites as *léperos* (street people).[69]

Over time, racial status became a function of culture and wealth rather than of birth, to the consternation of established Creole families. No discernible genetic differences existed between the "Indian" and "mestizo" categories, and villagers could fit into urban society simply by changing their patterns of dress, hair, and speech. More threateningly still, the boundaries between Europeans and mestizos began to erode as lower-class Spaniards lived among the *léperos*.[70] In an effort to shore up the racial hierarchy, Creoles developed an "almost pathological interest in genealogy," reflected in the *casta* paintings.[71] These works constituted a graphic record of elite views of colonial society. Each series contained a number of idealized family portraits cataloging the racially mixed castes, with labels such as "Spaniard and Indian beget mestizo" along with more bizarre combinations that included "coyote mestizo and mulatto woman beget *ahí te estás*" (there you remain). Foods composed an important part of this categorization scheme, as darker-skinned subjects appeared with native foods. The artists of two such series depicted tamales in scenes labeled "from *lobo* and Indian woman comes *cambujo*," and "from Indian and *barsino* woman: *zambaiga*." The most famous *casta* collection, executed in 1763 by Miguel Cabrera, included as the final panel a woman beating her husband—the ultimate social inversion stigmatizing these "unnatural" racial combinations.[72]

Colonial literature offers further evidence of Spaniards' scorn for native foods and mestizos in general. Most authors avoided all reference to the castes in their works. One notable exception, Mateo Rosas de Oquendo, provides a glimpse of mestizos through the eyes of colonial elites. This seventeenth-century poet mockingly related the amorous declarations of Juan de Diego:

> Oh, my Juanita,
> vision of beauty!
> Aren't you just dying
> for this "coyote"?

Although a poor coyote mestizo, Diego fancied himself an hidalgo of noble lineage, the grandson of conquistadors. His appetites nevertheless betrayed his lower-class origins.

> He carries tamales,
> and a few maize ears,
> passing like a gigolo
> through a sea of lovers.
>    And out in the pond,
> there is no salamander,
> nor frog nor fish
> he would not devour.
>    He enters the market
> with a dozen green chiles
> and ten avocados, to eat
> a hundred sweet potatoes.[73]

After this prodigious display of dining, no doubt could remain of his Indian heritage. Juan de Diego, with his two first names, his sexual promiscuity, and his taste for *animalitos*, exactly matched Spanish stereotypes of mestizo degeneracy.

Ruling over a multiracial society, Spaniards lived in mortal fear of losing the respect of the lower classes, for any appearance of going native could undermine the legitimacy of their privileged status. Even Indian *caciques* emulated European habits of riding horses, carrying swords, wearing wool clothes, and at times eating wheat bread.[74] Scattered archival records of food consumption confirm the vital importance of European cuisine as a status symbol. Mexico City restaurant owner Carlo Monti, in a lawsuit brought against Francisco Zapari in 1805, itemized a series of unpaid meals. The menus comprised exclusively Spanish foods such as *pucheros*, salads, and wines, and for Christmas Eve, the traditional Iberian dried cod.[75] A century earlier, the archbishop of Mexico City had recorded that a catastrophic wheat plague in 1692 reduced to eating tortillas more than forty thousand residents "who had not used this food before."[76]

The archbishop's assertion notwithstanding, large numbers of *blancos* (whites) subsisted on corn. This indicated not the abandonment of European prejudices, but rather the colony's ever-present downward mobility. In tropical Yucatán, where wheat refused to grow and even imported communion wafers "did bend like to wet paper, by reason of the extreme humidity and heat," settlers acquired a taste for corn out of necessity.[77] Even in Mexico City, immigrants who failed to strike it rich found themselves reduced to eating cheap tortillas, just as they were obliged to accept Indian or mestiza marriage partners, despite their preferences for wheat bread and Spanish women. So when the gentlemen of Chiapas went out on their doorsteps to brush bread crumbs from their ruffled collars, they affirmed both social status and Creole identity.

For *mole poblano* to have gained social status in colonial Mexico, therefore, it would have been seen as a Creole rather than mestizo dish. And notwithstanding the New World chiles lurking inside, *mole* would have seemed completely appropriate for any medieval banquet. Cookbooks preserved from European courts include fantastic but nevertheless familiar dishes. Their lavish use of expensive Asian spices served as a mark of conspicuous wealth, and a single recipe would include combinations of ingredients such as cinnamon, cloves, peppercorns, garlic, and sugar. Cooks based their sauces on meat broths, often mixed with wine, and added ground almonds for taste and texture. In short, these court recipes bore a striking resemblance to the foods of New Spain. To Creole tastes, *mole poblano* represented a New World version of medieval cooking.[78]

Cortés and his lieutenants, having gained noble status through their conquests, naturally wished to display all the trappings of Spanish lords, including their foods. Expensively spiced dishes, such as cardamom chicken and rosewater partridge, were introduced to the New World as rapidly as the conquistadors could import the ingredients. Spanish friars, in turn, disseminated these new spices among their Indian parishioners, as Friedlander hypothesized, adding new complexity to native festival foods. Colonial *moles* may well have grown more elaborate in the baroque seventeenth century as the expansion of Oriental trade brought additional spices to Mexican grocers.[79]

But the culinary exchange went both ways, for native cooks taught Creoles to incorporate chile peppers into European stews, and by the eighteenth century capsicums had become the defining characteristic of Creole cuisine. While New World elites fed their addictions to the fiery peppers in a wide range of *moles, chorizos, adobos*, and *chiles en nogada*, the French Enlightenment turned Europeans away from their medieval heritage of spicy tastes in favor of bland foods they considered more "natural" and "healthful." Indeed, the universal Mexican taste for chile peppers marked the first step in forging a distinctive national cuisine.

Nevertheless, the twentieth-century authors who glorified colonial *moles* as "mestizo" cuisine displayed the nationalist ideology of modern Mexico rather than the hierarchical mentality of the colonial period. The elites of New Spain viewed people of mixed blood as outcasts, economically necessary perhaps, but hardly human. Writers ignored the castes in their works, and painters depicted them in the same way they categorized flora and fauna. Foods gained acceptance only when they appeared to be Creole adaptations of Spanish dishes, for wealthy people scorned the Indian cuisine of corn, a snobbish attitude that persisted long after Mexico gained independence.

*THREE*

# Many Chefs in the National Kitchen

## *The Nineteenth Century*

❧

*El cocinero mexicano* (The Mexican Chef), published in 1831, a decade after independence, set the tone for Mexico's national cuisine. Possibly the country's first printed cookbook and certainly the most influential, it passed through a dozen editions and served as a model for cooking manuals throughout the nineteenth century. The anonymous author adopted a sharp nationalist voice in both linguistic and culinary matters. He denounced the Spanish Academy of the Language and insisted on using words of Mexican origins, even as he praised "truly national" spicy dishes and derided the delicate European palates unaccustomed to chile peppers.[1] The publisher, Mariano Galván Rivera, edited out the most chauvinistic phrases from future editions; nevertheless, the insistence on a distinctive national taste continued to flavor the work. The 1868 edition, for example, stated that foreign dishes appeared in the text, but only after they had been "Mexicanized," in other words adapted to Mexican tastes.[2]

Deciding what constituted the authentic national cuisine remained a source of ongoing concern. A few years after *The Mexican Chef* appeared, the *Nuevo y sencillo arte de cocina* (New and Simple Art of Cooking) advertised recipes specifically "accommodated to the Mexican palate," which supposedly had no use for "European stimulants."[3] Nevertheless, Narciso Bassols began his two-volume *La cocinera poblana* (The Puebla Cook) with the pessimistic claim that cookbooks contained an abundance of useless foreign recipes.[4] Vicenta Torres de Rubio reiterated this attack on irrelevant cookbooks, observing that Mexicans neither season nor condiment their food according to European practices.[5] A group of women from Gua-

45

dalajara declared that most cookbook authors copied recipes without concern for either quality or utility.[6]

These assertions revealed more than just the state of Mexican culinary arts. Certainly, they contained an element of self-promotion from publishers trying to increase sales at the expense of competitors. Yet they also reflected deep social divisions that persisted long after independence leaders abolished the colonial system of castes. Native American culture remained a marker of lower-class status, rendering many national dishes inappropriate for cookbooks of the *gente decente* (polite society). The volume claiming to be "accommodated to the Mexican palate," for instance, contained not a single recipe for tamales, enchiladas, or *quesadillas*.[7] Moreover, the term *tortilla* adopted its Spanish meaning of omelette unless specifically designated as corn tortillas. One manual even defined tortillas for the benefit of foreign readers, explaining that they appeared on even the most affluent tables in remote provincial cities; the recipes assured Europeans that sophisticated continental cuisine prevailed, at least in Mexico City.[8] And the *Diccionario de cocina* (Dictionary of Cooking), published in 1845, pointedly questioned the morals of any family that ate tamales — the food of "the lower orders."[9]

The striking biases of nineteenth-century culinary literature demonstrated the ambivalent attitude of Mexican elites toward the national culture. Liberal intellectuals sought to forge a sense of nationalism, but they conceived of the nation in European terms. Native Americans could gain citizenship only by sacrificing their traditional lifestyles and adopting the trappings of European civilization. Yet these same elites betrayed a sense of nostalgic yearning for many elements of the popular culture, particularly the foods. After all, the lack of corn-based recipes in cookbooks did not prove that elites never ate these dishes. The Indian servants who did the cooking hardly needed instructions for making enchiladas, and most were illiterate anyway. One must therefore read between the lines of this culinary literature and examine the contexts in which foods were eaten to discern the hesitant development of a national cuisine.

## Domestic Culture and Nation Building

Mexican nationalism, like an Aztec god, wore many masks. Creole patriots justified independence from Spain by wrapping themselves in pre-Columbian mantles, invoking the splendors of ancient civilizations and the valor of long-dead warriors. But confrontations with still-living Indians required a different mask, that of European civilization, which was the foundation on which nineteenth-century leaders hoped to build the Mexican nation. One of the great dilemmas facing these politicians was to gain the allegiance of mestizos and Indians who had been shunned by colonial elites. Intellectuals tried to overcome the divisions of the caste system and forge a common national identity through broadly conceived educational campaigns. Just as colonial missionaries had used religious festivals and icons to indoctrinate Native Americans into the Catholic faith, secular leaders fashioned patriotic celebrations and monuments to incorporate the lower classes into the Mexican nation.[10]

Political struggles between liberals, moderates, and conservatives compounded the difficulties facing the newly independent Mexico. Army revolts toppled governments with terrible regularity, as generals such as the flamboyant Antonio López de Santa Anna played out personal ambition at the expense of both tranquillity and the treasury. Internal strife also encouraged foreign invasions, in 1846 by the United States, which cost the country half its territory, and in 1862 by the French, who established a short-lived empire under the Austrian Archduke Maximilian. Mexico finally gained a measure of peace under the strong presidency and later dictatorship of Porfirio Díaz (1876–1911), but the resulting transformation of traditional agriculture and rise of urban industry brought new social upheavals.

To provide an anchor against the public turmoils threatening the nation, Mexican leaders perceived a desperate need for domestic middle-class values. Women therefore had an important although limited role to play as mothers of patriotic children and guardians of family morality. Liberal intellectuals embraced the Enlightenment ideal of educating women both to assure that they carried out these duties and to limit the influence of conservative clergy. Authors defined family values in a whole genre of instructional literature, including calendars and journals.[11] Cookbooks composed an important segment of the market for domestic guides because of the centrality of cuisine in nurturing a family. First, these books promoted the bourgeois ideal of balancing the household budget by preparing economical meals. They were also useful in guarding family health, with instructions for purchasing sanitary foods, filtering drinking water, and detecting adulterated milk. And if contamination should somehow slip past the household defenses, they taught women how to serve as family nurse, prudently dispensing remedies such as the ubiquitous *manzanilla* tea.[12]

But efficient management was not intended as a challenge to the basic separation between the house and the street. The ideals of domesticity

inherited from Mediterranean culture sought to keep women and children
locked safely behind heavy wooden doors and grated iron windows. Men
alone supposedly possessed the physical strength necessary to provide the
family with sustenance, which entitled the patriarch to unquestioned authority at home.[13] Nineteenth-century cookbook authors explicitly supported this subservient female role. In the introduction to one family manual, María Antonia Gutiérrez cautioned that a woman must "maintain
a pleasant and agreeable home so that her husband would not abandon
her."[14] Jacinto Anduiza elaborated this theme in a cookbook that attributed
many of the worst domestic calamities to failures in the kitchen. He warned
that men dissatisfied with their wives' cooking would seek their pleasures in
taverns and bordellos.[15]

The choice of appropriate foods for family meals not only helped assure a
stable domestic environment, it also served to foment patriotism within the
home. Cookbook authors often resorted to quite blatant nationalist language, preparing everything from stuffed onions to barbecued meat *a la
mexicana*, and dedicating dishes to national heroes, such as Moctezuma's
dessert, insurgents' soup, and Donato Guerra's cod.[16] They explored the
national taste for foods such as "patriotic" frijoles, and an 1886 banquet
attended by the minister of government and foreign dignitaries featured
*mole poblano*, identified as the "national dish."[17] Writers also celebrated the
recognition of their food in foreign countries. Newspapers announced
proudly that New York restaurants served *mole* and other Mexican dishes.[18]

The authors of this national cuisine came primarily from the liberal
intelligentsia. The anonymous author of *The Mexican Chef* employed many
themes of the Enlightenment and denounced Spanish conservatism. His
publisher, Mariano Galván, was a political moderate who produced Mexico's first almanac as well as countless editions of women's calendars, travel
guides, and textbooks. Although later jailed for supporting the French intervention, Galván had employed liberal ideologue José María Luis Mora
in the 1830s to manage his journals. Leading liberal newspaper editors
including Vicente García Torres and Ireneo Paz also entered the cookbook
trade. Vicenta Torres de Rubio, the first woman to publish a cookbook,
moved in liberal circles and even included menus from political banquets in
her work. Manuel Murguía dedicated a cooking manual to Mexican *señoritas* in 1856, two years after he printed the first edition of the Mexican
national anthem.[19]

Over the course of the nineteenth century, about fifteen separate cookbooks were published in Mexico. Multiple editions of these works bring the
number up to nearly forty, with perhaps a few thousand copies for each run,

for a total of between fifty and a hundred thousand cookbooks. Several of these works listed dual publication in Mexico City and abroad, principally Paris, which must have delighted Mexican patriots desiring foreign approval of their national cuisine. About four or five volumes, both new works and reprints of old ones, appeared each decade from 1831 until 1890, and at least eight cookbooks were published in each of the last two decades of the Porfiriato. Additional recipes printed in domestic manuals, calendars, and newspapers assured that cooking instructors reached a broad audience, at least among the middle and upper classes.[20]

Yet published recipes did not exhaust Mexican culinary literature; many women wrote their own manuscript volumes, particularly as educational opportunities increased toward the end of the nineteenth century. Fanny Gooch observed in the 1880s that affluent Mexican ladies took great pride in their handwritten volumes, although she noted that a hired cook often followed her own recipes and ignored her mistress's instructions.[21] Women likewise took ideas from published works, transforming them to fit their personal tastes.[22] One housewife copied a number of recipes from a published volume into her kitchen notebook. In the process she simplified techniques, removed extraneous ingredients, and on one occasion found it necessary to change "stirring frequently" to "stirring continuously," a lesson perhaps learned at the expense of a ruined dinner.[23] Moreover, women passed over impractical dishes such as Manuel Murguía's absurd recipe for stuffed *frijoles*, which involved cooking beans — "but not too soft" — slicing them in half, inserting a bit of cheese, dipping them in egg batter, and frying them in oil.[24] One cannot simply assume women adopted liberal ideals of a national culture, given the creative way they read these books and the diversity of regional cuisines across the republic.

## Many Mexicos, Many Cuisines

The liberal poet and politician Guillermo Prieto had few kind things to say about Antonio López de Santa Anna, but he did have to admit that the caudillo was, "like most *veracruzanos*, fond of a fine table."[25] The inhabitants of this Gulf Coast state, renowned for its fresh seafood, spoke endlessly about local delicacies such as fried *robalo* (snook), dogshark turnovers, and octopus stewed in ink. Other regions inherited their own distinctive culinary traditions from the colonial period. Puebla was known for its *mole* with turkey, while Oaxaca possessed its own special black *mole* sauce. Spatial divisions existed even within the boundaries of Mexico City between the popular cuisine of the streets and the elite foods consumed within private homes and exclusive restaurants. The enormous diversity of local dishes made it difficult to imagine a single national cuisine, just as devotion to *patrias chicas* (little fatherlands) confounded the search for national unity.

The strong sense of loyalty felt by Mexicans for their place of birth encouraged all sorts of regional rivalries, particularly between provincials and residents of the capital. A cookbook published in Mexico City and Paris asserted that lower-class Indian foods appeared on even the most affluent provincial tables. Vicenta Torres de Rubio refuted this slander in her book of Michoacán cooking by demonstrating the prowess of Morelia women in preparing French delicacies.[26] Another example of culinary chauvinism appeared among *jarochos*, who considered the tiny black *frijoles* of Veracruz, with their smooth texture and fragrant oils, to be the finest in the country. When forced to live in the capital, they willingly paid thirty to forty pesos per mule load to import them. *The Mexican Chef*, trying to overcome this regionalism, insisted that the black beans of central Mexico compared favorably to those of Veracruz.[27] And as late as 1916, Manuel Gamio asked for an imported beer in Mérida, and received a Dos Equis from Orizaba. When the anthropologist repeated his request, the waiter replied: "That's the only foreign beer we have; if you want a domestic, I'll bring you a Yucatecan brand."[28]

Nevertheless, many Mexicans also recognized the wealth of the country's diverse regional cooking styles. Nineteenth-century cookbooks included many local specialties, from the seafoods of Veracruz and Campeche, to the *moles* of Puebla and Oaxaca, and the roasted meats of Monterrey and Guadalajara. But by comparison with modern works, these books acknowledged only a handful of regional cuisines, in particular the centers of Spanish settlement. The virtual monopoly of Creole kitchens becomes apparent in the comparative treatment of *mole*. Puebla's chief rival in producing this dish, the southern state of Oaxaca, is known today as "the land of seven *moles*." Yet nineteenth-century cookbooks ignored the more indigenous versions of Oaxacan *mole* such as *verde*, a green stew perfumed with the incomparable aniselike fragrance of *hoja santa*. They focused instead on the black *mole* similar to Puebla's fabled dish. An 1834 volume explained that the *moles* of Puebla and Oaxaca "owe their particular good taste to the types of chiles employed; the first making use of a sweet chile called the *mulato*, and the second from a Oaxacan chile called the *chilohatle*."[29]

By defining even chile peppers in Creole terms, the nineteenth-century national cuisine ignored a gastronomic geography dating back to pre-Columbian times. Native culinary traditions centered around civilizations such as the Maya, Mexica, Zapotecs, Mixtecs, and Totonacs — ethnic groups that rarely corresponded to Mexican political boundaries. The Huasteca, for example, split between the states of San Luis Potosí, Tamaulipas, and Veracruz, seldom appeared on national maps. This heavily forested region contained only a small Hispanic population of rancheros with little political prominence. Nevertheless, large numbers of native communities thrived in the area and developed an enormously sophisticated cuisine. Modern ethnographers have counted forty-two distinct varieties of tamales, including the fabled *zacahuil*, a meter-long monster that required most of a tree of banana leaves for wrapping.[30]

Other culinary regions received little notice because of their native origins and local character. Culhuacán maintained two distinct gastronomic traditions in an obscure corner of the Valley of Mexico, southeast of the capital. The cuisine of the Chalco lakefront featured vegetables, fish, and ducks, while people living on nearby foothills dined on cactus, pork, and rabbits.[31] Along the Pacific Coast, the hominy stew *pozole* assumed countless forms among different native ethnic groups. Yet because of its indigenous associations, *pozole* was also ignored by elite cooking manuals.

Spatial divisions based on class and ethnicity existed even within the boundaries of Mexico City. An economic boom of the late eighteenth century attracted large numbers of immigrants from the countryside to the nation's capital. With housing deplorable or nonexistent, common people took their meals in the streets. The pre-Columbian kitchen of *metate* and *comal*, largely unchanged since the conquest, provided cheap and delicious food to help relieve the burdens of urban existence. A woman could set up a brazier on any street corner, and as soon as the coals began glowing, do a brisk business selling enchiladas to pedestrians. Expanding the operation required no more than a few stones to hold a *cazuela* of beans over the charcoal. These curbside kitchens were so pervasive that a government official complained that virtually every street and plaza in Mexico City had its own resident cook.[32] The upper classes objected to the spectacle of dirty, half-naked people crowded around pots of bubbling stews and beans. Nevertheless, in many places such as the Street of San Juan and the Plaza of San Pablo, improvised cafés became known for their superb dishes.[33]

Popular sector chefs also set up shop in drinking houses known as *pulquerías*. Decried by moral reformers as a social blight, these shops opened early in the morning and quickly filled to capacity, which might be more than five hundred occupants. Customers drank *pulque* from small clay bowls, then smashed the empties on the floor. They amused themselves by gambling, eating pickled chile appetizers, and dancing with waitresses to rowdy tunes. More substantial food was available, not from the management, but from women who set up small braziers at the back of the houses, filling the unventilated buildings with smoke. Once they started cooking, other aromas permeated the room, attracting numerous customers for foods such as *carnitas*, tasty bits of fried meat served with hot sauce.[34] Many *pulquerías* owed their reputations more to the delicious food than to the quality of their drinks, and despite their lower-class associations they often attracted an affluent clientele. Discriminating diners such as Guillermo Prieto and Mariano Otero favored the enchiladas served at the *pulque* houses of "Uncle Juan Aguirre" and "The Granny."[35]

Fiestas provided another focus for Mexico's popular cuisine, as they had since the days of Moctezuma. In the week before Christmas, people exchanged food and drinks in *posadas*, festive reenactments of the holy family's search for shelter in Bethlehem. All Souls' Day, or the Day of the Dead, was another popular holiday in which adults offered ritual foods to departed relatives while children devoured candy skeletons.[36] The most spectacular celebration of the year came during Holy Week, when great crowds converged on the capital from distant villages and ranches. From Holy Thursday to Easter Sunday throngs of people danced through the streets, in a movable feast of popular cuisine. Thirsty revelers guzzled *aguas frescas*, refreshing waters flavored with pineapple, melon, tamarindo, and *chía* seeds, dispensed by women from palm-frond and flower-decorated stands. Holy Week also marked the traditional start of Mexico City's ice-cream season, these frozen treats made with ice carried down from the slopes of Popocatépetl.[37]

In the early years of the republic, Mexicans of all classes participated in these festivals. But the process of modernization brought increasing attempts to remove disorderly people from the streets. By the 1880s, many fashionable residents left the capital to celebrate Holy Week in Tlalpan, where they dined in outlandishly expensive restaurants. Coffee houses also proliferated as an alternative to the undignified *pulquerías*. And street-corner enchilada women lost customers to restaurants such as "The Archbishop," managed by the redoubtable "Don Frijoles" (Mr. Beans). Spatial lines of class therefore became ever more apparent in the nineteenth century.[38]

## Etiquette and Transgression

Mexican cuisine varied not only between regions, but also over time, as different occasions demanded appropriate foods. Rules of etiquette served as temporal maps guiding interpersonal relations across the often tortuous social terrain of class, gender, and kinship. Appropriate behavior both depended on and determined an individual's status, making it difficult yet essential to situate oneself correctly within any given context. The etiquette of eating also helped to resolve social contradictions by affording members of the *gente decente* spaces in which to consume unfashionable yet desirable popular foods. Nevertheless, transgressing the boundaries between house and street posed grave dangers to polite society.

The memoirs of Guillermo Prieto fondly recalled the meals of his youth, illustrating the rich variety of Mexican meals in the nineteenth century. He had awakened each morning at boarding school anticipating a cup of succulent chocolate in bed. This essential stimulant, made with either milk or water and served with a roll or some candied fruit, composed the *desayuno* (breakfast). Serious eating did not begin until the *almuerzo* (brunch) served about ten in the morning. Still too early for visitors, this family meal proved substantial nevertheless, with grilled meat or chicken, stews, *moles*, or perhaps an omelet. And regardless of the main course, beans served as the regular accompaniment. Wealthy families drank imported red wine and the middle classes consumed native *pulque*.

The principal meal, *comida*, began around one or two in the afternoon, and Mexico City unfailingly observed its ritual. Offices closed early so that men could go home to eat with their families — they might return to work for a few hours after a siesta. The meal followed an invariable format, and each course arrived at the table separately. First came a broth of chicken or beef with limes for squeezing and chiles for garnishing. The next course consisted of a dry soup of pasta or rice, with tomato sauce either tossed over the former or cooked into the latter. Main courses had more variety, a typical choice being *puchero* stew, made with cabbage, turnips, garbanzos, ham, and assorted other ingredients. After *frijoles* and dessert, the family drifted into a siesta that lasted until the late afternoon.

Between four and five, another cup of chocolate stimulated appetites for the *merienda*, a late afternoon snack of rolls and sweets. Often served to visiting members of the extended family and other friends, it would tide them over until the *cena* (supper) was ready about ten at night. This meal, whether taken in the home or at a modest *fonda* (restaurant), might consist of stewed meat with salad or chicken covered in *mole*. Well-to-do Mexicans did not usually retire until quite late, having consumed remarkable quantities of food throughout the day.[39]

A skeptic might question whether this represented a typical diet, even for the wealthy. Prieto was, after all, a gourmand of unusual dimensions. His appetite shocked the boarding-school mistress, who exclaimed, "he eats like ten tigers."[40] Nevertheless, similar meals greeted foreign travelers from the beaches of Veracruz to the deserts of Sonora. Edward Tayloe characterized his first dinner in Mexico as "an incessant volley of dishes." Olive Percival recounted suppers in Mexico City that included twelve meats, eight sweets, and countless wines.[41]

These abundant meals not only sustained life, they also helped structure it. Keeping the family well fed occupied a great deal of a woman's time, regardless of whether servants did the actual work. Conscientious housewives went through a daily cycle of budgeting the groceries, planning the meals, overseeing the cooking, gathering the children, controlling the children, and organizing the leftovers.[42] Meals also regulated the city's life, closing businesses in the afternoon so that men could return home and share the *comida* with their families. Meanwhile, the *cena*, called the *mesa del amor* (table of love) and often taken in open-air *fondas*, formed part of the evening social life along with promenades through the Zócalo, the central plaza.[43]

The dinner table served as calendar as well as clock, changing over the year to reflect religious rituals and seasonal produce. Catholic dietary laws restricting the consumption of meat on Fridays and throughout Lent required the greatest adjustment. Guillermo Prieto reminisced that preparations for Good Friday dinners during his youth had called for a "genuine culinary congress" whose deliberations produced a lavish menu with several varieties of fish, lentils with pineapple and bananas, *romeritos* (dried shrimp fritters with greens) and *capirotada* (bread pudding). The feast of San Agustín, on August 28, demanded *chiles en nogada*, and for family celebrations such as baptisms and weddings, *mole* was essential.[44]

Social divisions revealed themselves in the foods chosen for such occasions; for the popular sectors important celebrations meant tamales. The villagers of Tepoztlán, Morelos, consumed these native treats on Christmas Eve after "putting the child to bed," ceremoniously placing a figure of the infant Jesus in a manger of hay. On June 24, the Day of San Juan, residents of Chavinda, Michoacán, ate *tamales tontos* (silly tamales) made of uncooked corn with only a little added pork fat. The people of Huejotzingo, Puebla, offered plain white tamales with *mole* to deceased relatives on All Saints Day. And in Acolmán, México, it was traditional to eat Judas tamales on the Saturday of Holy Week during the festivities in which crowds burned papier-maché effigies of the traitor Iscariot.[45]

For the *gente decente*, Christmas Eve supper, the most formal meal of the year, demonstrated the superior social status of European foods. The menu followed strict conventions in comfortable homes, with virtually nothing of domestic origin. First came the fabled *ensalada de la noche buena*, "the most pompous and magnificent of all salads," according to *The Mexican Chef*. He called it a miniature Plaza del Volador, and the riotous mixture of lettuce, carrots, beets, potatoes, raisins, almonds, peanuts, bananas, *jícamas*, oranges, limes, and pears did resemble the colorful market formerly adjacent to the Mexico City Zócalo.[46] Next came dried cod, a tradition dating back at least to 1804, when restauranteur Carlo Monti served this dish to his nonpaying customer Francisco Zapari on Christmas Eve. Cooks selected the whitest and fleshiest cuts, soaked them overnight, then cooked them in olive oil with finely chopped tomatoes, onions, garlic, and red bell peppers, as well as olives, capers, and pickled yellow chiles. The dish was always served with wheat bread rolls and wine. Indeed, much of its attraction lay in the conspicuous indication of wealth, for after spending outrageous amounts on the fish, housewives also had to buy imported wines, oils, and condiments.[47]

European food likewise dominated the most important meal of the day, the afternoon *comida*, pushing national dishes to the periphery. *The Mexican Chef* organized popular-sector dishes such as enchiladas and tamales into a chapter of *almuerzos ligeros* (light brunches), to be eaten privately in the morning.[48] A later edition of the cookbook explicitly distinguished between the situations for elite and common foods. Among family members and intimate friends, it explained, one could safely eat stuffed chiles, *mole poblano*, or even enchiladas and tamales. But for formal brunches, and always at dinner, one should adhere to European customs.[49] These rules were not limited to stuffy etiquette manuals. Guillermo Prieto, no stranger to lower-class enchilada makers, described *mole* as excellent for intimate family gatherings, but preferred the Spanish *olla podrida* for banquets.[50]

Location as well as time determined the appropriateness of certain foods; Mexico City required more formality than the countryside, where the affluent could relax and enjoy popular cuisine. The *tamalada*, a picnic expressly for eating tamales, was a regular feature of nineteenth-century social life. Families traveled to the suburbs of Tacubaya and San Angel to spend the afternoon in a quiet wood or beautiful garden, dancing, playing ball or croquet, or fighting *guerras de manzanas* (mock apple wars). In addition to tamales, refreshments included *atole de leche*, a sort of milkshake made with ground corn, and *chongos*, French toast with brown-sugar syrup and grated cheese.[51]

Travel provided another excuse for wealthy Mexicans to indulge in otherwise forbidden fruits, as it had since the colonial period. In 1695 an innkeeper, José de Rueda Montezuma, had complained that one María de Alsibar was selling tamales and chocolate from a crude hut on the roadside without a license, thus depriving him of business.[52] In 1910, an English-woman observed similar foods being sold in train stations on the route from Veracruz to the capital: "To my horror I saw these educated people lapping up dreadful little mixtures offered them on leaves, made with Heaven knows what ingredients."[53] The women of Tepoztlán, Morelos, climbed two hours to the nearest railroad station to sell their tamales. Tourists could achieve the ultimate pre-Columbian experience by eating tamales while exploring the newly uncovered pyramids of Teotihuacán.[54]

Thus, at times the elite shared in the culture of the popular classes, but only from a distance, secluded in remote picnic spots or disguised by the anonymity of travel. Another example of this reserve was the *jamaica*, a party in which upper-class girls dressed in peasant costume and went around selling each other candy, fruit, and lemonade. This playful imitation of street life took its name from a popular festival of the colonial period. Nevertheless, the "scandalous, profane" dances that provoked the outrage of eighteenth-century moralists had vanished from these elite affairs. Instead, the festival was trivialized to the level of a child's game, with play money from a "bank" and brightly decorated stands like those in the streets during Holy Week. A few girls dressed as ambulant vendors added further authenticity, and for a special touch, a boy with a burro carrying tropical fruits imitated the *fruteros* from the steamy lowlands.[55]

Mexican elites may have brought these street festivals into their homes to sublimate dangerous elements in society. Rather than allowing them free reign outside, they were kept under careful watch by family authorities. A painting by Agustín Arrieta of one such *jamaica* illustrated the nineteenth-century ideals of domesticity. The scene centered around a pretty young girl selling fruit drinks from a stand decorated with flowers and grasses. While she served a drink to her mother, maids worked at the *metate*, grinding and straining pineapple juice, and mixing it with water carried by another servant. Unlike the rowdy setting of Holy Week, solid walls protected this party from the dangers of the street, and the only scenery lay in a few landscape paintings. Finally, the patriarch stood by in a European top hat as guardian of family morality.

Constant vigilance was necessary because both tamales and the un-washed street people who ate them held a promiscuous allure for Mexico's *gente decente*. Carlos González Peña, in his 1915 novel *La fuga de la qui-mera* (The Flight of the Chimera), explored the forbidden delights of gastronomic transgressions. The dilemma centered around Sofía, the fashionable young wife of Don Miguel Bringas. Her temptation took place in the streets of San Juan del Río, north of Mexico City. The couple's journey by train, the symbol of modern life, sharpened the contrast with the filthy market and the street vendors. Miguel asked his wife if she wanted to taste them, but Sofía declined, fearing that somebody would see her in the un-dignified act of eating tamales. Miguel then goaded his wife across this line of propriety. She refused to buy the tamales herself, so he plunged into the market and came back with the popular confections wrapped in greasy paper. Sofía continued her protests, but when she finally accepted, her eager manner betrayed the feigned reluctance. A convenient case of dys-pepsia prevented Miguel from sharing the forbidden fruit. Instead he watched, a voyeur, as his wife "dispatched, with gluttonous face and linger-ing bites, the tamales of San Juan del Río. Chewing with satisfaction, her lips glossy with grease, she was filled with secret vanity knowing that her husband had solicited this caprice."[56]

González Peña wrote in the modernist style, which sought to portray the promiscuity of Latin American urban life. His association of the lower classes with dirt and sexuality corresponded to the middle-class morality of his time. Greasy lips, capricious indulgences, the ever-present threat of contamination through gastrointestinal disease, all appeared to the elite as natural elements of the streets. González Peña used Sofía's flirtation with tamales as a prelude to an adulterous affair and a tragic death. Purging Mexican cities of such dangerous forms of corruption, both culinary and sexual, became an important focus of nineteenth-century social reform.

## Cooking Classes as Social Reform

Laura Esquivel's best-selling novel *Like Water for Chocolate* dramatized the connection between cuisine and morality in Mexico. The heroine Tita was forbidden by custom to marry because as the youngest daughter she must care for her widowed mother. Worse still, her beloved Pedro, in order to be near Tita, agreed to marry her older sister. Unwilling to trade romance for respectability, Tita carried on an illicit affair through the medium of her cooking. Her dishes expressed her emotions: her sorrow brought people to tears, and her passion literally burned down the house. One of the most provocative scenes in the sensual screen adaptation depicted Tita grinding *mole* on the *metate*, the rhythmic swaying of her body nearly giving Pedro a heart attack. Such sexual electricity shocked Mexican elites as well, but for entirely different reasons. The lustful excesses they attributed to lower-class women seemed to threaten the nation's morality. Health authorities, meanwhile, began drawing connections between street foods and disease. Over the course of the nineteenth century, these two discourses of health and morality gradually intermingled, conflating legitimate concerns about public hygiene with a desire to instill middle-class values of domesticity among the urban poor. By the Porfirian period, elite fears of popular cuisine in the streets had escalated to the point that cooking classes became a national priority.

Mexicans have long associated the act of grinding corn on the *metate* with female sexuality. Pre-Columbian artists carved fertility symbols in the shape of lavish earth mothers bent over their grinding stones. Native women of the Huasteca still proposition men with suggestive claims that "my water is fresher, my *metate* tastier, and my sleeping mat hotter" than those of other women, and by urging potential lovers to "come taste my *cazuela*."[57] The kneeling exertions of tortilla makers certainly caught the eyes of nineteenth-century men, who paid particular attention to the blouses "that failed to cover their breasts." *Costumbrista* painters likewise lingered over this provocative subject of poorly clad yet graceful women.[58]

The popular press further aroused elite anxiety by using culinary metaphors in broadsheets attacking its genteel pretensions. José Guadalupe Posada, the woodcut artist best known for his satiric *calavera* skeletons, illustrated many of these works toward the end of the nineteenth century. In one scene he depicted two men sitting in the rain, protected only by the broad sombreros that marked them as commoners. As they watched, a well-dressed young woman crossed the flooded cobblestone street, her skirt pulled up to her knees. "Who could keep Lent?" asked one of the men, "and not trade the most delicious red snapper for those legs of pure *carne maciza* (chopped loin)."[59] Another broadside, entitled *El Pinche* (literally the scullery, but also an impolite word in Spanish), explicitly threatened bourgeois society. Posada drew the unshaven *pinche* waving a large knife over a string of *chorizones* (big sausages, with predictably rude connotations): a general, a banker, an industrialist, a foreigner, a priest, and an old woman symbolizing alcoholism. But the people feasting on elites remained largely a dream during the Porfirian period, when the reverse was more common. Posada once caricatured the governor of Puebla in the dress of a street-corner cook, grinding up *masa*, both corn dough and the common people, to make enchiladas for President Díaz, dressed as a peon. The *cocinera* also held a bundle of tamales, representing the municipalities of Puebla, waiting to be gobbled down by the dictator.[60] Cooking, the very

hallmark of domesticity, therefore posed a menace to society when practiced in streets.

Popular cuisine even threatened to subvert the patriarchal order, as
women resorted to kitchen secrets to defend themselves against their husbands. This tradition dated back to pre-Columbian and colonial times,
when food served as a medium for witchcraft. For instance, José de Ugalde
complained to the Mexican Inquisition in 1774 that his wife had bewitched
him by putting herbs in his food and drink. She allegedly fed him such
concoctions throughout their seventeen-year marriage, but he reported the
case only when she used supernatural powers to prevent him from exercis-
ing his right to beat her.[61] Another common display of machismo involved
the practice of maintaining a mistress, usually in a separate location, but at
times actually bringing her into the home. A disgruntled wife could negate
her husband's power to define the family in this way by refusing to feed the
other woman. And as a last resort, a woman could leave an abusive husband
and support herself, however precariously, by cooking on the street.[62]

Enlightened Mexicans of the nineteenth century may have scoffed at
stories of witchcraft or domestic insurrection, but they found other reasons
to fear street foods and the women who prepared them. Colonial authorities had long regulated municipal markets, but the first formal institution
dedicated to improving public sanitation, the Mexico City Board of Health
(Consejo Superior de Salubridad), was founded in 1841. One year later the
physicians and chemists of the Board issued their first ruling against unscrupulous vendors who adulterated chocolate with iron filings. When
merchants took advantage of a flood of dead trout in June 1856, the scientists called for a ban on the rotting fish as a public health hazard. The Board
also lobbied successfully for a regulation requiring poultry vendors to
slaughter chickens in the market, to prevent the sale of decaying carcasses.[63]
Other health hazards lurked in the candies sold to children throughout the
country. Mexicans used sugar to crystallize virtually every imaginable fruit,
vegetable, nut, and seed, with the ironic exception of chocolate. They particularly delighted in coloring these candies, and therein lay the problem.
To obtain brilliant hues of red, blue, and yellow, the vendors added mercury
bisulfate, powdered cromoxide, and aniline compounds, all toxic to humans. The Health Board recommended an immediate ban on such sub-
stances and provided a list of safe alternative dyes.[64]

Nevertheless, legitimate concerns about sanitation became conflated
with a general disdain for the lower classes and their foods. Guillermo
Prieto described a short-lived 1833 proclamation by the Federal District's

governor as filled with "tremendous prohibitions against fruits and other foods," banning even stuffed chile peppers.[65] In 1854 the Health Board again used the lack of hygienic practices among small-scale vendors as an excuse to outlaw the sale of fruits and vegetables in Mexico City. Public outcry against such outrageous restrictions quickly forced the district governor to reverse the decree.[66] In 1870 the Board launched a more limited offensive, this time against mushrooms. Allegations of frequent poisonings persuaded the *ayuntamiento* to ban the sale of mushrooms until scientists could prepare a guide identifying toxic species. Calls for such regulations dated back to 1831, when *The Mexican Chef* pointed with approval to Paris, where police vigilance allowed the public to eat mushrooms without fear. The prohibition also received the endorsement of Mexico City newspapers. Yet its implementation revealed the sanitary reformers' lack of regard for popular custom.[67]

By banning mushrooms completely, the Board provoked widespread opposition from the people of Mexico City. The city council therefore requested a list distinguishing safe and toxic mushrooms, but the scientists could not provide this and asked for a delay on the pretext that mushrooms were out of season. The police commissioner, besieged by disruptions in city markets, demanded immediate action: either list the acceptable spores or repeal the decree. Pressure continued to mount in city markets, and within two weeks the commissioner denounced the ban as completely unworkable, declaring that it was better to run "the remote and improbable risk" of a bad mushroom entering the market than to cut off the trade entirely. But two prominent Board physicians, Gumercindo Mendoza and Manuel Urbina, when called before the city council, scorned the demand for a quick answer. In a lofty discourse citing obscure German experts, they described the complexity of fungi and the difficulty of distinguishing between toxic and safe varieties. They then appealed for a grant to purchase several European monographs and for time to conduct a thorough study of regional specimens.[68] The scientists, if not so enamored of German texts, had local experts they could have consulted. Mexican folk healers had harvested mushrooms for thousands of years and knew an immense variety of specimens. But the thought of consulting such people, however efficacious, never occurred to the scientists, perhaps because the *curanderos* referred to the plants with Náhuatl rather than Latin names.[69]

Mexican leaders believed the solution to concerns about both public health and popular morality lay in the schooling of women; indeed, some considered a national campaign of domestic education as the only method of civilizing the masses, particularly the Native Americans.[70] The government of Benito Juárez took a step in this direction in 1871 by founding the Escuela de Artes y Oficios, an industrial school for women. Officials hailed the new school as a "powerful means of moralizing the people, inspiring love of work, and opening wider opportunities to *clases desvalidos* (helpless ones)." The goal was to "lift women from their current poor condition without arriving at the exaggeration of making them equal to men."[71] Similar institutions dedicated to working-class women opened in towns throughout the republic, often with the assistance of philanthropic donations from local elites.[72]

Behind the lofty rhetoric of moral improvement lay an attempt to ameliorate social tensions by transforming the working classes into replicas of the bourgeoisie. Historian William French has shown that Porfirian reformers sought to transform proletarian homes into cradles of the capitalist work ethic. Eliminating vice from the domestic sphere would encourage orderly behavior on the factory floor. Laborers who accepted middle-class values of progress through hard work would in turn be less likely to resort to violence. The stakes in this campaign were high for Mexican leaders, who hoped thereby to avoid the social upheavals that had erupted in Europe during the early stages of industrialization.[73] Teachers at the Escuela de Artes y Oficios praised their young students as "aristocratic plebeians," and encouraged them to participate in "spiritual fiestas" such as the *kermesse*, a ritual of respectable culture. Cookbook author Jacinto Anduiza summed up the belief that culinary techniques would contribute to the process of education that would level society.[74]

This social leveling did not seek to achieve genuine equality; instead, the goal was to eradicate practices seen as immoral by elites. Sociologists cited by *El Imparcial*, who "proposed the teaching of culinary arts as the obligatory base of female education," recognized that income differences would remain. Cooks in wealthy homes had to learn the art of truffling a turkey, while those in poor ones contented themselves with frying modest *frijoles*. Yet all were responsible for maintaining the good health of the family they served.[75] The founders of the Escuela de Artes y Oficios expressly rejected the concept of a liberal arts education for the masses, predicting that if workers gained a broad knowledge they would become insubordinate. This fear may also have motivated the people who took out newspaper classified ads for a cook "who knows her obligations."[76]

Efforts to change the attitudes of lower-class women focused heavily on their cooking techniques. The editors of *El Imparcial* proposed the establishment of worker kitchens, following a European model, to replace popular foods.[77] The Escuela de Artes y Oficios held special cooking classes as a method of attracting students. Police inspectors led in the recruiting campaign, an indication of its perceived importance to the Porfirian order. Instructors emphasized European styles such as modest French family cooking and inveighed against the "disgraceful habit" of eating spicy foods. They even advised the lower classes to eschew popular Mexican dishes in favor of simple English cooking—a drastic measure indeed.[78] These campaigns attained the status of official policy in a 1908 education law that held it "indispensable to modify the diet to which [the lower classes] are accustomed."[79] In this way the Mexican elite hoped the lower classes would follow them down a path to European civilization.

## European Fashions, Mexican Tastes

Fanny Calderón de la Barca, the Scottish wife of Spain's first minister to Mexico, wrote scornfully of the elite's clumsy attempts to imitate European cuisine. She described one of her first meals after arriving in port as "the worst of Spanish, Vera-Cruzified." Parisian chefs employed in the capital's wealthiest homes produced no better results; she likened one dish to mining slag. Mexican culinary skills, whether in carving meat, seasoning stews, or dressing tables, invariably fell short of her exacting standards. Yet eventually she stopped drawing comparisons with Europe, accepted Mexican cooking on its own merits, and on her departure in 1842 wrote that "Veracruz cookery, which two years ago I thought detestable, now appears to me delicious."[80] Fanny's experience revealed that even the most dedicated followers of European fashion imparted a uniquely Mexican flavor to their cooking.

Like the upper crust from New York to St. Petersburg, wealthy Mexicans cultivated a taste for French haute cuisine. France had begun to assert a gastronomic hegemony over Europe at the dawn of the eighteenth century, when the Sun King Louis XIV's absolutist policies had emasculated nobles of their political power. With few social functions beyond dueling and the salons, bored patricians turned for diversion to the arts, including music, painting, and cooking. This aristocracy of the spoon inspired a *nouvelle cuisine* based on the Enlightenment ideal that cooks should reveal rather than distort the true nature of foods. Following the rise of the restaurant industry in the decades around 1789, Chef Antonin Carême perfected the laborious and expensive techniques of classical French cuisine. Beginning with *fonds*, deeply flavored broths, he performed a complex alchemy of concentrating and reducing, adding and extracting, garnishing and gilding, to return in the end to a simple and unified whole. Although Carême worked for only the wealthiest aristocrats, his successors, such as Jules Gouffé, extended *la grande cuisine* to an international bourgeois audience, a process that culminated under Auguste Escoffier in the *fin de siècle* Age of Great Hotels.[81]

It is difficult to periodize French culinary influence in Mexico with precision. Many writers date the arrival of continental cuisine to the Second Empire of Maximilian, but this is too late by at least a decade. Eighteenth-century manuscripts displayed an affinity for French titles, but no mastery of the new techniques. The first published cookbooks of the Early Republic demonstrated much greater command of this difficult art, but Hispanic recipes still dominated the texts. Gallic styles seem to have gradually displaced colonial dishes of Iberian descent over the course of the nineteenth century, even as Spain itself declined in political and cultural influence. Indeed, the disastrous war with the United States that terminated Spain's empire in America coincided with the 1898 opening by Escoffier and César Ritz of the Carlton, Europe's most lavish hotel.[82]

The Mexican Chef, the anonymous author of the first published cookbook, had helped launch this penchant for Parisian cuisine as early as 1831. He began his work, in the tradition of classically trained French cooks, with a discussion of stocks, noting that these served as the foundation for all other preparations. Moreover, he admitted with rare humility that the most famous chefs' *fonds* were scarcely different from the broths of a common housewife. His allusions to French gastronomic culture included the saying that "man does not live on what he eats but on what he digests" — the same aphorism used by Alexandre Dumas in 1870 to begin his renowned *Dictionary of Cuisine*. The Mexican author likewise gave a recipe for "epigrams" of lamb, a dish invented in Paris early in the nineteenth century.[83]

French influences came to permeate nineteenth-century Mexican cooking literature. Kitchen manuals contained recipes for the basic sauces *espagnole*, *velouté*, *béchamel*, *tomatée*, and hollandaise; stylish appetizers such as quenelle soup and salmon genovese; classical entrees including veal blanquette and quail *en papillote*; and luscious desserts like mocha eclairs and the Gateau Saint Honore.[84] The women's pages of newspapers were filled with instructions for Parisian soup, truffled pheasant, duchess potatoes, vol-au-vent *à la financiere*, and *bifstec à la Chateaubriand*.[85] Mexicans could also enjoy the pleasures of Parisian dining vicariously through translations of French writings. Jean Anthelme Brillat-Savarin's *Physiology of Taste*, one of the masterpieces of culinary literature, appeared in its first Mexican edition in 1852, a few decades after its publication in French. In 1893 a Mexican press issued a special edition of the celebrated cookbook by Jules Gouffé, former chef of the Paris Jockey Club.[86]

Sophisticated women prided themselves on their ability to reproduce French haute cuisine when the occasion demanded. Vicenta Torres named as one of the most beloved foods of provincial Michoacán the *galatine*, a French dish prepared by boning poultry yet leaving the skin intact, then stuffing it with forcemeat and poaching it in broth. She recalled glowingly that in 1875 this dish had graced a banquet in honor of Governor Rafael Carrillo.[87] For women unwilling to invest hours in preparing such a dish and unable to employ a chef to do it for them, specialty shops sold gourmet pâté and pastry. Wine merchants imported hams, cheese, olive oil, and salted fish, in addition to barrels of Bordeaux wine and Jerez sherry.[88]

Aspiring gourmets also indulged their appetites for continental cuisine in Mexico City restaurants and social clubs. In the 1850s the Tívoli of San Cosme began offering fine dining in an idyllic setting. Tuxedo-clad waiters moved smoothly through the tree-lined courtyard with platters of *noix de veau diplomate* and *becassines à la cavaliere*. Chapultepec Castle, illuminated in the distance by moonlight, lent a romantic air unsurpassed even by the view of the Notre Dame Cathedral from La Tour d'Argent. In 1870 another Tívoli opened in Tlalpan and catered to wealthy people fleeing the urban hustle of Mexican City, particularly during the riotous celebrations of Holy Week.[89] By the end of the century, fine restaurants such as the Maison Dorée, Café Colon, Prendés, and San Angel Inn competed for the services of Paul Laville, V. Barattes, and other French chefs. Excellent kitchens also graced the numerous social clubs of the Spanish, British, American, and German colonies, as well as the capital's elite Jockey Club located in the fabulous House of Tiles.[90] Mexico's greatest coup in international dining came in 1891, when Don Ignacio de la Torre y Mier persuaded the celebrated Parisian chef Sylvain Daumont to come to Mexico City. The Frenchman caused such a sensation that within a year he left the Mexican millionaire to open his own restaurant.[91]

Banquet menus from these establishments testify to the cosmopolitan tastes of the country's leaders. An anonymous mid-nineteenth-century painting portraying a feast for a General León of Oaxaca reveals the symmetrical place settings, the multiple dishes, and the innumerable wine bottles of classical continental cuisine. A dinner for five hundred held in the National Theater to celebrate President Porfirio Díaz's birthday, in 1891, featured French food, wines, and cognac. Only men were seated for this banquet; their wives had to view the proceedings from a balcony, a significant indication of their exclusion from full citizenship in this patriarchal nation. Provincial elites paid lavish sums to rent French chefs from Mexico City restaurants for important events such as a 1903 Monterrey banquet for Governor Bernardo Reyes. The quest for imported civility reached its pinnacle in 1910, at the centennial of independence, in a series of banquets honoring President Díaz, cabinet members, and foreign dignitaries. Not a single Mexican dish appeared at any of the score of dinners dedicated to this patriotic occasion. Sylvain Daumont served most of the food, and G. H. Mumm provided all of the champagne. Even the Mexican colony in New York commemorated the centennial with French food.[92]

Notwithstanding this desire to appear cosmopolitan, Mexicans demanded a uniquely national flavor in their haute cuisine. Foreigners such as Fanny Calderón often made scathing comments about their inability to execute properly European culinary techniques. Critical Mexicans recognized that continental dishes underwent a process of creolization. Antonio García Cubas lampooned the pretentious Tívoli restaurant, wondering who had granted diplomatic credentials to a piece of veal and predicting that anyone who ate the horseman's snipe would receive spurs to the stomach. He noted that many dishes parading as French bore little resemblance to Parisian preparations.[93] These differences, while appearing outlandish to contemporaries, provide modern readers with valuable clues about the nature of Mexico's national cuisine.

Chile peppers constituted the greatest shock to foreign palates. Mexican *adobos*, for example, differed from the marinades used to preserve meat in Europe principally because they included chiles. The eighteenth-century French culinary revolution had banished such sharply spiced foods common to medieval and early modern Europe. The Enlightenment ideal of flavors — "exquisite but not strong" — left Mexican cuisine as a self-conscious anachronism. Patriotic authors bitterly refuted the European opinion of peppers as poisonous, and condemned the continental "war against stimulants, principally chiles."[94] The love of chiles had become a significant distinction between Mexicans and foreigners and thus formed part of the national identity.

Another characteristic of Mexican cuisine, at least among the elite, was the profusion of meat. A quick glance at any nineteenth-century cookbook reveals an enormous variety of seasonings and dressings for meat.[95] Nor was this creativity limited to cookbooks; women prepared these diverse recipes on a daily basis. One foreign traveler observed that wealthy families ate the same meats prepared in different styles several times a week.[96] Fanny Calderón de la Barca described plates filled with meat, fish, and fowl served indiscriminately at every meal. She recorded that the wealthy ate meat for virtually every meal and in astonishing quantities, more than in any other country in the world.[97] But visitors from Europe and the United States almost invariably criticized Mexican meat dishes as overcooked. An Englishman, lamenting the lack of juicy roast beef, blamed local butchers for cutting meat in a "slovenly and injudicious manner."[98] In fact, tradesmen carved beef to suit their customers' preference for well-done steaks. Mexicans abhorred the dripping, rare fillets served in Europe and cut their meat in thin strips, pounding and marinating to tenderize them. Such techniques often constituted the "Mexicanization" of European dishes: a recipe for *bifstec à la Chateaubriand* appears to foreigners like fajitas with French fries.[99]

National tastes therefore showed through even in the midst of foreign cuisine. The unique flavor that Mexicans imparted to their foods served as one way of forming a distinctive national identity. Yet patriotism ultimately derives as much from the devotion to one's own community as the distrust of outsiders. And the love of childhood food provides one of the means of acquiring this nationalist affiliation.

## Culinary Patriotism

A sense of national identity and patriotic loyalty ultimately derives from participation in the national community. The patriarchal Mexican nation based on Western European models envisioned by most domestic manuals may have held little attraction for women and the popular sectors, who were largely excluded from citizenship. After all, French cuisine never reached beyond a small elite, notwithstanding cooking teachers' attempts to make it accessible at least to middle-class families. Mexican women began to write their own manuscript and community cookbooks in the late nineteenth century, and in so doing they created their own visions of the Mexican nation. For them, domestic culture offered as valid a means for building communities as did politics. Yet the competition between European and Mexican models instilled a deep sense of ambivalence about the national culture.

The formation of a national community in the kitchen grew out of the basic sociability of Mexican women, for housewives carried on a brisk market in recipes as well as gossip. María Luisa Soto de Cossio, for example, a rancher's wife in Hidalgo, included in her personal cookbook dishes from her grandmother, Aunt Gabriela, and a neighbor Virginia. She also copied out recipes from the published *Recetas prácticas*, a volume she may have borrowed from a friend.[100] By the last decade of the nineteenth century, the exchange of cooking tips had reached beyond the extended family to become the focus for Catholic charities, one of the few legitimate female activities outside the home. A group of matrons in Guadalajara prepared a recipe manual to support the local orphanage, and several community cookbooks from Mexico City were dedicated to works such as cathedrals for Saint Rafael and Saint Vincent DePaul.[101]

In 1896, Vicenta Torres extended this community of cooks throughout the republic in her *Cocina michoacana*, a serialized guide to the cuisine of Michoacán. Printed in the provincial town of Zamora and sold by subscription, it began with local recipes submitted by women within the state. Nevertheless, she soon expanded her audience to reach cooks from all over the country. A woman from Celaya sent her recipe for "Heroic Nopales," from Guadalajara came a green chile lamb stew, a Mexico City matron offered her favorite meat glaze, and a reader in the border town of Nuevo Laredo even sent her "Hens from the Gastronomic Frontier."[102]

Torres and her collaborators conceived of their work as a community cookbook, first for the state of Michoacán and later embracing the entire nation. Members of this extended community shared the common oral culture of the kitchen despite the distances separating them. Confident that readers were familiar with the basic techniques of cooking, they provided correspondingly vague instructions. One woman wrote simply to fry pork chops in "sufficient quantities of pork fat" until well done and to serve with "hot sauce to taste." A contributor to another community cookbook listed among the ingredients for *mole poblano*: "of all spices, a little bit." A recipe for stuffed chiles read: "having roasted and cleaned [chiles], fill with cooked zucchini squash, onion, oregano, etc." It went without saying that cooks would adjust their seasonings to taste, for recipes served merely as written keys to a much fuller language of the kitchen.[103]

By printing recipes from throughout Mexico, Torres provided the first genuine forum for uniting regional cuisines into a national repertoire. Contributors exchanged recipes with middle-class counterparts they had never met, and began to experiment with regional dishes, combining them in new ways that transcended local traditions. In this way women began to imagine their own national community in the familiar terms of the kitchen, rather than as an alien political entity formulated by men and served up to them in didactic literature.

Women used cuisine as a means of defining a uniquely religious version of the national identity. Torres and her correspondents, while not afraid to experiment with the techniques of foreign haute cuisine, emphasized national dishes that often held religious significance. Most prominent were the colonial *moles*, "those essentially American dishes," which they considered indispensable for festivals such as the Day of the Dead. Another culinary tradition with patriotic affiliations developed around the Virgin of Guadalupe. Having first appeared to an Indian in 1531, the saint gained a universal appeal in Mexico that was even recognized by anticlerical liberals such as Ignacio M. Altamirano. The Porfirian regime acknowledged the Virgin's power as a national symbol in 1895 by formally crowning her the patron saint of Mexico. Vicenta Torres paid homage a year later by publishing a recipe for *gorditas* (small corn griddle cakes) from Guadalupe Hidalgo, the location of her shrine.[104]

The Virgin's incorporation into the national cuisine illustrated not only the religious character of female patriotism, but also the peculiar selection process that transformed local dishes into national symbols. Residents of Guadalupe Hidalgo made a living by selling the plump, sweet, silver-dollar-sized corn griddle cakes to visiting pilgrims. Among their own families they celebrated December 12, the Virgin's day, by eating barbecued goat with *salsa borracha* (drunken sauce). Nevertheless, the plaza *gorditas* ultimately gained recognition as the food of the Virgin, so that by 1926 a newspaper ran a cartoon showing a man refusing to accompany his plump wife (in Spanish, also a *gordita*) on a trip to the Virgin's shrine with the excuse: "Why take a *gordita* to *la villa*?"[105]

This exchange of recipes even began to cross established class and ethnic lines to create a genuinely national cuisine. Unlike the usual practice of segregating enchiladas into a ghetto labeled "light brunches," the *Recetas prácticas* integrated these foods among other recipes for meats and vegetables. Another cookbook prepared by a charitable women's organization in Mexico City gave more recipes for enchiladas than for any other type of food.[106] Vicenta Torres made a virtue of including recipes of explicitly Indian origin, assuring readers that these "secrets of the indigenous classes" would be appropriate at any party. Along with tamales, she included *gordita* cordials, *pozole* de Quiroga, and *carnero al pastor* (Shepherd's mutton), but out of deference to her Porfirian audience, she carefully set them apart with the label "*indigenista*."[107]

Ambivalence thus remained about the acceptability of the national cuisine. An 1897 editorial entitled "The influence of *mole*," signed by the anonymous Guajolote (Turkey), likewise wavered between nostalgic love and bourgeois scorn. "Baptisms, confirmations, birthdays, weddings, even last rites and funerals, to merit the name, have to be accompanied by the national dish, be it green like hope, yellow like rancor, black like jealousy, or red like homicide, but in abundance, in a broad *cazuela*, thick, pungent, with

metallic reflections, speckled with sesame seeds, a magical surface." Guajolote attributed both the genius and the defects of the national character to
the influence of chile peppers, then concluded with a warning. "Doctors
counsel parsimonious use, even if it be *en nogada*, of this other enemy of the
heart, that combined with *pulque* and tortillas, serves as fuel for the untiring
machine of the proletarians and even of some who are not."[108]

Fanny Calderón de la Barca, always the trenchant observer, wrote simply,
"all national dishes [are] unfashionable, but in reality much liked by the
natives."[109] Foreigners and exiles therefore became, by default, the leading
advocates of nineteenth-century Mexican cuisine. Manuel Payno wrote his
nationalistic novel *Los bandidos de Río Frío* in Europe, just as a century earlier
the Jesuit priest Francisco Clavijero had penned a nostalgic account of
Aztec foods after his expulsion from New Spain. Payno denounced the
etiquette that forbade the consumption of corn tortillas and stuffed chiles
because of their plebeian image, obliging fashionable Mexicans to eat English *rosbif*. Moreover, the nineteenth-century's finest collection of *mole*
sauces, *La cocinera poblana*, was assembled by a Spanish immigrant, Narciso
Bassols.[110]

The Mexican Chef likewise illustrated the interest in indigenous foods
shown by outsiders. Although his devotion to Mexican nationalism was
beyond reproach, he betrayed an unmistakable European attitude toward
Indians. Not only did he give recipes for tamales, he positively exalted the
primitive delicacy of Native American cooking. Steamed tamales, like the
barbecued elephant of African Hottentots and the grilled fruits of Tahitian
islanders, reflected the "simplicity and lack of artifice" common to all "savage nations." He lamented that "civilization, in trying to purify good taste,
had deprived it in some things."[111] In contrast to such liberal authors as José
María Luis Mora, who saw the rural masses as vicious brutes, the Mexican
Chef viewed them through the Enlightenment lens of the noble savage. His
language indicates a certain distance from Mexican society that may have
resulted from prolonged exile. Perhaps the anonymous chef resembled
another New World patriot, Francisco de Miranda. The Venezuelan free-
dom fighter had traveled widely in Europe, winning the favors of the Russian Queen Catherine the Great and becoming a general in the French
revolutionary army, before returning to fight with Simón Bolívar in the
liberation of Spanish America.

This gastronomic Miranda's vision of the Mexican national cuisine
proved far too radical for his publisher, Mariano Galván Rivera. In 1834,
when the first edition had sold out, the moderate Galván revised the work
drastically. He deleted the nationalistic language, adopted the Castilian

spelling of "Méjico," and wrote a new introduction apologizing for defects in the previous edition.[112] Subsequent versions incorporated other changes; by 1841 it had become the *Nuevo cocinero mejicano* and four years later it was reorganized in dictionary form. This 1845 edition wrote tamales completely out of the national cuisine. Corn confections gradually returned to the work over the decades, but a lower-class stigma continued to mark pre-Columbian foods.[113]

One last foreign salute to Mexican cuisine came from the Austrian Archduke Maximilian. The French-imposed emperor and his consort Carlotta adopted many aspects of the native culture, including *mole*. They first tasted the national dish in the village of Acultzingo, Veracruz, and although the chiles brought tears to their eyes, they nevertheless incorporated it into their banquet menus.[114] But such gestures were not always welcomed by conservatives eager for what they considered to be the civilizing influences of European culture. The *Calendario del cocinero* (Chef's Calendar) reflected the resulting confusion among the wealthy. First published in 1865 in the wake of the archduke's arrival, it celebrated the elite taste for such cosmopolitan dishes as Flemish leg of lamb and kidneys sautéed in champagne. But when national dishes began appearing on the imperial table, the publisher revised the 1866 calendar — inserting three different *moles*, *pipían* (pumpkin-seed stew), and even tamales — in an effort to follow this unexpected fad for Mexican food.[115]

Nineteenth-century Mexicans clearly recognized their national cuisine in the forms of pre-Columbian tamales and colonial *moles*. Women continued to prepare these foods, both within sheltered domestic spaces and in boisterous street festivals. Yet male leaders proved remarkably unwilling to acknowledge such dishes as legitimate expressions of the national culture, leaving European cuisine as the standard for public banquets. Moreover, after 1900 Mexican elites, who had once dismissed maize as simple Indian fodder, began to attach a sinister new meaning to the Native American grain, considering it to be one of the greatest impediments to national development.

Provincial banquet in Oaxaca, about 1850, with the geometrically placed dishes,
numerous wine bottles, and elaborate centerpiece of European haute cuisine.
*(Instituto Nacional de Antropología e Historia)*

Mexico City street corner restaurant, about 1900, equipped with *cazuelas*,
tortilla baskets, dishes, coffee cups, and a water bucket.
*(Archivo General de la Nación)*

*Florentine Codex:* Aztec kitchen with *metate, molcajete,* and corn basket on a woven reed mat.
(*Archivo General de la Nación*)

Colonial period: Roadside restaurant serving muleteers in the Tierra Caliente.
Sexual innuendos about women grinding corn were common.
(*Instituto Nacional de Antropología e Historia*)

About 1900: The technology of this lower-class kitchen in Mexico City had not changed since the Conquest.
*(Archivo General de la Nación)*

A century later: After the revolution of mechanical corn mills and automatic tortilla machines.
*(John F. Schwaller)*

Gorditas of the Virgin of Guadalupe. Corn and brown sugar
griddlecakes for sale to pilgrims outside the
basilica of the national saint.
*(Archivo General de la Nación)*

Enchilada maker with a basket of crisp tortillas and
two different chile sauces.
*(Archivo General de la Nación)*

Flirting with cooks in a well-furnished kitchen containing a *fogón* with two burners, several *cazuelas*, a rack of wooden spoons and paddles for fanning the cooking fires, a dish cabinet, and the essential water barrel.

*(Instituto Nacional de Antropología e Historia)*

Supplying an *aguas frescas* stand, decorated with flowers like those on street corners, but exposed to nothing more boisterous than landscape paintings.

*(Instituto Nacional de Antropología e Historia)*

*FOUR*

# The Tortilla Discourse

## *Nutrition and Nation Building*

❦

Senator Francisco Bulnes delighted in his reputation as the most controversial member of the Porfirian intellectual elite. While others composed eulogies to celebrate the 1906 centennial of Benito Juárez's birth, Bulnes derided the hero of the liberal reform as a dull and incapable president. His attack on the symbol of national unity followed an equally infamous condemnation of the national character. In *El porvenir de las naciones Hispano-Americanas* (The Future of the Hispanic-American Nations), published in 1899 in the wake of the Spanish–American War, Bulnes attributed Mexico's backwardness to a combination of Iberian conservatism and Indian debility. He explained the natives' weakness, using the recently developed science of nutrition, by dividing mankind into three races: the people of corn, wheat, and rice. After some dubious calculations of the nutritional value of staple grains, he concluded that "the race of wheat is the only truly progressive one," and that "maize has been the eternal pacifier of America's indigenous races and the foundation of their refusal to become civilized."[1]

Bulnes's provocative book catapulted the tortilla to the center of elite discourse. For the next half-century, the language of nutritional science largely shaped Mexican leaders' understanding of and attempts to control social relations and cultural practices. Porfirian intellectuals considered the Indians, whom they mistakenly conflated with the largely mestizo rural population, to be one of the fundamental barriers to Mexican development because of their apparent refusal to participate in either the market economy or the national community. Unlike Creole intellectuals of the Early Republic, who saw little hope for incorporating the indigenous masses into the national life, the Porfirian elite, composed of mestizos from President

77

Díaz down, were determined to transform the seemingly idle *campesinos* into productive workers. The *científicos* (scientific party) that dominated high administrative office found nutritional explanations of Indian backwardness particularly appealing. They adhered to the European philosophy of positivism, which described human societies as biological organisms subject to evolution and decay. The language of proteins and carbohydrates offered a scientific explanation of Indian underdevelopment that did not resort to the racist, deterministic doctrines of Social Darwinism. Mestizo *científicos* rejected the idea that their Indian ancestors were inherently unfit and embraced instead the notion that maize had oppressed pre-Columbian peoples. Salvation therefore lay in the adoption of European culture, especially the consumption of wheat bread.

Nutritional explanations of economic underdevelopment persisted even after the Revolution of 1910 tempered the Porfirian faith in imported progress. As *campesino* armies roamed the countryside, positivist certainty gave way to an ideology of romantic nationalism. Manuel Gamio, the archaeologist who excavated the pyramids of Teotihuacán, denounced Bulnes as a racist, while Daniel Cosío Villegas, a leading historian, described him as "one of the most evasive, designing, and deceitful writers that Mexico has ever produced."[2] Nevertheless, revolutionary leaders shared the Porfirian dream of incorporating natives into a fundamentally European national culture, and to achieve that elusive goal they found themselves returning to the fundamental issue of nutrition. When Gamio became director of the Interamerican Indigenous Institute, he worked to replace corn with soybeans.[3]

The tortilla discourse really served as a subterfuge to divert attention away from social inequalities. When scientists from the National Institute of Nutrition finally analyzed the national diet in the 1940s, they found wheat and maize to be virtually interchangeable. Rural malnutrition resulted not from any inferiority in tortillas; instead, poverty, particularly the lack of land, made it impossible to obtain a well-balanced diet. Unfortunately, an agrarian reform that allowed *campesinos* to feed themselves represented an unacceptable answer for Mexican governments trying to achieve economic modernization. Industrial development required both cheap labor to produce goods and large markets to consume them, neither of which existed when the vast majority of the people derived a subsistence livelihood in isolated communities. But while Porfirian development meant merely cutting off Indian villages at their roots — the maize fields that fed them — revolutionary governments genuinely worked to incorporate the *campesinos* into the national community.

## Porfirian Origins

In 1901, two years after the appearance of Francisco Bulnes's study of the national malaise, Mexican audiences applauded Ignacio Altamirano's novel of national romance. The title character of *El Zarco* was an elegantly dressed, blue-eyed bandit chief who terrorized the countryside south of Mexico City. In the heart of the Zarco's domain, protected only by their widowed mother, lived two Creole sisters, the fair but vacuous Manuela and the modest, dusky Pilar. A local blacksmith, Nicolás, adored the beautiful Manuela and offered to defend her family from the bandits, but she despised him as a humble Indian and secretly desired Zarco. Her wish was sadly fulfilled, as the dashing desperado carried her off to a life of ruin, providing an implicit warning to the Porfirian elite about the seductive dangers of their foreign infatuations. Meanwhile, the hardworking Nicolás married the long-suffering Pilar and produced a mestizo family symbolic of the Mexican nation. But to consummate this national romance in real life, the native masses had to be lifted from their primitive villages and integrated into the national community.[4]

The Indians of Porfirian stereotype were stooped and indolent peasants, unlike the broad-shouldered blacksmith Nicolás or the fiercely independent Yaqui of the north. Francisco Pimentel, a student of indigenous languages, described the typical native in 1864 as "grave, taciturn, and melancholy, phlegmatic, cold, and slow, suffering, servile, and hypocritical."[5] Ezequiel Chávez, one of Mexico's leading educators, wrote in 1901 that centuries of oppression had left the Indian conservative and fatalistic. Unable to overcome the Spanish conquistadors, they turned for escape to alcohol. "But drunkenness was transitory and the burden of life constant, so the Indian either chose suicide or remained indifferent."[6] Francisco Bulnes summarized the Native American, with less existential sympathy, as "disinterested, stoic, uneducated; he cares little for life or death, work or money, science or ethics, pain or hope. He loves only four things: land, liberty, idols, and alcohol."[7]

The apparent debility of the indigenous masses had grave implications for national development at the turn of the twentieth century, when a shortage of skilled labor constituted one of the major barriers to industrialization. Recent immigrants from the countryside, accustomed to the self-made pace of agrarian society, often had great difficulty adjusting to the demands of industrial work discipline. Factory owners interpreted their resistance to time clocks and production schedules as simple laziness, and complained bitterly when they abandoned their work to return home for the harvest or to celebrate a festival.[8] Moreover, these new factory hands constituted the elite of the Mexican workforce. The vast majority of rural inhabitants seemed to have no economic ambitions at all; they constituted, in the words of geographer Alfonso Luis Velasco, "an obstacle to civilization."[9]

To explain the unproductive nature of indigenous peoples, social scientists in Europe and the United States often pointed to biological inferiority. Herbert Spencer, following Charles Darwin's theory of natural selection, imagined a universal struggle for existence in which only the fittest survived. But the conclusion that the Indians were inherently unfit and would be driven to extinction like Tasmanian aborigines did not appeal to Mexican elites. They recognized that Indians composed a substantial and permanent part of the population and looked instead for ways to redeem them, particularly through intermarriage with Europeans. Vicente Riva Palacio even suggested that Native Americans, with their lack of facial hair and wisdom teeth, had entered a higher stage of development than Europeans. Porfirian *científicos* rejected his theory, but supported the ideal of incorporating the indigenous people into the national life.[10]

European immigration offered one possible answer that would simultaneously whiten the population and relieve labor shortages. Laws passed in 1883 sought both to stimulate foreign colonization and to increase agricultural productivity by surveying vacant land — as well as Indian communal property lacking proper titles — and making it available to private investors, immigrants, or agribusiness. Mexican leaders thereby hoped with a single stroke to exploit unproductive village lands and to create a rural middle class. Esteban Maqueo Castellanos speculated that the country would be thirty times richer if it could somehow replace the eleven million Indians with an equal number of foreign immigrants, regardless of their country of origin.[11] Less racist commentators praised the policy as a way of encouraging intermarriage between Europeans and Indians, thus contributing to the growth of the mestizo nation. Ultimately, the laws failed to establish a middle class and, instead, further concentrated landholding among a small elite. Late nineteenth-century migrations benefited Argentina and the United States far more than Mexico, whose 1900 census registered only sixty thousand immigrants in a population of thirteen million.[12]

Another proposed solution to the Indian problem, inspired by both the ideals of classical liberalism and the example of Benito Juárez, lay in universal education. Justo Sierra led a campaign in the 1880s to amend the constitution to require primary education for all Mexican children. Francisco Cosmes opposed the measure on the grounds that Indians in the countryside had no need for education, and sending their children to schools would only deprive them of workers. Providing a suitable environment for education did indeed pose a problem; Ignacio Ramírez had earlier proposed establishing agrarian communes in which the Indians could be indoctrinated in Western culture. Sierra agreed that educators had to adapt their message to the special conditions of the indigenous race. Nevertheless, his insistence that universal schooling was essential to national survival and growth failed to gain passage of the measure by a Porfirian congress little concerned with improving the plight of *campesinos*.[13]

The education debate did focus attention on environmental factors responsible for the natives' supposed inferiority. Some authors such as Julio Guerrero blamed the tropical climate for Mexican languor and pined somewhat facetiously for the snows that invigorated northern Europeans. Francisco Pimentel traced their degradation back to the barbarous religions, despotic governments, and cruel education of pre-Columbian times. Additional centuries of oppression by Spanish conquistadors and hacendados contributed further to the Indian ennui, according to Ezequiel Chávez. The lack of education explained their backward state to Justo Sierra. Even Francisco Cosmes, who doubted the Indians' capacity to benefit from education, attributed their uncivilized state to environmental factors.[14]

Diet offered a natural answer to *científicos* searching for environmental causes of indigenous underdevelopment. German scientist Justus von Liebig had already defined the basic elements of modern nutrition by the 1840s, and debates over physiological effects of cuisine dated back to antiquity. Nineteenth-century moral reformers in Germany, Britain, and the United States attributed all manner of vice to improper diet. Connecticut minister Sylvester Graham began preaching in the 1830s that highly seasoned food, particularly meat, provoked dangerous bodily stimulations that could only be countered by eating coarse, whole-wheat "Graham" bread. The radical English poet Percy Shelley, meanwhile, wrote that revolutionary France could have avoided the Terror had Parisian crowds eaten less meat, and that a vegetarian Bonaparte would never have aspired to conquer Europe. But while Victorian moralists tried to smother their lustful appetites with whole-grain bread, Mexican elites sought the opposite effect, to ignite vigor in the Indian masses through the consumption of wheat.[15]

Spanish attempts to wean the natives from corn had a long and haphazard history dating back to the sixteenth-century evangelization. Mexico City poorhouses of the 1830s offered charitable meals that included wheat bread, stewed beans, and a little meat. Porfirian prison regulations required that inmates receive a diet based on wheat bread. For breakfast they ate bread and porridge, their lunch consisted of bread with rice and meat, and they finished the day with bread and beans. Not even on festival days did officials allow such popular favorites as tamales and enchiladas.[16] Cooking classes offered to girls at the Escuela de Artes y Oficios, described in the previous chapter, likewise emphasized modest European dishes instead of spicy Mexican foods. By the 1880s, Justo Sierra and other commentators had begun to suggest a link between poor nutrition and Indian debility. Dr. Samuel Morales Pereira, in an 1888 study of hygiene in Puebla, condemned all aspects of popular eating habits including the dependency on corn tortillas, the lack of pure water, and the adult diet fed to small children. Morales even attacked the national penchant for snacking, which upset the digestive routine and produced gastrointestinal disorders.[17]

Thus armed with both Mexican and European authorities, Francisco Bulnes proceeded to elaborate the tortilla discourse by blaming Indian debility on their corn-based diet. Using the nutritional classifications developed by von Liebig, Bulnes gave a minimum daily requirement of 130 grams of protein—about twice modern recommendations, but similar to contemporary standards. He then estimated that to attain this level a person would have to eat 1,400 grams of wheat bread or 2,300 grams of corn, three loaves of bread or a hefty stack of tortillas. Although the former sounds excessive, Bulnes calculated that the percentage of protein in wheat bread most closely approximated that of a mother's milk, from which he deduced that "milk is the wheat of children, and wheat the milk of adults." Two and a half kilograms of tortillas nevertheless exceeded the limits of human digestion and was fundamentally "incompatible with human life." Moreover, he observed that Europeans consumed large quantities of meat, whereas Indians ate an almost exclusively vegetarian diet. Quoting the French scientist Geoffrey Saint-Hilaire, he concluded that without meat in the diet the human brain stopped functioning and civilization became impossible.[18]

Bulnes also placed diet within the evolutionary history so essential to positivist analysis. He asserted that the great civilizations of antiquity— Egypt, Greece, Rome, and Vedic India—all grew out of wheat fields. The corn-fed Aztec and Inca empires "appeared powerful, but [were] in fact so weak as to fall victim to insignificant bands of Spanish *bandoleros*." Similar faulty logic explained the success of British imperialism in Asia (against rice eaters) and Ireland (potatoes). Nutritional problems continued to the present and accounted for the inability of natives to perform industrial work. In a crude comparison of coffee harvests in Veracruz and Brazil, Mexican workers averaged one-third the productivity achieved by African slaves before their emancipation in 1888. The Indians came off even more unfavorably when contrasted with European factory workers. Bulnes argued most controversially that generations of malnutrition had "mineralized" the indigenous people, "inclined them to the immutability of rocks," and prevented any hope of future progress.[19]

Bulnes became quite notorious for his theories, particularly for maintaining that maize had left an irrevocable stigma on the entire Indian race. A review in the *Revista Positiva* cited Benito Juárez and Ignacio Altamirano as proof that the people of corn could rise above their humble village life. The newspaper *El Imparcial* agreed generally with the nutritional assessment of the natives, but insisted that their problems could be solved if maize were balanced with other foods such as beans.[20] Moreover, Bulnes often borrowed inconsistently from his scientific authorities. He cited the work of Geoffrey Saint-Hilaire in support of a carnivorous diet, yet attributed European superiority to wheat bread. Victorians, on the other hand, believed that wheat actually helped calm the stimulations caused by eating meat. But techniques for studying nutrition remained primitive throughout the century, and Bulnes derived his claims more from cultural prejudice than experimental data.[21]

While doubts remained about the full implications of the theory, nutritional arguments became a recurrent theme in elite discourse. Authors such as Francisco Flores and Esteban Maqueo Castellanos attributed the lack of industrial spirit among the indigenous peoples to their poor living conditions and diet.[22] In an attempt to measure scientifically the underdevelopment of Mexican youth, the Education Ministry began a program of anthropometric measurements. The initial results proved disturbing, because middle-class school children in Mexico City were shorter than those in the United States. Experimenters quickly realized that they would have to adjust their standards, but despite this lesson in cultural relativity, they expressed concern when poor children did not measure up to Mexican middle-class ideals.[23]

Even more dreadful to the Porfirian elite was the threat to public order posed by popular cooking. In the countryside poor diets led to nothing more serious than indolence, but in the cities the lack of adequate nutrition provoked deviant behavior, lawlessness, and alcoholism. Sociologist Julio Guerrero described, with lurid detail, the filthy living conditions of the urban poor and their "abominable" foods, such as mosquito larvae and tamales filled with unboned fish. To fill their stomachs, they turned to a life of crime. Moreover, the nutritious drink *pulque* composed an important part of the lower-class diet. Justo Sierra called alcoholism the "evil of the century," and a 1902 study by Demetrio Sodi described a direct relationship between crime levels and the quantity of *pulque* sold in Mexico City. Guerrero explicitly advised the lower classes to "shun the pleasures of the table and reduce themselves to a hygienic diet."[24]

The supposed nutritional inferiority of corn gained a prominent place in elite discourse because it fit within the dominant *científico* mentality. The language of carbohydrates and proteins appealed to positivists seeking objective, biological explanations for social phenomena. And unlike the Social Darwinism of Spencer, in which natural laws judged individuals and races without appeal, nutritional deficiencies could be corrected through human intervention. The deterministic nature of "survival of the fittest" was unacceptable to Mexican intellectuals, who, except perhaps for Bulnes and Cosmes, had a liberal faith in the efficacy of human agency. Finally, racial explanations had inherent limits in Mexico because the *científicos* were almost entirely of mestizo birth. The Porfirian Persuasion, the *fin de siècle* faith in imported progress, derived from an unstated premise that culture, not race, determined modernity. One did not have to be born a European, it was sufficient to act like one, dress like one, and eat like one.[25]

Nevertheless, the vast majority of Mexicans had little desire to act, dress, or eat like a European, much less be one. Indeed, that was the fundamental problem confronting Porfirian elites: the rural masses and even many urban dwellers did not always share their dreams of modernity. It is therefore necessary to examine the degree to which Bulnes and his fellows succeeded in spreading the tortilla discourse to the popular sectors.

## Diffusion and Dissent

The hegemonic value of any discourse ultimately depends on the extent of its popular acceptance. For elites to rule by consensus instead of force, they must convince the people that their objectives are valid and their authority is legitimate. Moreover, they must convey such messages in a language meaningful to the intended audience. Mexican rulers had great difficulty communicating their developmentalist ideology directly to the rural masses, who often had little appreciation for the benefits of railroads and factories, work discipline and bourgeois values. The tortilla discourse, by contrast, provided easily understood and widely accepted symbols. Its propaganda value lay not in the nutritional language and evolutionary analogies that *científicos* found so persuasive, but rather in the associations between Europeans and wheat on the one hand, and Indians and maize on the other.

Attempts by Porfirian leaders to spread the cultivation and consumption of wheat as a step toward assimilating *campesinos* into the dominant culture met with some success, but also inspired a subversive counterdiscourse.

Formulations of the tortilla discourse revealed a profound ignorance about the variety of Mexican rural life; nevertheless, they drew upon a genuine association between corn and identity. Many urban elites conceived of the countryside as populated by undifferentiated masses of indigenous peoples, although many aspects of mestizo culture had penetrated even Native American communities. Moreover, contrary to the stereotype of *campesinos* as ignorant of and apathetic toward life outside their village, most participated in regional markets and displayed great curiosity about mestizo society. Many had traveled great distances on religious pilgrimages and government petitions. Yet the tortilla discourse did recognize the deep significance of maize, both as subsistence crop and as a source of identity. As a newspaper observed in 1877, heavy rains rotted local wheat crops and caused a grave situation "principally for the priest and government minister, who like their wheat bread good and hot."[26]

Moreover, the goal of incorporating *campesinos* into the national life contained more rhetoric than reality. Justo Sierra's oratorical triumphs promoting universal primary education did not translate into the budgets needed to achieve that dream. The first federal law promoting rural education passed congress on May 30, 1911, shortly after Díaz's resignation. Railroad construction perhaps best illustrated the reality of late nineteenth-century rural modernization programs. The Díaz administration reported the ever-expanding track mileage as proof of economic growth, but rather than unifying the country to create genuine development, the new railroads served mainly to facilitate raw material exports to Europe and the United States.[27] In the case of wheat, although Porfirian agricultural experts emphasized the need for increased production, from 1892 to 1907 yields grew a modest 5 percent per capita. Some of this crop remained in rural areas, as bakeries opened in small mestizo towns such as San José de Gracia, Michoacán, but the majority of the harvests went to satisfy growing urban markets.[28]

Elite developmentalist ideology had its greatest impact in the cities, where positivist ideas dominated the popular press. Mexico City's leading daily, *El Imparcial*, enthusiastically promoted the tortilla discourse. In 1898, the editors quoted a prediction of future wheat shortages in Europe and explored possible solutions. Perhaps Europeans could eat bananas or tortillas, they mused briefly before rejecting these thoughts as absurd. They concluded decisively that wheat was the food of the civilized world. A year later they pointed to the spread of wheat as a measure of civilization's advance. *El Colono*, in a discussion of the low productivity of Mexican agricultural workers, described Indians as capable of planting corn and beans, but virtually useless for growing cash crops. *El Imparcial* likewise decried the low productivity of Indian farm workers and reaffirmed the belief that corn was unfit for human consumption. *El Economista Mexicana* stated that "inflexible laws" had condemned the country's Indians to a state of perpetual melancholy as a result of hard work and hunger.[29]

The Mexican middle class shared *El Imparcial*'s reverence for wheat, but whether they accepted the paper's nutritional judgment of corn remains uncertain. Vicenta Torres de Rubio, in her manual of Michoacán cookery, referred to wheat as "the first of the cereals," and she even believed "that precious grain" provided an indication of Divine Providence, for "having conceded to humanity such a delicate and noble fruit as wheat." While less effusive about corn, she did accept it at the table.[30] A Monterrey newspaper carried an advertisement stating: "Some people may be satisfied with tortillas, but if you really want to enjoy living order your groceries and wines from the American Grocery Store."[31] The persuasiveness of such ads on Mexican audiences seems questionable; indeed, they may even have proved counterproductive by inspiring associations between corn and nationalism. In any event, the tortilla discourse attempted not so much to eliminate maize from middle-class diets as to spread a taste for wheat among working-class consumers.

Modern consumer goods held a seductive allure for many urban industrial workers. William French has shown that some miners in Chihuahua spent their leisure time adopting many aspects of middle-class culture such as wearing starched collars and attending the theater in order to assert a form of social equality with their employers. Mexican workers also began eating more wheat, either bread or the increasingly common soda cracker. Although workers provided sorely needed markets for Mexican manufactures, members of the middle class often took offense at their presumption of equality. This unease resulted in part from the laborers' habit of carrying elements of popular culture into middle-class society — for example, whistling in the theater as they did in the bullring.[32]

The spread of wheat also resulted in new mixtures between European and native cuisines. It may have been some unknown Porfirian taco vendor who created the most popular use of bread in modern Mexico, the *torta compuesta*. The typical recipe for this now ubiquitous sandwich — cold cuts or hot pork or chicken along with beans, cheese, avocado slices, and pickled chiles, all stuffed into a *bolillo* roll—hints at the substitution of bread for tortillas in urban street food. The origin of the *torta compuesta*, like that of *mole poblano*, has passed into legend, but it is possible that the Mexican sandwich became common as wheat consumption spread about the turn of the century. Artemio del Valle Arizpe found perhaps the first references to *torta* vendors in Porfirian Mexico City. A *tortero* appeared as a character in the 1899 play "Las Luces de los Angeles" (The Lights of the Angels), and José Vasconcelos recalled serving *tortas* of chicken and sardines at a student party about the same time.[33] In 1902, the Health Board took notice of the possible hazards of unsanitary ingredients used in the *torta compuesta*. Scientists stated that "for some time and increasing every day," street vendors had been constructing stands to sell these sandwiches to workers and poor families.[34]

The growing popularity of the *torta* notwithstanding, some Mexicans began questioning the superiority of wheat and the ideals of consumer society in general. One of the first challenges to the emerging hegemony of Porfirian patriotism and bourgeois values appeared in 1894 in the workers' newspaper, *El Obrero Mexicano*: "It is time for our citizens to put their own interests before the music of parades, put the country before Bengal rockets, do some thinking instead of eating Salvatierra crackers."[35] Labor syndicalism grew rapidly in the next two decades, particularly in Mexico City bakeries, but their demands remained within the middle-class framework of higher wages and better conditions.[36] The most articulate response to the tortilla discourse appeared in the work of Andrés Molina Enríquez, a liberal intellectual and fervent nationalist. He considered mestizos to be the true representatives of the Mexican nation, and observed that "maize constituted the principal base of their daily diet, and represented in an absolutely indubitable manner the national cuisine."[37]

Molina Enríquez refuted assertions of wheat's superiority, and pointed to the true nature of Mexico's rural problems. First, he divided Mexican diets into three cumulative levels. The absolute poorest ate simply maize, salt, and water; when possible the Indians complemented their diet with chiles and *pulque*; finally, at the highest level Mexicans added meat, bread, and other foods to these basic staples. The simple diet of tortillas alone had sufficed for Indians and mestizos to carry heavy burdens as tirelessly as a horse and to fight bravely in the Wars of Independence and the Reform. Molina Enríquez instead blamed the national problems on the unequal distribution of land, which impeded economic development at the same time that it prevented Mexicans from consuming a more rounded diet. In calling for agrarian reform, he became one of the leading prophets of the Revolution of 1910.[38]


## Revolutionary Nationalism

The largely exclusionist policies of the Porfirian government — denying the middle class an effective vote and alienating the rural masses from their village lands — precipitated a decade-long social revolution. Beginning in 1910, *campesinos* rose up in arms, toppled the Díaz regime, and demanded the return of lands lost to large estates and survey companies. The military initiative of the peasantry notwithstanding, leadership of the movement fell to middle-class adherents of Porfirian developmentalist ideology. These generals, who dominated Mexican politics throughout the 1920s and 1930s, sought to continue many of Díaz's policies. They nevertheless derived legitimacy from service in the revolution, so they had to balance agricultural and industrial modernization with agrarian and labor reforms embodied in a revolutionary constitution of 1917. To facilitate these compromises, they sought to forge an inclusionist national identity incorporating *campesinos* as supporters for the new regime.

Three decades of revolutionary struggle contributed enormously to the growth of national unity. Frederick C. Turner, in his classic study *The Dynamics of Mexican Nationalism*, considered the revolution to be the crucible of social cohesion and political consensus in modern Mexico. In purging the Porfirian temple, revolutionary prophets cast out the sources of nineteenth-century disunity, regional parochialism, ethnic hatred, and class conflict. Military campaigns dragged *campesinos* out of their villages and united them in a revolutionary esprit de corps with people from distant parts of the republic. Local loyalties thus gave way to a sense of national community. And their patriotic service, in turn, forced governments to replace the exclusionist nineteenth-century image of a Creole nation with an inclusionist policy of *indigenismo* embracing the Indian as a vital source of Mexican culture. Organized labor likewise joined the fighting with "Red Battalions," and trade unions received recognition by the Constitution of 1917 and status within the official party. Yet while the revolution may have contributed to nationalist sentiment, Turner's conclusions about Mexican social and political consensus remain questionable. He had the misfortune to publish in 1968, the year that a massacre of hundreds of students at the Tlatelolco Plaza in Mexico City gravely undermined the vision of national unity.[39]

Revolutionary administrations certainly tried to foment such political and social consensus as a means of consolidating their power and modernizing the country. They sought nothing less than the complete transformation of *campesinos* into new revolutionary citizens. President Alvaro Obregón initiated a massive program of rural schools, in 1921, to teach the Spanish language and Mexican patriotism. His successor, Plutarco Elías Calles, carried this project to its furthest extreme, attacking the traditional culture of the countryside, and in particular the Catholic Church. A rabid anticlerical, he closed cathedrals, expelled priests, and hoped to eradicate the faith entirely, transferring Mexican loyalties from church to nation.[40] Even President Lázaro Cárdenas's expropriation of foreign oil companies in 1938, the defining moment of revolutionary nationalism, was largely motivated by domestic political calculation. Historian Friedrich Schuler has shown that in 1937 the Mexican government stood on the brink of bankruptcy as a result of expensive development programs. The oil expropriation promised to help finance further modernization at the same time that it allowed Cárdenas to blame the country's economic difficulties on foreigners.[41]

But revolutionary attempts at social engineering failed to overcome widespread popular resistance. Calles's anticlerical campaign provoked a Catholic guerrilla insurgency, the Cristero Rebellion (1926–1929). Although the fighting concentrated in the conservative heartland of central western Mexico, opposition to government iconoclasm extended all the way to the president's home state of Sonora. By the late 1930s, Calles had gone into exile and his red and black banners had given way to the traditional symbol of Mexican nationalism, the Virgin of Guadalupe.[42] The revolutionary government had more success at instilling nationalism through its rural education campaigns, yet even here disparities remained between the message sent from Mexico City and that received in remote communities.

## Educational Missions

José Vasconcelos, Minister of Education from 1921 to 1924, built Mexico's rural schooling program on the inspiration of sixteenth-century Spanish missionaries. He believed that friars had revolutionized pre-Columbian material culture by teaching advanced European agricultural and mechanical skills. Their educational success he attributed to spiritual zeal that made manual skills secondary to the goal of converting the Indians to Catholicism. According to Vasconcelos, twentieth-century Indians needed a similar evangelical program to overcome their primitive conditions. And like the Spanish friars, these modern missionaries needed a "religion," a source of enthusiasm that could only come from patriotism. Successive revolutionary governments pursued this goal of incorporating Indians into the national life, teaching them the accepted patterns of modern Mexican society, including the Spanish language, the capitalist work ethic, and the cuisine of wheat.

These objectives coincided with developmentalist programs of the Porfiriato; nevertheless, a decade of conflict — the First World War as well as the Mexican Revolution — had discredited Europe as a cultural model. Revolutionary governments adopted, instead, an ideology of *indigenismo* exalting Indians as important members of the nation. Manuel Gamio formulated the basis of this ideology in 1916, in his book *Forjando patria* (Forging the Fatherland), which proclaimed the goals of racial fusion, cultural convergence, linguistic unification, and economic equality. But unlike the Porfirian ideal of a mestizo in European clothes, Gamio recognized Native American contributions to the national culture. His archaeological work at Teotihuacán not only revived pre-Columbian monuments; it also paid tribute to living Indians by fomenting handicraft industries, although many of these had been introduced by Spanish missionaries. The mural renaissance, meanwhile, sought to infuse this popular aesthetic in new monuments exalting the revolutionary government. The masterpieces of Diego Rivera, José Clemente Orozco, and David Alfredo Siquieros featured prominent images of maize, and conflated the Indian heritage and revolutionary martyrs with Mexican nationalism.[43]

These cultural beacons notwithstanding, the practical challenge remained of disseminating this national vision and modernizing rural Mexico. Teachers entering the countryside were astonished by the magnitude of the problem before them. The 1921 census recorded more than 70 percent of Mexicans as illiterate, and 10 percent unable to speak Spanish.[44] Material poverty further precluded hope for change. Missionaries found villagers crowded into one-room adobe huts without plumbing or lighting. The door provided the only source of ventilation, and cooking fires filled the room with smoke that suffocated visitors, although village women ignored it with "marvelous forbearance." Moreover, the people lived at a bare subsistence level, eating a "terrible" diet of tortillas, *frijoles*, and chiles.[45]

Educational programs evolved over the span of two decades, but the underlying goals of improving material conditions and instilling national values remained constant. In 1921, Vasconcelos began recruiting missionary teachers to travel from one isolated village to the next building the first schools, called the *Casa del Pueblo* (House of the People or Nation). These modern-day apostles taught not only reading, writing, and arithmetic, but also agriculture, industry, and hygiene. By the time Vasconcelos resigned in 1924, they had built more than a thousand schools. The Calles administration likewise placed great emphasis on rural education, and four years later some four thousand new schools had opened throughout the nation, enrolling 250,000 children. To provide teachers for the growing number of students, the Ministry also created a series of Normal Schools. At the same time, traveling missions were expanded to include agricultural engineers, medical doctors, and social workers to provide remote villages with a crash course in modernization. Progress nevertheless came slowly, and in 1934 President Cárdenas implemented a prominent but controversial program of socialist education. Perhaps the greatest trouble arose over the inclusion of sex education in the curriculum, and by the end of his administration the program had been phased out.[46]

These rural schools took a broad cultural approach to instill national values. The first teachers immersed themselves in village life, encouraging community suppers, patriotic festivals, and family celebrations. Cuisine represented a fundamental aspect of this modernization program, reflecting the continued influence of the Porfirian tortilla discourse on revolutionary thought. Manuel Gamio, the father of *indigenismo*, agreed with Justo Sierra that rural backwardness resulted from poor diet and lack of education. Gamio considered soybeans the answer to dietary deficiencies, but others followed Bulnes in advocating wheat. One doctor, writing in *El Universal*, denounced the Mexican diet as the worst in the world and recommended educational campaigns to substitute wheat for corn. Another critic of the tortilla reiterated the Porfirian belief that malnutrition led to alcoholism.[47] Census officials in 1940 designated eating tortillas as one of the basic markers of poverty and backwardness. José Vasconcelos wrote that Mexicans would remain underdeveloped until they abandoned maize and adopted wheat. Rafael Ramírez, the director of rural education, explicitly demanded "that children not only learn the Spanish language, but also acquire our customs and lifestyles, which are unquestionably superior to theirs. They must know that Indians call us the *gente de razón* (people of reason) not only because we speak Spanish, but because we dress and eat differently."[48]

The Ministry of Education modeled many of its rural nutrition campaigns on programs that had originated in Mexico City. Perhaps the most basic and useful practice of all, providing free breakfasts to poor children, started in 1921 with voluntary contributions from professors at the National University. The government immediately assumed the costs of this program and soon provided breakfasts of bread, beans, and coffee with milk to more than three thousand students. Rural teachers with the resources to provide breakfasts witnessed a radical change in their young students, who stopped sleeping in class and became eager and attentive.[49] Radio broadcasts provided another means for fomenting a national cuisine. Clementina Cerrilla and Stella de Gamboa, home economics teachers in Mexico City, featured urban middle-class cuisine in cooking shows in the 1920s and 1930s, but failed to reach a broad rural audience simply because at that early date few villages had radios.[50]

Educational missions provided more direct means of inculcating these middle-class dietary goals in the countryside. Social workers' standard reports to headquarters specifically listed the number of bread recipes they had taught to rural women. Rural schools also received instructions for pasta manufacturing, so *campesinos* could eat macaroni and cheese. In extreme cases, the Education Ministry responded to instructors' urgent requests for the primary elements of civilization: aluminum casseroles went by express shipment to Tamatan, Tamaulipas; soup spoons to Champusco, Puebla; and dessert plates to Jalpa de Méndez, Tabasco.[51] While social workers instructed women on modern cooking techniques, agronomists taught men how to cultivate wheat. This campaign to replace corn with wheat reached its high point in the late 1930s, during the Cárdenas administration, which appears less ironic given the agrarian reformers' insistence that *ejidos* produce for sale to markets instead of for local consumption.[52]

The dedication of rural teachers notwithstanding, *campesinos* often resisted these efforts to transform their lifestyles. Even with higher incomes made possible by land reform, many people ignored teachers who advised them to abandon their adobe huts and build concrete block houses. They also retained their sandals and hammocks, better adapted to tropical climates than European shoes and beds. Bread making represented simply one more impractical suggestion to women already skilled in making tortillas and lacking the ovens necessary for baking. One discouraged field worker exclaimed that Mexico needed a "dictatorship" of rural education.[53] Yet after two decades, rural education had yielded significant benefits as well. By 1940 five million Mexicans had learned to read and hundreds of thousands who had spoken only an Indian language had become bilingual in Spanish. Thousands of communities had likewise acquired new schools and higher incomes.[54]

Moreover, consumption of wheat bread rose dramatically over the same period as urban values and consumption patterns spread through the countryside. In 1940, in the first national census to record dietary preferences, 45 percent of all Mexicans ate wheat bread at least occasionally, and a decade later 55 percent of the population reported eating it on a daily basis. The village of Tepoztlán, Morelos, demonstrated the suddenness with which this change often occurred. Only 30 percent claimed to eat bread regularly in the 1940 census, but within three years virtually everyone ate it at least once or twice a month, and it had become a favorite food among small children.[55] Yet the increased consumption of bread along with other manufactured goods reflected rising incomes and market penetration at least as much as the success of government education. And even as the tortilla discourse achieved its purpose, advances in nutritional science undermined its validity.

## Nutritional Science and the Tortilla Discourse

Francisco Bulnes's pseudo-scientific writings held enormous appeal for Mexican elites seeking to modernize their society, yet ultimately scientific progress discredited his speculations. When the government finally funded a National Institute of Nutrition in the 1940s, researchers announced the basic nutritional equivalence of wheat and corn. But by this point individual dietary preference was irrelevant; Mexico had launched itself inexorably on the path from isolated subsistence communities to urban industrializing nation. Once in the supermarket of modern life, it mattered little whether consumers filled their shopping carts with wheat bread or corn tortillas.

The concern demonstrated by turn-of-the-century Mexican elites about the social consequences of the tortilla may appear more comprehensible when compared with contemporary efforts in the United States to equate diet and national identity. Catharine Beecher founded the science of home economics, in the 1870s, on the premise that economy and nutrition should conquer rather than complement taste. Her successor, Ellen Richards, and chemist Wilbur Atwater established demonstration kitchens in Boston, in the 1890s, to teach working-class women to prepare affordable New England cookery. The program failed for lack of interest, but the ideal of bland chowders, baked beans, and white sauces as the national cuisine of the United States continued to guide nutritional reformers. New York City social workers, appalled by the spicy, "garlicky" foods of Eastern European and Italian immigrants, considered dietary change an essential element of "Americanization." Many believed the newcomers would never accept the social and political values of the United States until they abandoned the lifestyles and eating habits of the old country. One social worker described an Italian family as "still eating spaghetti, not yet assimilated."[56]

Moreover, the uncertain nature of nutritional science in the first half of the twentieth century prompted conflicting reports and exaggerated claims. Daily allowances of protein, for example, varied from 120 grams recommended by Wilbur Atwater to less than 45 consumed by food faddist Horace Fletcher—who, incidentally, came much closer to modern guidelines than the scientist. Early attempts to determine uniform standards also produced malnutrition scares, such as in New York City beginning about 1907, when anthropometric comparisons revealed immigrant Jewish and Italian children to be shorter than their native-born middle-class peers. The discovery of vitamins in the 1910s and 1920s led to further uncertainty, for while their absence led to diseases such as pellagra, scurvy, and rickets, no one could measure either nutritional requirements or levels in foods. The extent of the confusion became evident at the outbreak of World War II, when the United States government rejected one in four recruits as malnourished, and fed soldiers as much as five kilograms of food daily. These questions have not been resolved definitely even today, as debate continues over proper dietary intake.[57]

Serious research of Mexican diets started only in the 1930s and proceeded slowly for lack of adequate support. In 1939, Alfredo Ramos Espinosa published a pioneering study based on years of experience in treating malnourished children as well as on controlled experiments feeding chile peppers to laboratory rats. Although providing the first sound estimates of the vitamins and minerals contained in tortillas and other Mexican foods, Ramos Espinosa's primitive equipment could not give the accurate nutritional measures needed to define a balanced diet.[58] President Cárdenas had recognized the need for federal nutrition programs in a 1936 decree establishing the National Nutrition Commission as part of the Ministry of Health. Nevertheless, the committee's work remained limited to handing out informational leaflets and giving a few public lectures. Laboratory analysis did not begin until 1942, when the government funded a permanent Institute of Nutrition under the direction of Francisco de Paula Miranda. Even with this new budget, the Institute could not afford more than one full-time researcher in addition to Miranda, nor could it offer financial aid to train other investigators.[59]

Philanthropic organizations from the United States proved invaluable in supporting, without subordinating, early nutritional campaigns in Mexico. Beginning in 1942, the Rockefeller Foundation sent, first, William D. Robinson and, later, Richmond K. Anderson to Mexico, while the Kellogg

Foundation supported work by Robert S. Harris. The scientists hoped to identify and treat Mexican vitamin deficiency diseases, especially pellagra resulting from a shortage of niacin (vitamin B3) associated with inadequate maize diets. Pellagra had devastated poor farmers in the Deep South, who often had little to eat besides cornmeal, until the 1930s when doctors learned to treat it with vitamin supplements. In Mexico, by contrast, few cases of the disease appeared because the technique of soaking corn in mineral lime freed much of the bound niacin. Rockefeller scientists found even the poorest *campesinos* to have only subclinical symptoms of the disease, and in 1945 they moved on to treat more serious problems in famine-stricken Asia. The Foundation nevertheless contributed greatly by training and equipping Mexicans to study and treat their own particular nutritional deficiencies. Rockefeller fellowships supported the education of a generation of nutritionists including José Calvo de la Torre, who succeeded Miranda in 1951 as head of the Nutrition Institute.[60]

The process of surveying the Mexican people to determine their nutritional strengths and weaknesses continued for several decades. The Institute of Nutrition received its first test subjects in the form of army recruits shortly after Mexico declared war on the Axis powers in May 1942. Miranda, sharing the concern about undernourished soldiers, devised a special protein and vitamin-rich military diet, although in practice United States soldiers ate far more meat than their Mexican — or British — allies. Rockefeller scientist William Robinson extended the nutritional surveys later that year to include civilians in the Mexico City suburb of Tacuba. The volcanic eruption of Paracutín on April 1, 1943, determined the choice of a rural survey location, as both Miranda and Robinson rushed to the Mezquital Valley of Hidalgo to deliver emergency assistance and examine the tongues of Otomí Indian refugees. Calvo conducted a rural dietary survey four years later in the village of Chimalpa, near Cuernavaca, Morelos.[61]

Studies of Mexican diets produced their first significant results by demonstrating the basic value of maize, beans, and chiles. The pre-Columbian dietary complex, so long scorned by laymen and experts, did indeed provide adequate amounts of all essential nutrients. The complementary proteins of maize and beans, each of which provided amino acids lacking in the other, came as a particular surprise to researchers. Miranda wrote that "the superiority of wheat over maize is not as great as was supposed," while Robinson concluded that "diets of tortillas, beans, and chiles may be much more satisfactory than has hitherto been believed."[62] As this knowledge spread, maize appeared to be a more acceptable basis for the national cuisine, and the Mexican government changed its nutritional goals from replacing corn to supplementing it. An Education Ministry publication admitted, in 1947, that "it would be truly stupid to try to substitute beans and corn with equivalent foods. The important thing is to complement them with vegetables, salads, and fruits."[63]

Although Bulnes's calculations had been definitively refuted, rural Mexican diets remained far from ideal. Surveys by both the Mexican Institute of Nutrition and the Rockefeller Foundation encountered large numbers of subclinical deficiencies. Chile peppers might have satisfied the requirements of vitamin A, but low quantities of dietary fat — usually limited to small amounts of lard in the bean pot and an occasional avocado — prevented full utilization of the vitamin. As a result, the researchers found cases of inflammation of the membranes lining the eyes. The scattered practice of washing corn dough before making tortillas reduced the intake of vitamin B, producing occasional pellagra symptoms, and may also have contributed to anemia. Nutritional deficiencies took their worst toll among nursing mothers and young children. Surveys taken in Chiapas in the 1960s found children receiving only about 70 percent of recommended levels of protein. This deficiency not only stunted development; it also weakened immune systems and thus contributed to the spread of dysentery, a leading killer of Mexican children.[64]

Dietary problems predominated around the plantations of southern Mexico, precisely those areas where Porfirians had lamented the low productivity of agricultural workers. By 1910, Yucatán had become a virtual henequen plantation, with three-fourths of the population working in slavelike conditions to produce binding twine to sell to the International Harvester Company. Large numbers of peasants, most notably the Yaqui Indians of Sonora, were meanwhile driven out of their villages to grow cotton and tobacco in Oaxaca and Chiapas. Workers had only the most miserable rations as planters devoted all available land and labor to cash crops, and mortality rates from overwork and starvation were correspondingly high.[65] By contrast, free peasants could support themselves on even the poorest land, as the Otomí Indians demonstrated in the Mezquital. Although they inhabited land too arid for cultivating maize, and had to cure and sell *pulque* to buy corn for making tortillas, they nevertheless met their basic nutritional requirements by gathering and consuming every edible plant in the region.[66] The tortilla discourse thus achieved its most insidious effect by shifting debate away from the question of land reform, which could actually benefit *campesinos* nutritionally, and directing it toward a dietary change that promised only to make them dependent on markets without offering corresponding nutritional gains.

Mexican nutritional discourse, both Porfirian and revolutionary, sought not to fill the countryside with plump, contented peasants; instead, it aimed to support development programs by making those rural workers a productive part of the market economy. Even radical agrarian reformers and *indigenista* champions saw the *ejido* as a means of increasing rural production and financing urban industrialization. The tortilla discourse correctly recognized maize as the root of self-supporting communal life, and thus a barrier to modernization, although for cultural rather than nutritional reasons. Nevertheless, the ultimate incorporation of peasants into the national economy came not through the elimination of corn, but rather through its commodification. Once maize had changed from subsistence crop to market commodity, *campesinos* had no choice but to follow it into the modern world.

FIVE

# Replacing the Aztec Blender

## *The Modernization of Popular Cuisine*

❧

As dusk settled over the adobe schoolhouse, nineteen women sat awkwardly on benches built for their children. They had gathered that evening in the spring of 1936 to form the Women's Anticlerical and Anti-Alcohol League for the Rancho of Las Canoas near Lake Pátzcuaro, Michoacán. Delfina Jazo, president of the association, led the work of drafting a petition to a fellow native of Michoacán, General Lázaro Cárdenas, president of the republic. The women respectfully asked for help to obtain a mechanical mill to grind corn for making tortillas, and in this way to liberate them from the "bitter, black stone with three feet called the *metate*."[1]

Replacing the "Aztec blender," as the *metate* came to be called, with a mechanical mill freed rural women from a grueling daily chore and came to represent for many the emancipating dream of the Mexican Revolution. But realizing this dream entailed a host of other changes, as the women of Las Canoas acknowledged when they formed an anticlerical association to petition for a food processing appliance. Indeed, the revolution transformed Mexico far more profoundly than most insurgents had imagined when they took up arms in 1910. Just as agrarian reform undermined village independence by incorporating local *campesino* leagues into national political parties, the arrival of corn mills increased peasant households' exposure to market forces. Tortilla mechanization therefore helped incorporate peasants into the national economy, an ironic twist of the tortilla discourse, which had pursued the same goal by eradicating maize.

A number of technological and commercial advances contributed to the twentieth-century commodification of corn. Mexican engineers invented corn mills and tortilla machines, which automated the traditional female

99

duties of grinding and cooking. Agronomists, meanwhile, applied genetics and chemistry to produce high-yield varieties of corn along with fertilizers and pesticides, boosting crop yields and allowing large agribusinesses to displace small farmers. These innovations culminated in the creation of dehydrated tortilla flour; simply pour it into a machine, the Maseca model T-600, add water, and without further intervention from human hands, out come tortillas. Simultaneous developments in mass marketing encouraged the distribution of manufactured tortillas, along with a host of other processed foods, to even the most remote communities. By the late twentieth century, the high point of the business week for rural store owners had become the arrival of the soft drink and snack candy delivery truck. Mass production thus contributed to the standardization, if not the improvement, of Mexican diets.

Nevertheless, these changes did not mean the total annihilation of traditional peasant cooking by industrial processed foods. No simple opposition can be made between the two, for even the seemingly primordial *metates* used in remote Indian communities were in fact a form of technology. *Campesinos* rationally evaluated the implications of modernization, accepting those innovations that seemed advantageous while rejecting others that did not fit their society and culture. Instead of regarding peasants as inherently conservative, it is more useful to examine the process of culinary change within social, economic, and cultural contexts.

## Tortilla Technology

The tortilla discourse represented a comprehensive examination of the significance of maize in Mexican society. At the same time that Francisco Bulnes warned of the dire consequences of tortilla consumption, Luis de la Rosa considered the economic inefficiencies of production. He calculated that if 8 tortillas weighed 1.5 pounds, and 24 pounds fed 16 people, and 5,000,000 people ate tortillas, then by the laws of algebra, "312,500 robust and strong women were destined to make tortillas every day, [performing] in 365 days 115,062,500 tasks."[2] Such numbers sent Porfirian minds racing. Hundreds of thousands of robust and strong women were needlessly withdrawn from the industrial workforce while a potential market for mass-produced tortillas surpassed a hundred million in annual sales. Even as political leaders hoped to eliminate the tortilla from Mexican diets, entrepreneurs aspired to make fortunes off its mechanization. Nevertheless, it took decades for Mexican inventors to automate the skills of the *tortillera*, a tribute to the subtlety of tortilla making and to its significance in domestic culture.

The traditional techniques of tortilla making reflected the "hard but sure" nature of Mexican *campesino* kitchens. Twentieth-century anthropologists found that a woman cooking for a large family typically spent the entire morning, five or six hours, making tortillas. Work began the night before, when she simmered the corn in a solution of mineral lime to make *nixtamal*. The woman arose before dawn to grind the corn on the *metate* into a dough called *masa*. Immediately before each meal, she deftly patted the dough into flat, round tortillas and cooked them briefly over the *comal*. Tortillas could not be saved for the following day, or even the next meal, because they became hard and inedible in a few hours. The dough likewise would not keep more than a day before it began to ferment. So each morning she returned to the stone on hands and knees, with back sloped as if she herself were a *metate* wielded by some tyrannical maize goddess.[3]

Patting tortillas into shape required as much finesse as grinding required strength. The cook began by rolling the moist dough into balls called *testales*, about the size of a golf ball for an average tortilla. She then slapped one of these gently between her hands, flattening it out, and rotating to achieve a round shape. Success in this endeavor depended on the consistency of the dough; if it were too dry the edges of the tortilla cracked, while a tortilla that was too moist stuck to the hands. Even at the ideal consistency, the dough tended to stick, and could only be removed by scraping it off and starting over. Moreover, inexperienced persons, trying to keep the tortilla light on the fingers, usually sent it flying across the kitchen like a frisbee. Skilled hands could nevertheless mold — in about thirty-three pats — a perfectly round tortilla, ready for the *comal*.[4]

Cooking the tortilla, like patting it out, required a practiced hand and a careful eye. First, the *comal* had to be heated to the temperature of a clothes iron, hot enough to sizzle a drop of water, but not so hot as to burn the tortillas before they had cooked through. The cook gave a final pat to a tortilla, and with it resting lightly on her fingers, palm up and just above the griddle, she smoothly slid her hand out from underneath. The tortilla had to be slid into place, not dropped, for any trapped air would create cool spots and prevent a thorough cooking. A deft touch was also essential to avoid embarrassing creases and folds. The tortilla began to dry at the edges after about thirty seconds, whereupon the cook peeled it off the *comal*, quickly, to avoid burning her fingers, and flipped it onto the other side to cook for another minute. After the second turn, if all went well, water in the dough would turn to steam causing the tortilla to inflate suddenly. Reluctant tortillas could sometimes be tickled into puffing up, but if they stayed flat the surface would burn before the interior cooked properly. The cook made a few more quick turns to assure that both sides had a nice brown speckling, then tucked the tortilla into a warm towel. Although quite stiff when just off the griddle, they softened after a few minutes into a delicious flabby texture that kept for an hour or two, then grew stale and brittle.

This procedure, which was second nature to millions of peasant women, proved extremely difficult to reproduce mechanically. Grinding maize into *masa* represented the pre-Columbian kitchen's most physically demanding and time-consuming task. Although Europeans had harnessed wind, water, and draft animals to milling wheat for thousands of years, mechanical mills failed to work with corn. Old World grains in dry form passed easily through the stone wheels to produce flour, but the American staple had to be soaked first in a lime solution and ground wet into dough. Even if the moist corn did not gum up the works, stone mills ground the *nixtamal* far too coarsely to make an acceptable tortilla.[5]

Only in the second half of the nineteenth century did inventors finally overcome the hurdles to mechanical corn milling. On July 26, 1859, Julián González registered the first patent for a *nixtamal* mill, consisting of a rectangular chute mounted on a large table that fed corn between two steam-driven rollers. How well it worked remains a mystery, for liberal victory in the War of the Reform forced the Spanish-born inventor to flee the country a year later, before he could market the device. He returned to Mexico in 1865 to renew his patent with the French-imposed government of Maximilian, but once again conservative defeat thwarted his commercial ambitions.[6] The next patent was filed in 1876, and the onset of the Porfirian peace fueled a boom in corn-mill inventions. In the 1890s these mills went from blueprints to factory production, and newspapers soon advertised economical *nixtamal* mills for as little as ten pesos. By the end of the century more than fifty electrically powered mills were operating in Mexico City alone.[7]

Corn mills gained rapid acceptance among urban women, who were already accustomed to buying tortillas from street vendors. Commercial tortilla markers, often recent immigrants from the countryside, began buying *masa* from millers, but while they saved themselves work in this manner, their financial independence actually had declined. Machines made it culturally acceptable for men to take over the management of *tortillerías*, once an exclusively female occupation. The taste of the tortillas may also have deteriorated with the use of coarse machine-ground corn. Nevertheless, Mexico City consumers had limited tolerance of low-quality tortillas, as aspiring industrialists soon discovered.[8]

Numerous inventors attempted to mechanize the entire process of tortilla making and build fully automatic factories in the late nineteenth and early twentieth centuries. Julián González, the ill-fated Spanish inventor, may have conceived the first design for a mechanical tortilla maker, which fed *masa* down a chute, between two rolling presses, and out onto a large table. The rather crude plans filed with the Mexican patent office did not indicate how exactly González intended to cut the tortillas into shape, nor did they include a *comal* for cooking them. Nearly two decades passed before the next tortilla patent went to Pedro Cortés, in 1884, for a tortilla machine that resembled a tabletop drill press. Neither González nor Cortés succeeded in marketing their creations, but their dream of mass-produced tortillas inspired many others, such as an innovative woman from Veracruz, María de Mejía, a Constitutionalist politician from Coahuila, Vito Alessio Robles, and even a Connecticut Yankee from New Haven, Herbert Collins.[9]

One of the most colorful and inventive figures in the development of the tortilla industry was Don Luis Romero Soto. Born in 1876 in San Juan del Río, the site of Sofía de Bringas's fictional flirtation with tamales, Romero had already displayed his mechanical ingenuity at the precocious age of seven. To his mother's chagrin, he built a Rube Goldberg–style alarm clock with string and candle that woke him up in time for school by knocking over a pile of kitchen utensils. At nineteen, he gained the attention of Porfirio Díaz with an automatic postage machine; the president personally canceled the first stamp. Romero also had an artistic talent for ironwork and helped decorate the Palacio de Bellas Artes, the Supreme Court building, and numerous wealthy homes in the exclusive Colonia Roma. But he had a higher mission in life, he later explained, to "redeem the women of our nation from the slavery of the *metate.*"[10] He obtained his first patents for a tortilla machine in 1899 and a year later formed a corporation called "La Malinche" after Cortés's native mistress, who had assisted the Spaniards in conquering the Aztec capital of Tenochtitlán. In September 1902, Romero announced the grand opening of his first tortilla factory. He predicted a rapid expansion to twenty-five outlets and even home delivery, but unfortunately for Romero, "La Malinche" did not conquer the taste buds of Mexico City tortilla connoisseurs.[11]

The possibilities of mass production so engrossed Romero and his rivals that they entirely overlooked the utility of a modest hand-operated press. This simple device — two square boards hinged together, with a lever to

provide torque and banana leaves to avoid sticking — allowed anyone, however clumsy, to flatten out a perfectly round tortilla in seconds. The genius
who created the handpress, Ramón Benítez of Puebla, obtained patent
rights in 1905.[12] Luis Romero, on hearing of this sublime invention, set
aside plans for a tortilla factory and began work on his own home model. By
July of 1906 he had built a far more complicated prototype consisting of a
vertical cylinder with a tortilla-shaped mold at the bottom that opened like
a drawer. The *masa* was placed in the tube, then pressed down into the mold
with compressed air from a bicycle pump — not Romero's most successful
invention. But in 1908, Miguel Bernardo perfected Benítez's basic idea by
reversing the lever, attaching it to the bottom plate at the opposite end from
the hinge and then folding it back over the top plate, a design that remains
in use in countless Mexican kitchens.[13]

Mechanically pressed tortillas still had to be peeled away from the lining,
a delicate operation that continued to frustrate the progress of automa-
tion. The problem of sticky tortillas stimulated numerous schemes, such as
Alberto Altamirano's idea of installing a spring-loaded spoon to dislodge
reluctant tortillas. Luis Romero toyed briefly with using hot plates to
press the *masa*, which obviated the need to move the dough while still
moist, but his waffle-iron approach did not produce a decent tortilla. He
finally resolved the sticking problem in 1911 with a system of three rolling
presses. The first two presses flattened the corn dough and fed it into a
round mold impressed on a third, which then rolled against a pair of wires
to peel away the tortilla. Although the wires tended to leave a rough edge,
Romero's rolling mold became an essential component of future machines.
Still, the challenge remained of automatically cooking tortillas to the
proper consistency.[14]

Conveyor belts offered an obvious way of passing tortillas through an
oven, but inventors found it fiendishly difficult to fine-tune this system. For
two decades after experiments began about 1900, tortillas emerged from
the ovens in a desiccated, inedible state. To prevent scorching, Guillermo
Albino of Mérida tried building an elevated conveyor belt that lifted the
tortillas to the top of an oven, away from the heat source. Luis Romero
resorted to cooking with steam in search of a moist tortilla. But a solution
evaded researchers until 1919, when Enrique Espinoza of Mexico City
combined three separate conveyor belts, flipping the tortilla as it dropped
from one belt to the next, to imitate the turns given on a traditional *comal*.
By carefully regulating the timing and temperature, Espinoza finally solved
the mystery of how to mass-produce an edible tortilla.[15]

After two decades of work, automatic tortilla makers combining Romero's rolling mold with Espinoza's "endless *comal*" finally reached the market. Romero himself came out with a model called "La Rotativa" (The Rotator) in 1926, and soon met with competition from Octavio Peralta, another early manufacturer. But their models achieved only modest sales, and by 1945 an industrial census recorded no more than 2,215 tortilla factories in the entire country. Fausto Celorio, for example, who entered the business in 1947, managed to sell only about one machine per month in the early 1950s. Then in 1954, Alfonso Gándara, a mechanical engineering student at the National Polytechnic Institute, made a breakthrough in tortilla technology. By modifying Romero's tortilla mold, Gándara dispensed with the cutting wires and thus produced a tortilla with smooth edges and a superior texture, rendering all previous models obsolete. Celorio wisely offered the young engineer a partnership, and their sales soon jumped to forty machines per week. Between 1960 and 1980, Celorio sold forty-two thousand tortilla machines, more than double the output of his largest competitor, Oscar Verástegui.[16]

The third major step in the industrialization of tortillas came with the invention of *masa harina* or *nixtamal* flour. Luis Romero pioneered the technology for tortilla flour, registering the first patent in 1912 and encouraging his son to study the process in the chemistry school of the National University. Romero even had plans drawn up in 1946 to build a *masa harina* plant in Naucalpan, Mexico.[17] But once again, commercial success fell to another. Roberto M. González opened the first dried *nixtamal* factory in 1949 in Cerralvo, Nuevo León, under the trade name Molinos Azteca, S.A. (Maseca), with an output of scarcely fifteen tons a month. The following year, a state-supported enterprise, Maíz Industrializado, S. A. (Minsa), built a rival plant in Tlalnepantla, Mexico. *Nixtamal* flour, like corn mills and tortilla machines, required decades of research and development before yielding a marketable product. Maseca and Minsa could not afford to expand their operations and build new processing plants until the mid-1960s. To assure markets for the new product, Maseca invested heavily in the T-600, a tortilla machine that ran on *masa harina* and water, obviating the need for milling. In 1975, tortilla flour production surpassed 500,000 tons, 5 percent of all the corn consumed in Mexico, and by the 1990s the industry had tripled its output, reaching 1.5 million tons and placing Maseca's president on the Forbes list of billionaires.[18]

But the industrialization of tortilla making depended on more than just the technical skill of inventors, for consumers also had to be persuaded to buy machine-made tortillas. Each step in the process, from corn mills to tortilla machines to *masa harina*, entailed noticeable differences in the quality of the final product. Moreover, tortilla making was the most basic domestic skill of the peasant household. The transformation from hand-crafted to store-bought tortillas therefore constituted a genuine revolution in the lives of Mexican women.

## Modernizing the Campesino Kitchen

Although Mexicans had pioneered the industrial production of *nixtamal*, some of the country's first rural corn mills were established about 1900, in the distant Soconusco region of Chiapas, by German coffee planters. The foreigners had already installed electric generators on their plantations to power coffee-processing machinery, and so it was a simple matter for them to hook up corn mills and provide seasonal workers with a cheap source of food. Such itinerant workers usually brought their wives along to prepare tortillas while they harvested the crop. When the employers sent the women home, preferring to hand out tortillas to the men alone rather than twice as much corn to married couples, the workers protested loudly. Similar complaints greeted Morelos sugar planters who tried to free women for agricultural labor by mechanizing their domestic work. These early attempts to industrialize rural food production succeeded, as one German observed, only "where the authoritarianism of the owner" overcame the objections of the workers.[19] Resistance to corn mills demonstrated the importance of tortilla making to traditional domestic culture; acceptance of the new technology finally came as part of a revolutionary transformation of rural life.

Because tortilla making demanded so much time and effort — as much as a third of a woman's waking life — the activity acquired a corresponding significance in her personal and family identity. Historian Wendy Waters has examined these social implications using the field notes of anthropological studies conducted from the 1920s to the 1940s in Tepoztlán, Morelos. Tortilla making was so essential to domestic life that no woman in the village became eligible for marriage until she had demonstrated this skill. Men complemented women by praising their tortillas, and some even claimed to be able to identify the unique taste and texture of their wives' corn grinding and tortilla making. Women, in turn, expressed affection through their role of feeding the family. Although they avoided direct demonstrations of maternal love after weaning children, mothers offered subtle displays of tenderness by giving them extra helpings of beans or reserving for them the best tortillas. As a result, children were sensitive to the size of their portions and to the order in which they were fed. Food served to communicate anger as well as love; a wife could burn her husband's tortillas if she suspected him of infidelity, while children could throw their food to show disgust with mother. Women therefore became inextricably connected with the food they cooked.[20]

The spread of commercial *nixtamal* mills to Mexican villages, beginning in the 1920s, thus challenged women's established domestic roles. Technical flaws in the first mills allowed women to demonstrate their superiority over machines and assert their place within the family. Because villages lacked electricity, early models operated on gas engines, which caused the tortillas to come out tasting like high octane fuel. Even when gas generators were separated from electric motors, the corn acquired a metallic taste and rough texture. Women could avoid these unpleasant side effects by briefly regrinding the *masa* on the *metate*, yet they refused to patronize the mills, indicating deeper social concerns about grinding corn. Gossip in Tepoztlán questioned the femininity of anyone who carried her corn to a commercial mill. Many women feared that neglecting the *metate* would lead to a dangerous swelling of the joints called "laziness of the knees."[21] While the arrival of a *nixtamal* mill often worried village women, it absolutely infuriated men. Many forbade their wives and daughters from patronizing the new establishments, fearing a direct challenge to their patriarchal authority. Without the discipline of the *metate*, some believed women would become lazy and promiscuous. As one old-timer from the Yucatán explained, the mill "starts early and so women go out before dawn to grind their own corn the way they used to at home. They meet boys in the dark and that's why illegitimacy is caused by the *nixtamal*."[22]

Rural women nevertheless overcame these objections, and mills gradually gained acceptance as a natural tool of housework. Some of the first customers in Tepoztlán were women who had lived in Mexico City, where they had become accustomed to the new technology. Financial considerations also played a role in determining who patronized the mill. Relatively poor women with little land, contrary perhaps to expectations, often had the greatest incentive to pay for machine-ground corn. Although this service required a few centavos, it freed women from several hours of daily work. They could use that time to engage in artisanal crafts or to become petty merchants, traveling to nearby towns to buy cheaper products, and thus earn enough money to offset the cost of the mill. Wealthier families who could easily afford the added expense of the mill were among the last to give up the *metate*. Some considered home-ground corn a status marker, a way of asserting that they lived better than their neighbors because they

ate better tortillas. But they could also pay poorer women to do the actual grinding.[23]

Once mills gained acceptance they offered communities numerous advantages, social as well as economic. Mills opened a new space for women
to gather each morning and exchange gossip while waiting in line. They
served as a catalyst bringing other material improvements to villages. The
electric generator used to run the mill could also provide lighting for the
town square, and mill owners often reinvested profits in the community,
either for material improvements or to finance festivals. The acquisition of
a mill by one community could have a cumulative effect through inter-
village rivalry. Women from neighboring towns might see the machine in
action on market day and begin clamoring for one of their own. And when
one pueblo had several competing mills, entrepreneurs often left their
homes in search of more isolated villages where they could enjoy monopoly
profits. This plan often failed, however, because acceptance depended on
a degree of familiarity with the new technology. When the first mill in
Tepoztlán was opened in 1925 by an outsider, the suspicious villagers refused to patronize it. Nevertheless, a few years later local entrepreneurs
established their own mills, and supported themselves on their own land
until they had won over regular customers.[24]

More isolated communities had greater difficulty affording mill charges
because of monopolist practices by unscrupulous businessmen, union rack-
eteers, and municipal presidents. The women of Atequiza, Jalisco, for example, formed a cooperative to purchase a mill only to have their power cut
off by a nearby hacienda administrator who wanted to assure his own monopoly. Political bosses, called *caciques*, such as the hated José León Mon-
tero of Becal, Campeche, monopolized local *nixtamal* mills. In order to
dominate the townspeople he sent armed hoodlums to terrorize them by
night. Some women had to fight their own husbands to escape the chains of
the *metate*. The men of one agricultural cooperative locked the mill away
from their wives, and a member of another physically assaulted women who
attempted to organize for their right to a mill. *Nixtamal* cooperatives had to
maintain constant vigilance, as the Women's League for Class Conflict
of Huecorio, Michoacán, discovered in 1949. Businessman José Dongo
opened a competing mill in 1949 and drove the women out of business,
then raised prices to twice the level charged in a nearby town, forcing many
back to the *metate*. Not until 1963 did the village poultry association break
Dongo's monopoly.[25]

The activism needed to acquire and maintain a *nixtamal* mill plunged women into the political ferment of the 1930s. Senator Rubén Ortiz proposed making corn mills a basic public utility guaranteed by the Cárdenas administration. The motion failed to pass, despite his exclamation that "we still live in the Stone Age!"[26] Populists leaders may have denied support for the measure because they were using *nixtamal* mills as a form of patronage, like *ejido* land grants. The followers of Emilio Portes Gil donated one to a women's group in Tamaulipas, and after their fall from regional power tried unsuccessfully to repossess the machine. An example of a new brand of *nixtamal caciques* appeared in Torreón, Coahuila, a hotbed of agrarian radicalism. *Licenciado* Gabino Vázquez organized a number of women's leagues in 1936, supplying them with all the trappings of modern bureaucracy, including a Social Action Secretary and a "Lic. Gabino" letterhead. He functioned as a political broker, showing women how to work through the government apparatus to apply for a loan from the Ejido Bank, which failed, and then to petition President Cárdenas directly, this time successfully. By 1937 his followers controlled almost half of the mills of nearby Gómez Palacio, in blatant violation of federal antitrust laws.[27] President Cárdenas himself used grants of *nixtamal* mills to encourage membership in the official party and discourage rival church organizations. Women learned to phrase their requests for mills within the dominant developmentalist discourse; thus the use of anticlerical and anti-alcohol rhetoric by the women of Lake Pátzcuaro may have reflected political expedience rather than popular attitudes about either pulpit or *pulque*.[28]

Postrevolutionary rural modernization, resulting from both government projects and market forces, offered peasant families a broad menu of new attitudes and consumer goods. Educational missionaries conceived this transformation as a *prix fixe*, a complete package comprising the Spanish language and sewing machines, anticlericalism and household furniture, personal hygiene and radio programs, nationalism and wheat bread. Most *campesinos* preferred to order *à la carte*, accepting useful items like *nixtamal* mills while rejecting unwanted intrusions such as socialist education.[29] But once seduced by the money economy, even traditionalists found themselves drawn inextricably into the web of a consumer lifestyle. Children readily exchanged the peasant values of their parents for the allure of store-bought clothes, radios, and foods. The acceptance of wheat bread typified this triumph of the cash economy over subsistence production. Although rural teachers tried to show women how to bake bread at home, children in Tepoztlán valued bread in part because it had to be purchased from a bakery, and therefore demonstrated the wealth and modernity of the family. And even conservative parents saw the advantages of some consumer goods; canned milk could save an infant if a mother fell ill after childbirth and was unable to nurse.[30]

The willingness of *campesinos* to purchase relatively expensive goods while rejecting cheaper and seemingly more useful material improvements frustrated rural modernization programs. Manuel Gamio's campaign to replace corn with soybeans offered significant advantages to the impoverished Otomí Indians living in the Mezquital Valley. The Asian legume not only contained high levels of protein, it also flourished in arid soil that withered the American grain. Although native farmers agreed to plant seeds they received from agents of the National Indian Institute, the experiment failed in the kitchen. Otomí women simply could not prepare a decent soybean tortilla and eventually gave up trying. Scientists from both Mexico and the United States noticed little difference in taste between genuine corn tortillas and substitutes such as soybeans and sorghum. As they explained it: "after all, the tortilla doesn't have too much taste," but *campesinos* did not share this opinion.[31]

Another promising innovation, a solar cooker developed at the University of Wisconsin, likewise failed to gain acceptance among Mexican peasants. The cooker consisted of a tripod-mounted reflector panel that focused the sun's rays onto a cooking surface. Initial tests conducted in Denver, Colorado, by a Mexican restaurant owner demonstrated the need for a special griddle to diffuse the heat and prevent tortillas from burning, and with this adaptation Rockefeller scientists carried the cooker to Mexico for field tests. Northern Mexico offered the most promising conditions: virtually cloudless skies prevailed for most of the year; firewood was scarce in many locations, and cooking was usually done about midday for an afternoon *comida*. Mexican peasants greeted the device eagerly at first, the men anxious to show off their mechanical skills by setting it up and the women curious about how well they could cook on it. Even the poorest families asked to buy one of the cookers immediately. But when the representatives returned for follow-up interviews, the initial enthusiasm had vanished. Peasants issued a stream of complaints about the glare from the panel, the discomfort caused by cooking in the sun, the inability to cook tortillas properly, the flimsiness of the stand, and the constant peeling off of the reflector material.[32]

One might attribute the failure of solar cookers and soybean tortillas to simple conservatism, but this does little to explain the changes that did take place in peasant kitchens. For women living in deforested regions, the solar cooker might have saved as much time gathering firewood as the *nixtamal* mill saved grinding corn. Rockefeller scientists concluded that they should have concentrated on the poorest segments of society, who had the most to gain, but if peasants had come to associate the cooker with poverty, their rejection would have been almost certain. More significantly, the Foundation agents admitted that they did not follow up their demonstrations sufficiently, an error that commercial distributors, whether of corn mills or soft drinks, carefully avoided.[33]

More interesting than *campesino* conservatism are the ways peasants have incorporated new technology into their lives. Hermann Bausinger observed that "traditional" cultures have always evolved, utilizing new forms of technology, and that this innovation stops only when "modern" outsiders attempt to preserve the "primitive" folkways as a means of rejuvenating their own seemingly decadent societies.[34] The arrival of tortilla machines in the Mexican countryside in the 1960s perfectly illustrated both this innate process of adaptation and the desire of outsiders to experience more "traditional" ways. Ordinary *campesinas* began to purchase tortillas for everyday consumption and used the time saved to earn outside income. On the other hand, relatively wealthy peasant women, who could afford to devote themselves exclusively to domestic work, rejected machine-made tortillas as "raw" because they stuck together. In addition, commercial cooks continued to pat out tortillas by hand at tourist attractions such as Janitzio Island on Lake Pátzcuaro. But even in this latter case, the native cooks adapted creatively, starting with Maseca brand *masa harina*, then regrinding it on the *metate* for the tourists' benefit. In much the same way, the arrival of refrigerators in the Mexican countryside did not change the pattern of buying fresh foods daily. Instead, the peasants used the new appliances to store new foods, soft drinks, and beer.[35]

The so-called conservatism of Mexican peasant life represented not an innate opposition to change, but rather a measured evaluation of new ideas. The *metate* itself represented a form of technology that gained acceptance as a historical process. Until the middle of the twentieth century, *campesinas* considered the grinding stone to be one of the basic elements of their domestic identity. When the *nixtamal* mill presented itself as a viable alternative, women shelved the *metates* for special occasions. A woman might now begin a description of her daily work routine with the statement, "I go to the mill to grind the *nixtamal* and come home to make tortillas."[36] And this new work pattern was likewise subject to change, as technological change accelerated in the postwar Mexican countryside.

## From Agrarian Revolution to Green Revolution

The Mexican Revolution pursued agrarian reform through the creation of collectively owned and individually farmed *ejidos*. Land distribution reached a high point in the administration of Lázaro Cárdenas, when international agricultural surpluses compelled the United States government to pay farmers to destroy excess crops. With agricultural prices so low, the Mexican government could easily afford to swing the scales of social justice in favor of small cultivators. But by 1940, Mexican farm production had already begun to decline and cities were experiencing food shortages. Prices rose even higher with the onset of World War II and the resulting diversion of land from food to oilseed crops needed for the Allied war effort.[37] Mexican politicians, forced to choose between adequate incomes for small farmers and cheap food for urban markets, sacrificed the *ejido* to feed the voracious demands of industrialization. In the pursuit of economic modernization and political stability, the federal bureaucracy under Cárdenas and his successors established urban subsidies and encouraged large agribusiness, policies that devastated Mexico's peasantry and forced their entry into the industrial economy.

Mexican agriculture developed into an essentially dual system divided between a handful of commercially oriented and highly productive enterprises and large numbers of precariously situated and technically backward cultivators. The majority of farmers, particularly in the center and south, struggled for a subsistence income by raising corn and beans for their own consumption and for sale to local markets. In the revolutionary land distribution, most *ejido* farmers received plots smaller than the legal limit, and lacking security of tenure they had little incentive to make material improvements. Even if they tried to improve productivity, they had limited access to credit and technical assistance.[38] Meanwhile, many wealthy commercial farmers either maintained their estates intact or repurchased land after 1940. They circumvented the hundred hectare legal limit on farms by dividing land titles among members of their extended family, then operating the whole as a single business. These enterprises, concentrated in the northwestern states of Sonora and Sinaloa, raised commercially profitable crops such as wheat and produce for export to the United States or for sale to urban Mexican markets. In this way, the colonial division between wealthy northern wheat farmers and impoverished southern corn farmers persisted long into the twentieth century and even received official sanction from postrevolutionary governments.[39]

Federal intervention in agricultural markets, which began in the 1930s with modest attempts to support wheat producers, grew into a vast bureaucratic empire dedicated to subsidizing urban food prices. Historian Enrique Ochoa has described the evolution of this State Food Agency and its role in diffusing political unrest. Government efforts began with a network of wheat storage facilities established in 1931, and six years later resulted in the creation of an independent agency to guarantee grain supplies and preempt private speculation. A 20 percent drop in wheat production in 1938 sent bread prices soaring and led to widespread unrest among urban workers. Cárdenas responded to anti-inflation protests by reorganizing the State Food Agency, eliminating wheat producers from its board of directors, and subsidizing urban food prices, first for wheat, and then for corn and beans as well. Moreover, the new agency disregarded the president's goal of incorporating small producers into national markets. Instead, the bureaucrats usually purchased grains in bulk from large producers located near rail lines. This preference for agribusiness continued as the agency expanded its operations during World War II and the subsequent industrial boom.[40]

Improvements in agricultural productivity, even more than government intervention in markets, transformed the Mexican countryside in the postwar era. Mexican agronomists had been working since the 1920s to raise farm output, but their research had achieved only modest results before the arrival in 1943 of a team of specialists supported by the Rockefeller Foundation. These scientists set about increasing Mexican productivity through the application of genetics and chemistry. Dr. Norman Borlaug, a graduate of the Iowa Agricultural College, later Iowa State University, developed hybrid wheat varieties resistant to stem rust, a parasite that had long plagued Mexican farmers, devastating whole regions in wet years. By crossing seeds gathered from several different countries, he developed a highly resistant strain, Lerma Red, which alleviated this former plague. Improved varieties, assisted by chemical fertilizers, grew so large that they actually keeled over before the harvest. This new problem confounded researchers until they added genetic material from Japanese dwarf wheat, so the plant grew thick instead of tall. Increased productivity, in turn, attracted large numbers of insects and required the heavy use of chemical pesticides. The use of improved seed, fertilizers, and pesticides yielded enormous harvests in Mexico and spread throughout the world under the label of the Green Revolution.[41]

Agricultural science therefore held the promise of freeing *campesinos* from their subsistence farms, thus realizing the dreams of development contained in the tortilla discourse. Ramón Fernández y Fernández, a leading agronomist of the Cárdenas era, voiced these aspirations in a poem he composed to corn. He began by cursing the plant as the "father of pellagra, mother of hunger." But unlike Bulnes, who saw corn as nutritionally inferior, Fernández attributed the problem to low productivity, which could be overcome through science. "It will give me great pleasure to see the geneticists imprisoning your noble organs with cellophane paper. They will force you to be more generous. But even in the hands of scientists you are a troublesome and traitorous plant. Only science, with all of its power, is capable of chaining you a little bit. And you will have to go back to being the slave of man."[42] The guarded optimism of Fernández's conclusion reflected a transition taking place within the tortilla discourse in the 1940s. The redemption of Mexico's *campesinos* lay not in the replacement of corn by wheat, but through the transformation of corn through science and technology.

Unfortunately for *campesinos*, the benefits of the Green Revolution accrued primarily to large agribusinesses that could afford this expensive new technology. The small farmer's first problem was gaining access to government extension agents, who played an essential role in carrying innovations from the laboratories to the fields. Farmers in the United States learned to demand these services from conveniently located land grant colleges, and as historian Deborah Fitzgerald has demonstrated, the Rockefeller agricultural research program took a similar view toward extension in Mexico. As a result, the limited number of agents concentrated on affluent wheat farmers who resembled their counterparts in the United States, and largely ignored the large numbers of peasants who most needed education. Moreover, *campesinos* growing corn could not afford to purchase any of the needed seed and chemical inputs to take advantage of the Green Revolution.[43] Government irrigation projects likewise contributed to the advantage of large agricultural enterprises. A bold program begun in the 1940s had doubled the total area of irrigated land by the 1960s. But once again, affluent farmers growing wheat and vegetables for urban markets derived most of the benefits; fully 40 percent of the country's irrigated land lay in the states of Sonora and Sinaloa.[44]

By 1960 the Green Revolution had achieved phenomenal but lopsided results. Wheat production had more than quadrupled over two decades, and in 1958 Mexico no longer needed to import the grain. The country actually began exporting hundreds of thousands of tons of surplus wheat in the 1960s. Corn production increased as well, although at only half the rate of wheat. But this golden age of Mexican farming soon passed.

The owners of agribusinesses in Sonora and Sinaloa, apparently believing that the profits of the 1960s would continue indefinitely, engaged in awesome displays of conspicuous consumption, purchasing the latest model Caterpillar tractors as if they were Cadillac Sevilles. By the 1970s, profligate spending and inefficient production had driven a large percentage of these agricultural enterprises into bankruptcy. Agricultural stagnation combined with population growth then reversed the favorable balance of trade, forcing the government to import massive quantities of corn to feed the poor.[45]

This crisis notwithstanding, Mexican agricultural policies of the postwar era achieved their primary goal of supporting urban industrialization. From 1940 to 1970, the economy grew at an average rate of more than 6 percent per year, but this growth was financed by low wages for workers. At a time of soaring business profits, personal incomes for the poorest segments of Mexican society actually declined in real terms. Farmworkers suffered the greatest dislocations as modern agricultural machines imported from the United States replaced the human labor abundant in the Mexican countryside. Since fewer workers could produce more food, rural incomes dropped sharply, a problem compounded by rapid population growth. Unable to support themselves on the land, *campesinos* flooded into the cities, where the situation was scarcely better because the same capital-intensive methods dominated Mexican industry. The influx of rural workers added to an already excessive urban labor force, depressing industrial wages still further. In this way, businessmen benefited from the miserable squatter settlements that sprang up around Mexico City and other manufacturing centers. Industrialists in the United States also profited from Mexican rural poverty, as large numbers of immigrants crossed the border, authorized under the *bracero* program from 1943 to 1964, and after that time as undocumented laborers.[46]

Rising disparities between rich and poor increased the importance of the State Food Agency as an agent of social control. Subsidized food provided to urban consumers not only helped restrain union demands, therefore assuring business profits, but also muffled calls for democracy and an end to single-party rule. The crisis in Mexican agriculture of the 1970s forced the government to extend food subsidies to the countryside by establishing rural grocery stores. The political goals of this program became obvious during election campaigns, when the government flooded opposition strongholds with food to win votes for official party candidates. Moreover, the State Food Agency carried a strong urban bias, contributing to the rise of a national cuisine based on industrial food.[47]

## Popular Cuisine and Mass Consumption

Industrial processed foods have become fixtures of Mexican popular culture in the postwar era, appearing ubiquitously in even the most remote indigenous villages. The Tzotzil Indians of San Juan Chamula, Chiapas, provide an extreme example with their fanatic devotion to Pepsi Cola. The local *cacique* established a Pepsi distributorship and boosted sales among impoverished residents by encouraging them to use the soft drink for ritual occasions, such as giving cases of Pepsi as brides' dowries. Religious leaders celebrated church services with Pepsi instead of wine, telling parishioners that carbonation drives off evil spirits and cleanses the soul. The natives even hung Pepsi posters in their homes beside the family crucifix, for as one person explained to an anthropologist: "When men burp, their hearts open."[48] While the veneration of Pepsi reached absurd heights in Chamula, soft drinks built up a large and devoted following throughout the country. By 1990 the average Mexican consumed a little more than one twelve-ounce soft drink a day in addition to excessive quantities of snacks and beer. Industrial foods had clearly become a significant part of both the gross national product and the national cuisine, thus fulfilling the goals of the tortilla discourse. But Mexican diets, rather than improving as Bulnes had predicted, have simply changed from the heavy carbohydrates of corn and beans to the empty calories of fat and sugars, a transition that caused serious new health problems without corresponding nutritional gains.[49]

Food processing technology, developed in nineteenth-century Europe and the United States, reached Mexico in the final two decades of the Porfirian era. Although sugar mills had operated on an industrial scale since the sixteenth century, perhaps the first of the nineteenth-century industries was beer. By the end of the century Mexico boasted seventy-two breweries producing for regional markets. Chronic shortages of pure water also supported a market for bottled mineral waters; Pedro Treviño tapped the springs of Topo Chico near Monterrey, and José Peñafiel established a bottling plant at Tehuacán, Puebla. Clemente Jacques y Compañía, meanwhile, founded a food canning operation in Mexico City. And Fernando Pimentel y Fagoaga opened Mexico's first modern dairy farm on a Tlalnepantla hacienda, which produced pasteurized milk and excellent European-style cheeses such as Gruyère, Camembert, and Edam. While these entrepreneurs relied largely on imported technology, foreign capital predominated as well in other industries. Chicago interests backed John Wesley DeKay in his bid to dominate the Mexican meat market with "El

Popo" brand refrigerated and canned meats. Porfirians also witnessed the arrival of that ambassador of American capitalism, Coca Cola.[50]

Despite a strong urban base, Mexican industrial food processors needed half a century to expand into rural markets. Revolutionary fighting and the Great Depression hindered economic expansion for decades, although road construction assisted businessmen in reaching new consumers. In the 1920s and 1930s many new food processing companies were established, such as the "Búfalo" canning operation in Monterrey and the Tres Reyes (Three Kings) dessert factory in Zamora, Michoacán. Nevertheless, domestic production of canned goods remained low, and expensive imports dominated the market until the end of World War II. Vegetable oils, another important sector of the food industry, were likewise limited mainly to urban consumers. Production expanded enormously as a result of Allied wartime needs and investment by multinational companies such as Anderson Clayton, but a 1960 study estimated that a third of the population still had little access to either animal or vegetable fats.[51]

Although foreigners had provided the technology for food preservation and mechanization, Mexicans needed to develop their own solutions to problems of transportation and retailing. Some perishable items, such as tortillas and bread, remained local craft industries in rural areas, for baker's ovens, *nixtamal* mills, and tortilla machines could be established in any community with the cash to purchase these services. Nonperishable, relatively high value goods including coffee, sugar, and spices could be safely transported — by mules if necessary — from factories to consumers, and also fit within customary marketing networks that in some cases extended back to the pre-Columbian era. Perhaps the first great challenge to this marketing system came from the soft drink and beer industries. Minimum standards of road maintenance and truck suspensions were needed to bring the glass bottles safely from regional plants to consumers and then to return the empties for refilling — an essential step to keep prices affordable. As a result, soft drink and beer distributors were among the first entrepreneurs to profit from the highways constructed in the 1920s and 1930s. Both Coke and beer arrived in the village of Tepoztlán within six years after the opening of a road to Cuernavaca in 1936. The appearance of Pepsi in the 1940s and the concentration of the Mexican beer industry assured a fierce competition for local markets.[52]

These distributorships fulfilled a vital role in supplying the small-scale grocers who continued to dominate Mexican commerce. Merchants in both the countryside and the city depended on distributors for credit as well as such business supplies as display cases and refrigerators. One shop-keeper considered the Coke deliveryman so important to his livelihood that he invited the driver to his daughter's fifteenth birthday party. Distribution networks were just as vital from the perspective of corporate giants. The enormous investments needed to establish and maintain these delivery routes encouraged centralization of the Mexican food processing industry with industrial groups. For instance, the largest Coke franchise in the world, Fomento Económico Mexicano SA, also included Cervecería Cuauhtémoc within the Monterrey-based Garza Sada conglomerate. Pepsico meanwhile diversified into the complementary snack-food industry, merging with Frito-Lay in the United States, then acquiring Mexican chip makers Sabritas and Bali.[53]

The State Food Agency, although ostensibly in competition with these private enterprises, has actually supported their expansion. Rural stores established in the 1960s and 1970s helped extend the reach of industrial products to remote markets. The goods sold in these government outlets either resembled commercial counterparts, such as animal crackers, or actually came from private producers, as in the case of soft drinks. In either case, they helped incorporate rural consumers into larger national markets.[54] As another example of the State Food Agency's support for private enterprise, the public company Minsa worked together with the Monterrey firm Maseca to develop the technology for *masa harina*. Maseca executives conceded a minority market share to the state producer to avoid claims of monopolistic practices, for the company's real competition lay in fresh corn tortillas. Moreover, the Ministry of Commerce and Industrial Development helped the industry increase market share by requiring many corn millers to sell *masa harina* despite the millers' vigorous protests about the inferior quality of such tortillas. Perhaps the most nutritionally irresponsible example of state assistance to private enterprise lay in the subsidies on flour and sugar given to snack-food producers, which made this business, in the words of one health official, a *"negociazo"* (scam).[55]

Mexican politicians have simply lacked the will to use their power to improve the nation's nutritional health. Granted, state intervention often fails to achieve the desired results; indeed, government handouts provide one of the least effective means of solving nutritional problems because recipients usually resell the food. One group of investigators chemically marked an aid shipment of powdered milk, then proceeded to follow it into commercial channels — not only as powdered milk, but also in bottles of "fresh" milk, cases of ice cream, and numerous other products.[56] Nevertheless, cheaper and more effective methods of improving nutrition, such as vitamin enrichment, have also been foregone. For the nominal cost of ten dollars a ton, Maseca could enrich its *masa harina* with enough protein and vitamins to satisfy minimum daily requirements. While the company has gained government support largely because of such possible nutritional gains, it has nevertheless resisted implementing the strategy. Although vitamin and protein enrichment would make little difference in taste beyond the already significant change from fresh to dehydrated corn, the politically powerful company feared that any additives would undermine its market share.[57]

The government has also conceded to food manufacturers the educational power of the mass media. Although private channels such as Televisa have included nutritional advice on women's programs, the networks have given far more time to soft-drink and snack-candy advertising. Their only concession to public health was small-print advice to eat fresh fruits and vegetables.[58] The government's most successful educational program came not over mass media, but from community-level efforts to improve neonatal care. Investigators found that rural mothers waited up to a year before introducing their children to solid foods. Supplementing the infants' diets at the age of three months greatly enhanced early childhood development and at a trivial cost to the family.[59] In this and other ways, nutritional advice has been incorporated into popular culture. For example, an anthropologist recorded the following sales pitch of a Zapotec fruit vendor: "Look, girls, tortillas are great—food for the heart—but you need vitamins. Fruits are full of vitamins. With vitamins you cure yourself and you don't get sick."[60]

Yet education has only limited effect without corresponding economic improvements, as the high incidence of gastrointestinal disease demonstrates. Native Americans had always shown concern for hygiene, despite efforts of Spanish friars to stop them from bathing. Women in rural areas displayed a genuine mania for sanitation in the kitchen, washing their hands religiously before preparing foods. Moreover, they attributed most kitchen disasters (not obviously caused by the evil eye) to a lack of cleanliness. But their efforts usually went in vain because of the lack of pure water. Shortages of firewood limited their ability to purify water by boiling, while a corresponding lack of money slowed the spread of modern plumbing to rural areas.[61]

Unfortunately for nutritional health, the modern remedy for contaminated water became bottled soft drinks, while shortages of firewood encouraged the consumption of packaged food. Studies by the National Nutrition Institute as well as by numerous anthropologists documented enormous changes in Mexican lower-class diets from 1960 to 1990. The fundamental trend has been the replacement of corn and beans by sugar and fats. The most exaggerated examples of this pattern have emerged in the urban lower class and the rural middle class, two groups with close connections as a result of internal migration. Well-to-do Yucatecan peasants and working-class Mexico City residents both derive an average of 20 percent of their calories from processed foods, including soft drinks, beer, chips, and candy. The rural poor, unable to afford such snacks except on special occasions, dump heaping spoons full of sugar into weak coffee; those who lack the means to buy coffee get their energy by drinking a thin syrup of sugar boiled in water. So pervasive has sucrose become that one study recommended vitamin-enriched sugar as the most efficient means of improving rural nutrition.[62]

The incorporation of processed foods into rural diets began at the periphery of the culinary system, as did the use of European ingredients in sixteenth-century Indian cuisine. The main meal of the day usually remained tortillas, beans, and chiles, while bread rolls, sweet coffee, and animal crackers were eaten for breakfast. In keeping with traditional patterns of *pulque* consumption, most *campesinos* celebrated special occasions with the expensive, high-status beverages such as beer, or as in San Juan Chamula, Pepsi.[63] Canned sardines, tuna, and eggs added protein to the diets of rural dwellers. Yet the convenience of processed foods often came at the expense of nutrition, as when cooks used dried consommé instead of tomatoes and onions, in effect replacing vegetables with salt. Poverty further distorted the diets of *campesinos* subsisting on the fringes of the market economy. The rising price of beans forced many poor families to buy cheaper wheat pasta, with grave dietary consequences. While corn and beans together formed a complete amino acid, corn and spaghetti did not.[64]

Adolfo Chávez, director of the Community Nutrition Division of the National Nutrition Institute, has described an epidemiological trap in which Mexicans have fallen victim to the dietary diseases of the rich world without escaping the nutritional deficiencies of the poor world. Serum cholesterol levels among residents of the wealthy, meat-consuming areas of northern Mexico average higher than those in the United States. Heart disease has become a serious problem throughout Mexico, and ranks as the leading cause of death even among indigenous peasants in Yucatán, Campeche, and Hidalgo. Excessive sugar consumption has meanwhile created an epidemic of diabetes, the fourth leading cause of death nationwide. Hypoglycemia, hypertension, arteriosclerosis, and various forms of cancer have likewise grown more common. These diseases seemed all the more tragic given the continuing prevalence of serious malnutrition in Mexico. Although the increased availability of calories helped lower infant mortality rates and extend life expectancy, junk foods did not provide the vitamins, minerals, and proteins that children needed for full mental and physical development. As a final irony, Mexican adults often suffered from both obesity and anemia at the same time.[65]

The development of a Mexican food industry therefore brought not a shift from corn to wheat, as predicted by Bulnes, but from starch to sugar. Anthropologist Sidney Mintz documented a similar transformation in British diets over the course of the industrial revolution. Observing that sugar excelled all other foods in providing maximum energy at minimum cost, Mintz concluded that the British transition from peasant soups to sweetened tea helped assure a supply of energetic workers at depressed wages.[66] Twentieth-century Mexican nutritional discourse served much the same ends. Nevertheless, the commodification of corn did not cause the grain to disappear from Mexican diets. Instead, the creation of mechanical tortilla makers guaranteed the survival of this peasant food in an industrial world, although not with its former predominance.[67] But even as maize declined in the countryside, it became a symbol of nostalgic nationalism for the urban middle class.

*SIX*

# Apostles of the Enchilada

## *Postrevolutionary Nationalism*

ᡓᡕᢀᢦ

Josefina Velázquez de León, the daughter of one of Mexico's most distinguished families, published a thick book in 1946 entitled *Platillos regionales
de la República mexicana* (Regional Dishes of the Mexican Republic).[1] This
classic work collected for the first time the country's diverse regional cuisines in a single volume. Moreover, she exalted enchiladas, tamales, and
other popular corn dishes as culinary expressions of the national identity.
By unifying culinary traditions that had formerly been divided by geography, ethnicity, and class, she created the modern form of Mexico's national cuisine. In a career spanning three decades, from the late 1930s
until 1968, she published more than 150 cookbooks. But her enormous
energy notwithstanding, she owed much of her success to the industrial and
urban transformation of Mexican society during this period. These changes
seemed to promise a new era of Mexican history, one dominated by the
middle-class ideal of consumerism rather than the Marxist class conflict
of Cardenismo.

For three decades, beginning in the late 1930s, the Mexican economy
grew more than 6 percent annually, a rate higher than any other country in
the Americas and exceeded only by postwar Japan, Korea, and a few others.
This economic "miracle," as contemporaries labeled it, coincided with a
period of political stability under the authoritarian Institutional Revolutionary Party (PRI). The election of Miguel Alemán in 1946 ushered in a
new generation of civilian, professional politicians who sought to manage
policy by peaceful compromises among interest groups rather than by divi-
sive electoral battles. Nevertheless, nationalist agreement could not rest
simply on political accords. To achieve a genuine social consensus, Mexi-

cans had to feel a sense of belonging within the national community. Mass media and school curricula provided obvious channels for forging a national culture, but television shows and civic lessons often had limited connection to everyday life. Political rituals in particular, such as rallies and elections, held little real significance in an authoritarian government.[2]

Middle-class housewives were more likely to perceive the meaning of *lo mexicano* in the food they prepared for their families. And urban consumers in the postwar era could sample the wide variety of Mexican cuisines to an unprecedented degree, thanks to improved communications. Highway construction lowered the cost of shipping exotic ingredients across the republic, making daily visits to the market into explorations of regional cuisines. The exchange of recipes between neighbors took on a new meaning as internal migration brought together people from all parts of the country. This dialogue expanded still further with the spread of cookbooks, and culminated with the creation of a self-conscious Mexican national cuisine.[3]

The cookbooks of Velázquez de León and her contemporaries served to define a specific middle-class nationalism based on conservative religious and family traditions. This domestic view of *lo mexicano* differed from the ruling party's version of the national history, but at the same time it validated sharp social inequalities and the exclusion of large sectors of the population from the benefits of economic growth. Popular dishes were appropriated into the national cuisine as a means of transforming elements of lower class and ethnic culture into symbols of unity for an authoritarian regime. Yet ultimately, although Mexico's political consensus broke down after the massacre at Tlatelolco in 1968, the national cuisine could at least provide comfort in the troubled times that followed.

## The Labyrinth of Sisterhood

Nobel laureate Octavio Paz wrote *The Labyrinth of Solitude* as a portrait of the Mexican's lonely existence. The poet found his national identity in the role of the macho, who perceived all social relations as struggles of dominance and submission. Shamed by his own heritage of submission, as the offspring of an Indian woman raped by a Spanish man, the macho masked his emotions and derived satisfaction from conquering other women.[4] While rightly critical of such attitudes, Paz defined this national spirit exclusively in male terms.[5] Mexican women also lived in a labyrinth, but not one of separation or solitude. Instead of closed walls, their maze comprised open networks that united people through bonds of family and friendship.

This alternative experience, an equally valid expression of Mexican identity, made up the essence of domestic culture.

These labyrinths of family networks were maintained by the work of "centralizing women," a term used by Larissa Lomnitz and Marisol Pérez-Lizaur to describe particular women who devoted their lives to preserving cohesion within extended families. Using the example of an elite clan they called the Gómez, the two anthropologists demonstrated that such women fulfilled an essential role in the management of Mexican businesses. Women's social networks served as an informal, but nonetheless vital, "interlocking directorate" that coordinated diverse companies managed by family members.[6] In other studies, Lomnitz has shown the importance of similar networks within the public sector as well as the informal sector, where people survived in desperate squatter settlements by relying on family contacts.[7]

The use of the term *family traditions* does not imply that domestic values and rituals existed unchanged since the colonial period; urban middle-class life represented a new experience for large numbers of Mexicans. The growth of university enrollment and government employment allowed working-class youths a chance to gain professional status. The concentration of jobs in the nation's capital fueled a massive internal migration, drawing people from provincial towns to the metropolis. Those who escaped the burgeoning slums found Mexico City to be a consumer wonderland, with supermarket aisles full of canned goods and frozen foods undreamed of in village plazas. Women also raised their expectations in this new world as they entered the workforce and received the vote. To maintain stability, families reshaped old traditions and invented new ones to fit the rapidly changing times. Cookbooks and family magazines dealt with middle-class aspirations and experiences, ranging from the prosaic consumer demand for durable stockings to the life-threatening danger of homicidal bus drivers.[8]

Mexico's culinary library expanded greatly in the postwar era, a reflection of the spread of literacy, from 40 percent of the population in 1940 to 72 percent three decades later.[9] Cookbook authors catered to downscale audiences by publishing inexpensive paperback editions containing economical dishes. Josefina Velázquez de León wrote many books with titles such as *Popular Cooking: 30 Economical Menus* and *How to Cook in Hard Times*.[10] More affluent readers, meanwhile, demanded greater variety and specialization. While nineteenth-century volumes had attempted to meet virtually any need from roasts and desserts to medicines and detergents, twentieth-century works sought to build markets through product differentiation.

Authors filled entire books with highly specific recipes for holidays and diets, for vegetarians and carnivores, for children and the infirm, and most recently for microwave ovens and vegetarian aphrodisiacs.[11]

The growing market and increasing diversification of cookbooks reflected a larger spread of consumerist values among the middle classes. The United States not only set the example with a binge of postwar spending, it also exported technology and marketing techniques to foment Mexican consumer-goods industries. By the mid-1950s, with the assistance of import restrictions, Mexican appliance manufacturers boasted annual sales of 140,000 stoves and 45,000 refrigerators, although many came from local subsidiaries of General Electric and American Refrigeration.[12] United States supermarket chains such as Piggly Wiggly, meanwhile, inspired the opening of Mexican chains SUMESA in 1945 and Aurrera in 1958. Unlike the mass marketing of United States chains, Mexican supermarkets were located predominantly in upper-middle-class neighborhoods and stocked luxury goods beyond the reach of working-class consumers, who continued to patronize small grocers.[13]

Mexicans even began to accommodate their eating habits to the United States workday, creating a boom in the restaurant industry. From 1940 to 1965, the total number of restaurants in Mexico jumped from fifteen thousand to twenty-five thousand. These included several tourist spots in the Zona Rosa (Pink Zone) along Reforma Avenue, but the majority were small establishments catering to blue- and white-collar workers. Nineteenth-century professionals had gone home each afternoon about two o'clock for an extended lunch, then returned to work until about seven o'clock, but this became increasingly impractical with the growth of commuter traffic in Mexico City. Although workers refused to move their meals forward to the twelve noon lunchtime favored north of the border, they did take shorter breaks at nearby cafeterias and *fondas*, forsaking the pleasures of a home-cooked meal and subsequent siesta in return for a five o'clock quitting time.[14]

Middle-class families faced a still more serious transition as their daughters began entering the workforce. This change came slowly, with trepidation and hostility from both men and women. A scowling father would scrutinize the prospective place of employment—"casing the joint"—before allowing his daughter to work, and even then she went with the understanding that once married she would revert to accepted standards of domesticity.[15] But women had raised their expectations, and continued to enter the workforce despite being confined to jobs such as bank tellers and office girls.[16] They also expanded their educational goals, although enrollments at the National University likewise perpetuated job discrimination. Women composed only about 20 percent of university enrollments from the 1940s to the 1960s, and they were concentrated in fields such as nursing, social work, teaching, and the humanities.[17]

Although the Mexican middle class resembled its counterpart in the United States, deep cultural differences make it risky to generalize across the Río Bravo. Simple household appliances demonstrate these subtle but important distinctions. For example, Mexicans used their newly purchased refrigerators to store soft drinks and beer instead of a week's worth of groceries. And while the most valuable appliances north of the border may have been electric toasters and cake mixers, Mexicans preferred the electric blender, the juice press, and the pressure cooker. The blender's facility in grinding chile sauces relegated the *metate* to the status of a kitchen curiosity, and the juicer turned Mexico's ubiquitous oranges into daily glasses of fresh juice. The pressure cooker solved the age-old problem of boiling water at high altitudes in central Mexico. Beans can now be prepared in less than an hour, saving on fuel costs as well as time, and the toughest beef can be made edible in minutes.[18] Even these innovations demonstrated the comparative "underdevelopment" of Mexican kitchens: housewives continued to shop for groceries everyday and spurned such conveniences as canned beans and frozen orange-juice concentrate. Yet the Mexican woman's skepticism of the doctrine that time is money may reflect a more realistic view of the limitations of household technology. Ruth Schwartz Cowan observed that mechanizing housework in the United States had the ironic effect of creating "more work for mother." Time saved by laundry machines, for example, was spent in the automobile working as the family chauffeur.[19] Mexican women at least had the satisfaction of feeding their families fresh food.

Emphasis on kinship and friendship also balanced commercialism in the production of cookbooks. The most prominent cooking teacher in the United States, Betty Crocker, was actually the invention of a General Mills advertising worker, Marjorie Husted. The Betty Crocker radio show, which premiered in 1927, offered a disembodied friend to housewives needing advice in the kitchen.[20] Mexican authors occasionally resorted to such tactics; Adela Mena de Castro advertised her cookbook as the solution for young women whose mothers did not have time to teach them to cook. She also forbade readers to pass the book along to others, warning that anyone who wanted to try her recipes must pay for them.[21] But this contrasted sharply with the hospitality of another author, Faustina Lavalle, who invited readers to her Mexico City home to explain personally any unclear directions in her written recipes.[22]

Josefina Velázquez de León combined religious and family values with entrepreneurial skill and energy to become one of the most influential cookbook authors in modern Mexico. Doña Josefina came from a distinguished family dating back to the conquistador Diego Velázquez and the eighteenth-century founder of the national school of mines, Joaquín. In the nineteenth century her family had taken a political misstep—her great grandfather, also named Joaquín, while serving as Minister of Development under Santa Anna, had authorized the Gadsden Purchase, ceding southern Arizona and New Mexico to the United States. Nevertheless, they kept the family hacienda in Aguascalientes, where Josefina was born in 1899. A few years later the family moved to Mexico City, and along with her three younger sisters, she received a traditional domestic education centered on cooking, drawing, and sewing. About 1930, she married Joaquín González, a successful businessman of about fifty, against her mother's wishes. Her mother seemed to be right, for the marriage lasted less than a year before González died. But as a widow, Josefina could pursue her own goals without deferring to the authority of either husband or father. At first she attempted to run her deceased husband's business, but she disliked the work and sold out to his partners. She had to do something, however, because agrarian reformers had confiscated the family hacienda. To keep the house on Abráham González Street, about 1935 she transformed the downstairs into a cooking school and obtained sponsorship from General Electric. Over the "Caldroth" stove posters she hung an image of her true patron, Saint Eduviges, and she devoted many works to Catholic charities. Josefina soon won a loyal following among society ladies, at first through word of mouth from enthusiastic students. About 1940 she began submitting recipes to the Poblano women's magazine *Mignon*, and six years later she was publishing books on her own press, Ediciones Josefina Velázquez de León. As the classes grew, two of her younger sisters entered the business. Nevertheless, she continued to work with enormous energy for the rest of her life, teaching classes in the morning and evening, experimenting with recipes in the afternoon, and writing and illustrating books until late at night.[23]

Doña Josefina and other cooking teachers owed their success not only to hard work and creative recipes, but also to the importance of cuisine in defining family identity. A sociological study in Querétaro, for example, found that members of the upper-middle class considered eating well as more important to good living than having fancy automobiles or expensive clothes.[24] Families in the northern state of Sonora, meanwhile, expressed their solidarity through the ritual of *carne asada*, not simply a grilled steak, but an entire social event.[25] Within the Gómez family studied by Lomnitz and Pérez-Lizaur, weekly dinners united the various branches to plot business strategy or to discuss an upcoming baptism. The recipes prepared for these reunions were closely guarded secrets, passed by centralizing women only to daughters by blood, not those by marriage. Relatively poor women assured invitations to their wealthier relatives' parties — and by extension their status within the clan — through gifts of *buñuelos* and other desserts.[26]

These family rituals reproduced and reinforced the rituals that bound together the national community. Gómez women regarded colonial recipes as expressions of patriotism, similar to their veneration of the Mexican saint, the Virgin of Guadalupe.[27] Independence Day celebrations acquired their own ritual foods, often newly invented traditions such as tricolor rice.[28] Connections between family, food, and fatherland were made most explicitly by "Gourmet," a food and society columnist for the Mexico City daily *Excelsior* in the late 1940s. Her columns followed an invariable narrative of a high-society woman entertaining her family and distinguished friends with some special dish that evoked Mexican patriotism. "Gourmet" concluded with the recipe so that her middle-class readers — who would never actually dine with the likes of ex-president Emilio Portes Gil or composer Carlos Chávez — could at least share the national cuisine with their own family and friends.[29] These efforts to build a national cuisine were hardly new, but divisions of ethnicity, class, and region had frustrated these efforts in the nineteenth century. Twentieth-century responses to these questions reveal much about the evolving nature of Mexican nationalism.

## The Taste of *Indigenismo*

Diego Rivera and Frida Kahlo reigned notorious over Mexico's intellectual vanguard, outraging bourgeois morality with their revolutionary paintings and scandalous behavior. The couple delighted in their Bolshevik reputations — he placed Lenin's portrait in a mural at New York City's Rockefeller Plaza and she had an affair with Trotsky — but they preferred to cloak their radical ideas in nationalist, particularly Native American, mantles. For a dinner honoring former Agriculture Minister and patron of the arts Marte R. Gómez, Rivera suggested an Aztec main course of stewed human flesh, although he eventually deferred to his colleagues' preference for chicken.[30] Kahlo wore indigenous costumes accented with pre-Columbian jewelry and sought out traditional foods in native markets to serve at her parties.[31] Their *indigenista* taste ultimately became one of the foundations of Mexican nationalism, but only after it had been shorn of all radicalism and made palatable to the middle class they had worked so hard to disturb.

Foreign recipes continued to dominate Mexican culinary literature throughout the 1920s and 1930s, an ironic continuation of Porfirian tastes through the revolutionary period. María Aguilar de Carbia, who wrote some of the best selling cookbooks of the 1930s under the pen name Marichu, offered international cuisine to Mexican housewives, although her English-language cookbook, *Mexico through my kitchen window*, presented national recipes to an international audience.[32] Even Josefina Velázquez de León began her publishing career with cake recipes in a women's magazine. The illustrations featured imported figures such as Santa Claus and the Easter Bunny at first, but in 1940 she added national scenes of the China Poblana and mariachi musicians. International recipes likewise filled her first major book, *Manual práctico de cocina y repostería* (Practical Manual of Cooking and Pastry).[33]

Another expression of ambivalence toward native cooking appeared in the original 1926 account of the legend of *mole poblano*. Carlos de Gante first published the story of the nuns of the Dominican Santa Rosa cloister in Puebla who concocted Mexico's national dish. In this version, the mother superior asked the devotees to create a new dish in honor of their benefactor, an archbishop. One sister suggested cooking a turkey, which brought gasps of horror from others. "It's a dirty, stinking animal," they protested. "That's precisely why I have chosen it," responded the first. "Surely we can make something good and original." This dialogue reflected the *indigenista* program for redeeming Mexico's Indians, represented by the "dirty, stinking" turkey, cleansed by indoctrination in the ways of Old World civilization, the spices, to create the Mexican mestizo nation, *mole poblano*.[34]

Nevertheless, folklorists had already begun to replace this contempt with a genuine interest in Indian cuisine. In the 1920s Eugenio Gómez published a number of recipes gathered from villages near the great pyramids of Teotihuacán. These dishes, which he termed Mexico's "vernacular cuisine," included cactus paddles and peasant soups along with various tamales and *moles*.[35] Virginia Rodríguez Rivera became the most prolific scholar of traditional Mexican foods, publishing a now classic volume on nineteenth-century dishes drawn from oral-history interviews.[36] Other students of indigenous cuisine included Agustín Aragón Leyva, José Farías Galindo, and Lt. Col. Santos Acevedo López.[37] Perhaps the most prominent collector of village recipes, Mayita Parada, made a fortune as the leading caterer in postrevolutionary Mexico. From her kitchen on Juantepec Street, she introduced peasant cuisine to the nearby mansions of Lomas de Chapulte-pec and even the Presidential Palace of Los Pinos.[38]

By the mid-1940s class snobbery against indigenous foods had dimin-ished noticeably. Tamales and other *antojitos*, once deemed fit only for the "lower orders," provided the subject for entire volumes. Josefina Velázquez de León even declared chicken enchiladas the "regional dish of Guana-juato."[39] And *pozole*, formerly one of the "secrets of the indigenous classes," became the symbol of Guadalajara's cuisine.[40] The legend of *mole poblano* changed to reflect this new attitude. Melitón Salazar Monroy emphasized the delicacy of the "turkey fattened on chestnuts and hazelnuts to finish the dish with such a delicious broth and appetizing meat."[41] Moreover, authors recognized indigenous contributions to the dish in the name *mole*, which came from the Nahua "*molli*," meaning sauce, rather than the Spanish "*moler*," to grind.[42] Maize also lost the former stigma of its Indian origins and came to be seen as the most civilized of the world's grains because its tough outer husk allowed it to reproduce only with human assistance.[43] In the early 1950s, one newspaper announced the end of antagonisms between corn and wheat, explaining that sociologists no longer considered the Eu-ropean grain essential to Mexico's development.[44] A leading nutritionist, Alfredo Ramos Espinosa, formulated the simple equation that people who ate only corn were Indians, those who ate only wheat were Spaniards, while Mexicans were fortunate enough to eat both grains.[45]

But upper- and middle-class consumers still demanded a ritual cleansing of indigenous foods such as the black corn fungus *cuitlacoche*, literally "ex-crement of the gods." As late as the 1940s, cosmopolitan Mexicans consid-ered eating this spore to be a disgusting Indian habit.[46] Gourmet Jaime Saldívar first devised an acceptable way of presenting *cuitlacoche* rolled in *crêpes* and covered with *béchamel* sauce.[47] This association with French haute cuisine removed the lower-class stigma, and by the 1960s Feodora de Rosenzweig Díaz, wife of the subsecretary of foreign affairs, was serving *cuitlacoche* soup to foreign dignitaries. Within a few more decades Mexicans considered it one of their nation's great contributions to international haute cuisine, a sort of Mesoamerican noble rot.[48]

Middle-class acceptance of indigenous contributions to the national cui-sine came at a significant moment in Mexican history. Although this inclu-sive nationalism had appeared hesitantly in community cookbooks of the late Porfiriato, particularly the work of Vicenta Torres, European styles continued to predominate culinary literature in the 1920s and 1930s. Only after the threat of Cardenista populism had ended in the late 1930s did

cookbook authors embrace Indian foods as a national standard. As postrevolutionary governments downplayed class conflict in favor of social har-
mony, folklorists rushed to the countryside to collect oral traditions before
they were drowned by mass-media advertising and replaced with packaged
foods from the United States. Native ingredients and recipes then became
the basis for a uniquely Mexican national cuisine.

## Traveling Gourmets

Postrevolutionary governments from Calles onward based their nationalist
program on highways as much as on education. Roads unified the country
to a previously unthinkable extent by facilitating internal migration and by
carrying national markets, and if necessary the federal army, to the most
remote regions.[49] One of the most colorful nationalist champions to use the
Mexican highway system in the 1940s was Josefina Velázquez de León.
Determined to experience Mexico's diverse regional cuisines, she purchased an automobile, hired a chauffeur, and set off with her loyal servant
and traveling companion Luisa. She ventured across the country for more
than a decade, giving cooking classes, collecting local recipes, and eating
virtually anything.[50] The result, a series of cookbooks describing the foods
of most Mexican states, reflected broader movements of migration and
markets that unified regional recipes into a national cuisine.

   In the 1920s, as political bosses jealously guarded their autonomy against
federal interference, loyalties to local cuisines remained strong. Francisco J.
Santamaría included in a 1921 dictionary an enthusiastic portrait of his
home state Tabasco's tamales, which supposedly contained the finest dough
and fillings, far superior to those of central Mexico.[51] Manuel Toussaint
displayed even more chauvinism when describing the cuisine of Oaxaca
with its "succulent" tamales as opposed to the leathery ones made in Mexico City.[52] Salvador Novo perhaps best explained such culinary jingoism, in
his history of Mexican cuisine, when he spoke of the revolutionary conquest
of central and southern Mexico by *norteño* wheat tortillas.[53]

   Yet the increasing integration of the Mexican nation soon replaced ag-
gressive attitudes with curiosity about other regional cuisines. Faustina
Lavalle, a native of Campeche living in Mexico City, wrote a cookbook in
which she admitted little knowledge of "Mexican" cooking styles, and offered personal recipes so that her new neighbors could appreciate the distinct culture of her home state.[54] Josefina Velázquez de León went to great
lengths to explain the correct usage of herbs and chiles that were often

unknown outside their place of origin.[55] Women could reproduce these recipes because improved highways made it economical to ship diverse ingredients to Mexico City and other urban markets. The transportation industry allowed the transformation of regional cuisines from strictly local knowledges to potentially cosmopolitan cooking styles. The national cuisine therefore owed as much to capitalist development as to a search for *lo mexicano*.

The commodification of regional cuisines reached a peak in the tourism industry, one of the most important sectors of the Mexican economy. While promoters could lure tourists with beaches and pyramids, they also had to offer good food, and the 1950s became a golden age for Mexican gourmet restaurants. Chefs at César Balsa's Presidente Hotel in Acapulco introduced wealthy tourists to *cebiche*, a dish once made only by poor fishermen of freshly caught seafood "cooked" in the citric acid of lime juice.[56] The Gulf Coast port of Veracruz, meanwhile, attracted such celebrities as film director Emilio "El Indio" Fernández to dine on the delicious stuffed crab.[57] Cuernavaca, the vacation home of Mexico's elite from Moctezuma to Maximilian, enticed twentieth-century tourists to the Casa de Piedra for the highly acclaimed cooking of Doña Rosa Trías. This Catalan beauty transformed her Stone Castle into a restaurant and hotel when her husband, the Spanish Marques de Castellar, abandoned her. Spain's loss was Mexico's gain, and people flocked from the capital to sample her *mole poblano* and almond chicken.[58]

But with all due respect to the marquesa, the culinary heart of the republic lay in Mexico City, particularly in the Pink Zone, where some of the finest regional chefs gathered to exhibit their skills. José Inés Loredo, the most flamboyant of these restauranteurs, had already served as municipal president of Tampico before moving to Mexico City in 1943. His most famous creation, *carne asada a la tampiqueña*, butterflied filet served with grilled cheese and green enchiladas, took the capital by storm, and he soon parlayed his initial restaurant, the Tampico Club, into a gourmet empire.[59] Delicious regional cuisine could also be found at the Círculo del Sureste, featuring Yucatecan *cochinita pibil* (pit-barbecued pig), and at the Restaurante Los Norteños, specializing in Monterrey's *cabrito al pastor* (barbecued goat). Restaurants such as the Fonda del Refugio, Café de Tacuba, and Prendes blended a variety of traditional dishes from different regions.[60]

Fiestas provided another natural meeting ground for Mexico's regional cuisines. The society columnist "Gourmet" reported that a distinguished Oaxacan accountant living in Mexico City, Antolín Jiménez, celebrated his birthday with a Guelaguetza danced in traditional folk costume, followed by a buffet of Oaxacan regional foods. At another gathering, the Coahuilan General Alfredo Breceda invited the Yucatecan gourmet Benito Guerra Leal to prepare a *cochinita pibil* that guests could combine with Mexican dishes prepared by the hostess Nena Roth de Breceda. This particular party was intended to welcome some intimate friends returning from Europe with an *"ambiente tan mexicanismo,"* a very Mexican ambience that continued long into the night and did not end until after the governor had danced *la bamba* with the Swedish minister's wife.[61] This mixing of traditions from throughout the republic broke down regional divisions to create an inclusive national identity open to all Mexicans — and to Scandinavians as well.

The combination of regional dialects into a national cuisine was most evident in the culinary literature of the postwar era. Josefina Velázquez de León's influential volume *Platillos regionales de la República mexicana* made it essential to include recipes from each state in any work attempting to represent the national cuisine. Perhaps the most crudely patriotic of these cookbooks derived from the collaboration of a number of senators' wives during the administration of Adolfo López Mateos (1958–64). Each woman provided recipes from the foods of her constituents, but because so many of them were actually natives of Mexico City they collaborated on the dishes of the Federal District.[62] This pattern conveyed a subtle civic lesson to women, transforming their conceptions of space. By arranging dishes in neat categories from Aguascalientes to Zacatecas, the books reformulated a state's symbolic meaning from a unique *patria chica* to an interchangeable federal entity. This change in perspective also facilitated the growth of national identity by emphasizing distinctions between Mexican cuisine and the foods of foreigners.

## Confronting International Cuisine

The proliferation of industrial packaged foods in the twentieth century prompted fears that mass culture from the United States would overwhelm local traditions, reducing diverse national cuisines to the bland uniformity of a McDonald's franchise. The theory of cultural imperialism gained credence not only from the significant share of food markets held by multinational food companies, but also by the virtual domination of the Mexican advertising industry by United States firms.[63] Yet Mexicans are not in any imminent danger of abandoning their traditional cuisine, notwithstanding the efforts of Pepsico and its subsidiary Taco Bell. Immigrant cooks have made important contributions to modern Mexican cuisine, and contact with foreigners may even have stimulated new interest in indigenous ingredients once shunned by elites.

Wealthy Mexicans maintained their infatuation with continental haute cuisine, from the Porfirian gilded age to the postrevolutionary miracle. Tourist guides boasted a number of exclusive international restaurants, most notably the San Angel Inn, Ambassadeurs, Alfredo, and Papillon. These establishments kept up with the latest European fashions, shifting from the stuffy Parisian standards of Carême and Escoffier to the sunny Mediterranean cuisines of Provence and Italy. Antonio Costa, the midcentury counterpart of Porfirian chef Sylvain Daumont, fled the German occupation of France in 1940 to open Papillon, where he introduced Mexicans to the finest cassoulet and civet from the south of France. Alfredo Bellinghieri, a flamboyant Sicilian, maintained equally high standards of Italian cooking and living in his eponymous restaurant.[64]

Members of the middle class, meanwhile, adopted culinary standards set by mass media and food manufacturers from the United States. A 1945 newspaper advertisement for Aunt Jemima–brand pancake mix exemplified this process of culinary influence. The first scene depicted a cartoon figure suspiciously eyeing a stack of pancakes; he chewed the foreign food thoughtfully in the next panel, then finally broke into a broad grin of approval. By the late 1950s, anthropologist Oscar Lewis found that pancakes had become an established tradition among middle-class families, replacing the old breakfast of fried beans, tortillas, and chiles.[65] Many misguided consumers also abandoned fresh crusty *bolillos* (rolls) from neighborhood bakeries in favor of chewy, plastic-wrapped *pan de caja* (bread from a box). The Ideal Bakery came out with the first Mexican version of Wonder Bread in the 1930s, but after 1945 it lost customers to the current market leader, Bimbo Bread. Housewives not only began making geometrically precise sandwiches instead of lush *tortas compuestas*; they also conducted bizarre experiments with mass-produced ingredients to create such hybrid dishes as shrimp and cornflakes, calf brains with crackers, macaroni and milk soup, and pork loin in Pepsi Cola.[66]

These examples may well illustrate a dark side of mass production, but they do not depict the complete annihilation of Mexican gastronomy. Indeed, many foreign manufacturers won customers by demonstrating the utility of their products for making national dishes. Glasbake Cookware ran a series of newspaper advertisements featuring recipes for Mexican regional dishes such as *mole michoacano*. Appliance makers depicted giant *cazuelas* simmering on top of their modern stoves, and an advertisement for pressure cookers made the justifiable claim that "Mexican cooking enters a new epoch with the *Olla presto*." Even that agent of cultural imperialism, Coca Cola, appealed to Mexican customers with nostalgic scenes of *tamalada* picnics.[67]

Moreover, Mexicans often appropriated elements of foreign culture to their own purposes. Domestic soft-drink manufacturers such as Mundet competed with Coke and Pepsi by introducing lines of soda flavors adapted to Mexican tastes for orange, mango, and apple cider. Hollywood movie stars were unknowingly drafted into the service of Mexican culture; for example, the "My Best Recipes" page of a women's magazine paired photos of Jane Powell with Tlaxcalan *barbacoa* and Lucille Ball with tortilla soup.[68] The habit of eating eggs for breakfast, when transferred from the United States to Mexico, stimulated creative experimentation rather than slavish imitation. In searching for national counterparts to Eggs Benedict, Mexican chefs served *huevos rancheros* (ranch-style eggs) fried with tomato-and-chile sauce, *huevos albañiles* (bricklayers' eggs) scrambled with a similar sauce, and *huevos motuleños* (from Motul, Yucatán) fried with beans, ham, and peas.[69] Soon, no hotel with pretensions to luxury could neglect its own "traditional" egg dish on the breakfast menu.

Mexico also enriched the national cuisine through its open door to refugees, particularly Spanish Republicans after the Civil War and Middle Easterners fleeing turmoil in their homelands. Although Spanish cuisine was already well established in Mexico, immigrants from the Eastern Mediterranean brought new traditions such as the *gyro* method of roasting lamb on a portable cooker made up of a vertical spit next to a small gas flame. In the 1930s, Lebanese immigrants to the city of Puebla began selling this meat with flour tortillas, similar to pita bread, under the name *tacos arabes*. Elsewhere in Mexico, street-corner vendors adopted these cookers to make *tacos al pastor* (shepherd's tacos), originally a name used for a rustic form of *barbacoa* served with corn tortillas in the sheep country of Hidalgo.[70] Young people in Mexico City took this Middle Eastern and Mexican blend one step further, with a play on the German shepherd, to call them *tacos de perro* (dog tacos). German immigrants to the Pacific Coast state of Tepic naturalized their own traditions in the form of herring. Just as descendants of Spanish conquistadors celebrated Christmas Eve with Iberian dried cod, German settlers keenly anticipated the annual ship bringing canned fish, which along with Christmas cookies recalled life in the old country. Nostalgic immigrants cared little that people in Germany never thought of eating an everyday food like herring salad under the *Tannenbaum*.[71]

Moreover, the authors of national cookbooks needed foreign foods to distinguish against their own creations. Indeed, the emotional fulfillment of nationalism, a person's pride in the value and legitimacy of their national community, may depend in large part on acceptance by this "other."[72] Mexicans certainly sought such approval of their national cuisine. The food writer "Gourmet," for example, trumpeted the conquests of *mole* over French taste buds when the nationalist painter Dr. Atl (Gerardo Murillo) brought his cook to Paris. In another column she praised the visiting Austrian Prince Kilmanzay, who reportedly preferred Mexican *antojitos* to the most exquisite continental delicacies. "Gourmet's" newspaper, *Excelsior*, noted in 1945 that the Baltimore-Ohio Railroad offered tortillas and other Mexican foods on the daily menu, but added with chagrin that these were intended for migrant workers rather than passengers.[73] Within a few decades, however, the tables turned as Mexican restaurants gained popularity in the United States.[74]

But the foreign role in creating Mexico's national cuisine went far beyond polite applause. The nineteenth century's finest collection of *mole* recipes, *La cocinera poblana*, was written by Catalan immigrant Narciso Bassols. Another Spanish chef, Alejandro Pardo, arrived in Mexico about 1912, and while his European confections dazzled society women, he soon became intrigued by Mexican recipes and his columns in leading women's magazines began featuring *tortillitas* and *chalupitas*.[75] The modern apostle of Mexican food, Englishwoman Diana Southwood Kennedy, has achieved such renown in spreading the gospel of popular cuisine that she received the Order of the Aztec Eagle, the Mexican government's highest honor open to foreigners. The work of these immigrants did not detract from the invaluable research of Josefina Velázquez de León, Virginia Rodríguez Rivera, and many others. Nevertheless, foreigners have taken an undeniably important role in exploring the country's gastronomic traditions. This resulted in part from the almost religious enthusiasm of converts to a new cuisine, but also because they did not share the Mexican elite's disdain for the Indian masses and anything pertaining to them.

The eventual acceptance of native foods such as *cuitlacoche* may derive largely from the search for distinctively Mexican contributions to international cuisine. The 1980s *nouvelle* Mexican fashion of using European techniques to prepare indigenous ingredients owed its modern origins to Jaime Saldívar's corn fungus *crêpes*. Exclusive restaurants offered elegant plates of *chapulines*, tiny grasshoppers, cooked with chipotle chiles and garnished with guacamole. Chefs also prized *gusanos*, worms from the maguey plant, which were usually sautéed in butter to disguise the fact that they did not come fresh from the fields. Eating bugs became a source of national distinction, even pride, offered by middle-class families to visiting students from the United States. After centuries of neglect, Moctezuma's dinner finally made a comeback as Mexico's contender in the highly competitive restaurant world. This revaluation of popular cuisine represented part of a broad attempt to come to grips with the nation's past.

## Cooking History

Virtually all Mexican politicians of the 1920s and 1930s attributed their legitimacy to national service in the Revolution of 1910. These officials used the label "reactionary" as a political anathema even as they pursued increasingly conservative policies, stifling the radicalism of peasant and labor movements. To resolve this dissonance, they sought to reshape the popular memory of revolutionary leaders. Eulogies of Emiliano Zapata, for example, downplayed his support for village democracy and depicted him instead as an agent of the revolutionary state.[76] Even traditional conservatives could employ parts of the revolutionary past for their own purposes, viewing Francisco Madero as the true spirit of 1910 while representing Lázaro Cárdenas as a communist corruption of this democratic movement.[77] History thus became a tool of ideologues seeking to forge a national memory suited to their own political ends.

Cookbook authors likewise imagined the national cuisine in historical terms, and often began their works with brief accounts of Mexican gastronomic history. These narratives, together with a few longer essays, illustrated many of the beliefs and aspirations of middle-class housewives. Adela Fernández, daughter of "El Indio" Fernández, perhaps best articulated this distinctive ideology in a description of her culinary education in the 1940s. María Elena Sodi de Pallares wrote a well-known essay on Mexican culinary history in 1958 for a food industry trade fair sponsored by the Ministry of the Economy. Two book-length studies appeared in the late 1960s, one by Salvador Novo, Mexico City's official chronicler, and the other by Amando Farga, a Spanish immigrant and editor of the Mexican Restaurant Association's trade magazine.[78]

The periodization of this culinary history followed a predictable course, beginning with pre-Columbian foods. Authors glorified Tlatelolco's market and Moctezuma's banquets, reverently quoting the accounts of Spanish conquistadors and priests. Food critic Miguel Guzmán Peredo paid homage to the Aztec ruler as America's first gourmet, comparable to the French author Brillat-Savarin. Cooking teacher Florencio Gregorio even attempted to date the invention of certain Mesoamerican foods to successive rulers of Xochimilco. He imaginatively associated Xaopantzin (1379–1397) with the vegetable dish *huauhtzontles*, Oztolt (1397–1411) with enchiladalike *chilaquiles*, and Tilhuatzin (1437–1442) with herb-stuffed *quiltamales.*[79]

The colonial period constituted the second great age of Mexican cooking and the origins of the mestizo cuisine that became the national standard. Salvador Novo declared the first mestizo dish to be pork tacos, which he imagined were served at a banquet for Fernando Cortés. The greatest triumph of the "baroque" kitchens of New Spain was of course *mole poblano,* the heavenly dish of the sisters of Santa Rosa. This association gained added tourist appeal in 1968, when the former Dominican convent, closed down by the Reform, was converted into a museum of regional folk art. Another component of mestizo cuisine came from the romantic voyages of the Manila galleon, which sailed once a year between the Philippines and Acapulco. This majestic ship supposedly carried to Mexico both rice and *mancha-manteles* (tablecloth stainers), delicious mixtures of tropical fruits and spicy chiles reminiscent of Chinese sweet and sour sauces.[80]

With independence in 1821 came the first national dish, *chiles en nogada.* The people of Puebla created this dish of green chile peppers, white walnut sauce, and red pomegranate seeds to honor the tricolor flag of Agustín de Iturbide, first emperor of Mexico. The Second Empire of Maximilian and Carlota introduced still another influence in 1864, French cuisine. Although Mexicans expelled the invading French army three years later and executed the unfortunate archduke, European dishes continued their occupation of the country throughout the presidency of Porfirio Díaz. The development of Mexico's mestizo cuisine culminated in the revolution with the expulsion of French banquets and the mixing of various regional foods by *soldadera* camp followers, who carried wheat tortillas from the north and corn tamales from the south. This new national cooking style incorporated elements from America, Asia, Africa, and Europe, forming a universal cuisine that mirrored the "cosmic race" of mestizos.[81]

The significance of these culinary narratives lay not in their (often quite dubious) historical accuracy, but in what they revealed about modern Mexico. Cookbook authors paid little attention to traditional civic heroes such as Benito Juárez and Emiliano Zapata. Instead, they enshrined conservative religious figures as founders of the national cuisine. The seventeenth-century nuns who invented *mole poblano* became the symbolic mothers of the mestizo nation; the often-reviled first emperor Agustín Iturbide received credit for *chiles en nogada*; and the misguided Second Empire of

Maximilian and Carlota was recalled for its glorious European court life. This domestic construction of the past differed noticeably from the official PRI version of Mexican history, embracing instead a more conservative vision of the national past.[82]

Eric Hobsbawm has attributed such "invented traditions" — and nationalism more generally — to a search for stability in times of modernization.[83] Mexican women of the postwar era displayed a mania for preserving their culinary past, even as it began to slip away. When electric blenders finally allowed women to make *mole poblano* without a grinding stone, the food columnist "Gourmet" warned women to save their *metates*, "because this Mexican cooking utensil has still not been supplanted by any modern appliance."[84] Josefina Velázquez de León, in a guide to domestic appliances, made special efforts to create links with the past by juxtaposing modern housewives with stereotypes of historical figures. The cookbook's illustrations showed fashionable women effortlessly using blenders and pressure cookers to make tamales with peasant girls, *pulques* with maguey planters, and sweets with colonial nuns.[85] Editorial houses turned out facsimiles of nineteenth-century cookbooks, and magazines included whole sections devoted to archaic recipes.[86] A few people even published manuscript cookbooks they inherited from their grandmothers.[87]

The invention of tradition is particularly apparent in the creation myth of *pozole*, a hominy stew of the Pacific Coast. Cooking legends, like fairy tales, follow a set formula including an accident and an important personage. This story, set in eighteenth-century Chilapa, Guerrero, told of the dilemma facing women preparing for the visit of the Archbishop of Puebla. They had too much corn to grind, so instead of making tortillas they simply cooked the *nixtamalized* kernels with pork to make a stew, *pozole*. The choice of a *poblano* prelate is important, because in Mexican gastronomic mythology Puebla was the home of *mole*. The bishop's benediction thus sacralized *pozole*, giving it a legitimate place in the nation's culinary pantheon.[88]

Cookbooks also helped foment national consensus by downplaying class and ethnic struggle. They portrayed the conquest not as a brutal war of cultural genocide, but as a "happy encounter" of two culinary traditions. Cuisine even provided symbols for the cold war against international communism. A 1947 editorial cartoon in the newspaper *Excelsior* depicted the spread of communism in Chile as a voracious Joseph Stalin about to devour a pepper. The caption, however, warned him away, saying, "it's very hot and causes indigestion."[89] Latin American food thus served as a metaphorical defense against foreign influence. But the real threat of communism in the hemisphere lay not in outside agitation by Russian agents, but in the disaffected masses who rallied behind Fidel Castro. In Mexico, the middle classes themselves ultimately began to question the success of their authoritarian system.

## The Miracle's End

As hosts of the 1968 Olympic Games, Mexicans hoped to exhibit to the world their economic development, but instead revealed to themselves the failure of their "miracle." The political consensus of revolutionary nationalism began to unravel in the summer of 1968, when university student demonstrators began calling for democracy. Fearing disruption of the games, the government responded with repression, and confrontations escalated between protesters and police. On October 2, 1968, about five thousand students and spectators gathered at Tlatelolco, site of the great pre-Columbian marketplace and of the Aztec ruler Cuauhtémoc's last stand. When the students refused orders to disperse, army units attacked them with billy clubs and tear gas. Shots were fired, either by student snipers or government *granaderos*, and then the carnage began. Soldiers opened fire with high-caliber machine guns, killing more than three hundred men, women, and children. At least two thousand people suffered injuries in the fighting and as many more were arrested, beaten, and tortured.[90]

The massacre of Tlatelolco struck a grave blow to the ruling party's legitimacy, and it was only the first of many. The gains of the previous decades had gone primarily to the wealthy. In 1950 the poorest 20 percent of the population received only 6 percent of the national income; by 1987 their share had fallen to less than half that figure.[91] Glaring inequalities encouraged leftist guerrilla movements in the 1970s, which the army suppressed with terror tactics. At the same time economic growth faltered, forcing major devaluations of the peso beginning in 1976. By the mid-1980s, the foreign debt had increased to nearly 100 billion dollars and the peso plummeted to a rate of 3,000 to the dollar.[92]

Under these circumstances, Mexicans of all social classes questioned the viability of one-party politics and trickle-down development. The wealthy protected themselves by sending tens of billions of dollars abroad to United States and European banks, further compounding the country's economic crisis. The middle class, their savings wiped out by devaluations, gave up beach vacations and luxury goods. The poor simply ate less, especially after the government cut food subsidies as part of an International Monetary Fund austerity program. Economic hardship, in turn, fueled support for opposition political parties. The conservative National Action Party (PAN) began winning local elections throughout northern Mexico, while leftist members of the PRI defected under the leadership of Cuauhtémoc Cárdenas, son of the former president. It is widely suspected that the ruling party resorted to electoral fraud in the 1988 election to assure the victory of Carlos Salinas de Gortari over the Cardenista opposition. And as president, Salinas repressed attempts to open the party, thereby broadening the split between technocrats and populists. Demands for democracy and social justice grew violent on January 1, 1994, when the Zapatista National Liberation Army launched a rebellion in the southern state of Chiapas. Four months later, the PRI's reformist presidential candidate Luis Donaldo Colosio was gunned down at a campaign rally in Baja California. The possible implication of party members in the assassination wrote the requiem for the peace of the PRI.

With the end of the miracle came the close of another era in Mexican history. On September 19, 1968, just two weeks before the massacre at Tlatelolco, Josefina Velázquez de León passed away. At sixty-nine, she had already slowed down in her work, but had agreed to give a three-day cooking class in the city of Veracruz for Catholic charities. She fell ill in the port city and died a short time later. Her sisters attempted to carry on the business, but eventually closed the school and sold the rights to her books. The ground floor of the family house on Abraham González Street, where Doña Josefina had given her first cooking classes, was rented out as an auto parts store.[93] Nevertheless, her culinary legacy remained as a source of comfort for the Mexican people. Some of her first books to be reissued in the late 1980s were *How to Cook in Hard Times* and *How to Use Leftover Food*.[94] And when an earthquake devastated Mexico City in 1985, one of the first projects to aid the victims was, not surprisingly, a charity cookbook.[95]

*SEVEN*

# Recipes for *Patria*

## *National Cuisines in Global Perspective*

CYXYD

"If there is anything we [Chinese] are serious about," wrote Lin Yutang in 1935, "it is neither religion nor learning, but food." The philosopher went on to define patriotism as a "recollection of the keen sensual pleasures of our childhood. The loyalty to Uncle Sam is the loyalty to American doughnuts, and loyalty to the *Vaterland* is the loyalty to *Pfannkuchen* and *Stollen*, but the Americans and the Germans will not admit it."[1] Mexicans have tended toward the Chinese gastronomic impulse rather than Anglo-German reticence; poet Ramón López Velarde began the first act of his *Suave patria* (1921) with the words "Fatherland: your surface is maize," and architect Fernando González Gortázar cited cuisine along with art, language, and landscape as among the things most evocative of the national identity.[2] Although this Proustian notion requires historical and comparative perspective, it nevertheless helps explain the sense of belonging that inspires nationalism.

The first qualification arises from the need to distinguish nationalism from bonds of family, religion, or native land. Nations are communities of people who claim the right to self-government based on shared and distinctive cultures, which are themselves modern constructions. National political rituals, from the mass rallies of fascist states to the election days of parliamentary democracies, therefore emphasize the unity of the people.[3] Benedict Anderson noted that an essential step in the rise of national identity was the eighteenth-century decline of loyalties to older communities such as monarchies and religions.[4] Yet the nation need not be an individual's only, or even primary, affiliation. In the same way, tamales convey many levels of identity. Individual quirks of taste and texture allow Mexican

143

families to distinguish the neighbors' tamales from their own by particular blends of chiles and herbs or by subtle flourishes in spreading corn dough on the wrapper. Basic ingredients locate tamales on a regional level, sometimes broadly, with banana leaves in the south and east, corn husks in the center and north, and at other times point to a more precise *patria chica*, iguana in Chiapas, *gusanos* in Morelos, head cheese in Chihuahua. Tamales even range beyond the national borders, throughout the Gulf of Mexico and the Caribbean Basin, from Venezuela to Mississippi. Nevertheless, with the creation of a Mexican national cuisine, tamales have also become identified with *lo mexicano*.

A second analytical requirement is to distinguish between the many historical variants of nationalism. Two basic distinctions exist between ethnic and civic nationalism, on the one hand, and between official and popular nationalism, on the other. Although these categories do not exhaust the complexity of nationalist movements, they do pose important questions about the nature of modern politics. Proponents of ethnic nationalism, most notably the National Socialists in Germany, attributed their identity to racial characteristics, and accepted only those who claimed pure lineage. By contrast, civic nationalism acknowledges its modern origins in an act of political will, the French Revolution of 1789, for example, and theoretically anyone can gain citizenship by embracing the national ideals. Neither category is absolute; Germany grants naturalization although with some hesitation, while France has excluded many immigrants considered to have unacceptable ethnic origins. Mexico actually defied European logic in the twentieth century by formulating an inclusive ethnic nationalism based on the cosmic race. Nevertheless, definitions of citizenship have profoundly influenced the character of modern states.[5]

Nationalism has also lent support to the diverse interests of both government officials and the popular masses. The ideal of national unity often cloaked social-engineering programs aimed at eradicating local languages and cultures. Ernest Gellner attributed such educational and mass-media efforts to modern industrial societies' demands for interchangeable workers sharing a common culture and language.[6] Porfirian and revolutionary governments' developmentalist projects certainly pursued this goal, as have nationalist industrialization schemes elsewhere in Asia, Africa, and Latin America. But at the same time, nationalism opened spaces for lower-class political participation and provided the means for satisfying popular demands. Nineteenth-century Mexican civic militias used patriotic service in the wars of the Reform and of the French Intervention to justify local autonomy. Though often stifled by authoritarian governments, the popular sectors continued to demand effective participation in national politics.[7]

A comparative examination of cuisine helps elucidate the complex relations of gender, class, and region that merged in the construction of national identity. Nationalist ideologies have incorporated these specific identities, reformulating each to bolster the power and legitimacy of the state. Women were reified in the role of selfless, patriotic mothers, then denied a genuine voice in politics. Class differences seemingly vanished within the camaraderie of citizenship, even as development programs magnified social inequalities. And diverse regional cultures were cast into a few stereotypical molds — in Mexico, the silver-buckled *charro*, the white-bloused *china poblana* — that lent nostalgic authenticity to industrializing societies. Yet subordinate groups throughout the world have appropriated elements of national culture, twisting them to their own ends. Middle-class women wrote cookbooks expressing personal visions of the nation, while maintaining an air of domestic respectability. Popular-sector cooks created their own culinary art, and ridiculed the pretensions of their supposed social superiors. Finally, all cooks preserved distinctive regional dishes while situating them within emerging national cuisines.

## A Woman's Place?

The Virgin of Guadalupe evokes profound feelings of national loyalty from Mexicans partly because, as the symbol of motherhood, she embodies three of the most basic elements of nationalism. First, the self-sacrifice exemplified by the Indian Virgin's devotion to her Mexican children also nourished the patriotism of the *niños heroes*, who plunged to their death in 1847 rather than surrender Chapultepec Castle to the northern invaders. Second, the antiquity of the Virgin's appearance in 1531 established the permanence of the Mexican nation, just as motherhood linked successive generations of the national community. Third, the purity of *marianismo*, the Porfirian cult of female moral superiority, imparted an essential respectability to middle-class liberals' claims to be legitimate representatives of the nation. Women clearly had a vital role in the nation, but a passive one of self-abnegating, virtuous maternity. Nevertheless, the moral superiority of *marianismo* offered a potential challenge to the male monopoly of the public sphere, for the female duty of nurturing the nation could also justify political participation.[8]

Patriarchal Western societies since the archaic states of ancient Meso-
potamia have excluded women from civic participation and devalued their
social contributions. The twin functions of military service and property
ownership defined citizenship in classical Greece and Rome, feudal aristocracy in the Middle Ages, and the revival of citizenship in modern nation-
states. Neither function possessed an exclusively gendered nature; women
have long served the military in noncombatant support roles that exposed
them to as much danger as regular soldiers. A sharp distinction between
male battlefield and female home front nevertheless arose because, as Cynthia Enloe has shown, the image of defenseless women at home helped to
reconcile men to military discipline.[9] Although the uncertainties of human reproduction precluded the development of exclusively male property
rights, female sexuality did become exclusively male property in Mediterranean society. The creation of patriarchy, in turn, marginalized women from
religious participation. The Mother Goddesses Isis, Tiamat, and Namu of
ancient Near Eastern mythology were dethroned or destroyed by male
gods Osiris, Marduk, and Enki, at the same time that male priests usurped
power from rival temples run by women. Moreover, the exclusion of He-
brew women from the Covenant with Yahweh set the precedent for a male
monopoly of the Christian priesthood.[10]

European and Asian men reserved the right not only to speak with the
gods, but to feed them as well, taking over tasks ordinarily assigned to
women. Chinese emperors as early as the Chou dynasty (1032–480 B.C.)
represented the power of the state through the image of a cooking pot, and
they derived much of their legitimacy from the ritual feeding of gods and
ancestors — such delicacies as a raw fowl with tail feathers unplucked and
the entrails draped around its neck.[11] Wall paintings from the tomb of
Ramses III depicted males working in the kitchens of the Egyptian Pha-
raoh. From this time forward, European and Mediterranean royalty employed male chefs for the work of transforming ordinary foods into court
cuisine. The Topkapi Palace of Istanbul established a clear sexual division
of labor between pleasures of the table and of the bed by placing a great
courtyard between the kitchen and the harem.[12]

Jack Goody attributed the differences between male haute cuisine and
female domestic cookery to highly stratified, literate societies. He noted
that African kings and chiefs made no such distinctions; the duties of both
kitchen and bedroom rotated between wives, who prepared the same basic
foods as everyone else in the community. Although the Arabic written language had entered some parts of Sub-Saharan Africa, cooking remained
largely egalitarian before the onset of colonization. In Europe and Asia,

by contrast, cuisine developed as a literary field that distinguished elites from commoners. The first cookbooks written by the Greeks and Romans exemplified this search for social distinction through conspicuous consumption. The renowned although possibly fictitious gourmets of antiquity, Apicius and Athenaeus, spared no expense to obtain exotic ingredients, including spices from the Orient and game from Africa, as well as to perfect culinary techniques, for example, dressing up one meat to resemble another.[13] Chinese philosophers and poets, meanwhile, developed an even richer and more formal gastronomic literature. Confucius showed his priorities, when questioned about military tactics, by answering that while he knew how to arrange a meat platter, he had no advice for generals. More recently, French chef Antonin Carême, author of some ten thick cookbooks, attributed much of his success to the daily journal he kept.[14]

Although literary traditions separated professional chefs from the oral culture of domestic cooks, this does not imply the superiority of one over the other. A French woman who ventured to pen a cookbook in the 1930s illustrated this difference when she expressed the fear that her grandmother's recipes might "spoil in the writing." She advised readers not to worry about the arithmetic common to many cookbooks, but rather to "think a little about the things you are preparing, imagine the cauliflower in the garden in all its beauty, you can no longer let it burn!"[15] The term *oral culture* tends to mislead if it implies a simple opposition with written culture. Words, whether written or spoken, represent only one-dimensional approximations of what might be called more broadly "sensual culture." Chef Paul Bertolli has described cooking as "a richly shaded language understood by all the senses — the degrees of a simmer, the aroma of a roast telling you it's done, the stages of elasticity of kneaded dough, the earthy scent of a vegetable just pulled from the ground."[16]

This interactive process between cook and food makes it impossible to speak of cuisine, however traditional, as conservative. All cooking, at least before microwave ovens and frozen dinners, involved experimentation, a constant process of adjustment to transform a unique set of ingredients into a completed dish. This innovation need not be apparent to the final consumer; a tourist visiting a Mexican fiesta or an anthropologist investigating a remote community may complain of the repetitive nature of the food, the seemingly identical *flautas* or *pozoles* produced by every cook in sight. But, in fact, each *cazuela* bears a unique signature of technique and seasoning that is readily apparent to the discerning consumer, for only the most practiced coordination of hand, eye, ear, nose, and tongue can bring a dish to perfection — *al punto*.[17]

However much was lost in distilling this language to paper, cooks did gain the ability to communicate their recipes to a broader audience, making possible the conception of national cuisines. In Mexico, Vicenta Torres de Rubio and Josefina Velázquez de León invited collaborators from diverse parts of the republic to contribute recipes to their cookbooks, which began to codify the nation's many cuisines. Arjun Appadurai described a similar process of middle-class cultural construction in the cities of modern India. Women from throughout the subcontinent published the recipes of family and friends in English-language cookbooks. While affirming regional and ethnic traditions, these volumes also created a national repertoire of dishes available to all Indians.[18] In Thailand, Penny Van Esterik observed a unique variation of culinary literature in the form of cremation books, published as memorials to the deceased and distributed to funeral guests. These volumes, which often contained favorite recipes from the deceased person's home village, gained wide circulation through elaborate funerals held by elite families. Along with more traditional cookbooks, they formed the basis for a Thai national cuisine.[19]

Cookbooks inspired national loyalty less by any didactic content than by fostering a sense of community among women. The limitations of nineteenth-century Mexican instructional literature was discussed in chapter Three. For a twentieth-century example, consider the series of beautifully illustrated cookbooks created by artist Martha Chapa and sponsored by various state governments. A volume entitled *Taste of Independence* featured the foods of Querétaro, the home of La Corregidora, a Spanish official's wife who saved Father Hidalgo from arrest on September 16, 1810. These cookbooks contained explicit history and civics lessons in the introductions, and also made elegant Christmas presents from state governors.[20] Appadurai gave comparable examples of nationalist ideology in Indian cookbooks, but he discounted their rhetorical value and considered the seductiveness of regional variety more effective in fomenting national identity.[21] Eric Hobsbawm agreed that "deliberate propaganda was almost certainly less significant than the ability of the mass media to make what were in effect national symbols part of the life of every individual."[22]

The transformation of household practices into national symbols encouraged women to take more active roles in the national life. Precedents for this transcendental use of domestic symbolism reached back to female saints of the High Middle Ages, many of whom expressed their religiosity through the ritual of the Holy Eucharist. Some supposedly fasted for years, subsisting on nothing but communion wafers, and had mystical visions in which they nursed and were nursed by Christ. The religious significance of food to medieval women, who were denied more conventional forms of spirituality reserved for the male clergy, was described by Caroline Bynum. "God, like woman, fed his children from his own body. . . . Thus woman found it very easy to identify with a deity whose flesh, like theirs, was food. In mystical ecstasy, in communion, in ascetic *imitatio*, women ate and became a God who was food and flesh."[23]

In seventeenth-century Mexico, Sor Juana Inés de la Cruz also drew on food imagery, this time to challenge the exclusion of women from scriptural knowledge and their confinement to religious mysticism. In her 1690 response to "Sor Filotea," actually the Bishop of Puebla who had censured her for scholarly activity unbecoming of a woman, she reversed the usual association between women and ignorance. "What could I tell you of the natural secrets I have discovered while cooking?" she asked rhetorically, before launching into a lecture on the laws of chemistry revealed by cooking eggs. She concluded that "had Aristotle cooked, how much more he would have written."[24] But despite the cloak of domestic respectability, assertions of knowledge or religiosity were dangerous, for male priests ultimately decided whether female visions indicated sainthood or witchcraft. Sor Juana was driven to renounce her books and died a few years later while nursing the victims of a plague.

As the rise of nationalism transferred sacred ground from church to state, domestic roles also offered women a voice in this new religion of the people. French feminists of the 1890s adopted "pot-au-feu," "motherhood," and "*patrie*" as slogans in their campaign for limited reforms, while Egyptian contemporaries claimed a right to education on the grounds of patriotic sentiment and domestic efficiency.[25] In the Mexican Revolution of 1910, women cooked for and often died with their soldier husbands, yet official monuments celebrated only the male troops and devalued *soldadera* contributions.[26] Another opportunity for civic service came with the oil expropriation in 1938, when President Cárdenas's declaration of economic independence from foreign capital left the government heavily indebted. Filled with national pride, Mexicans donated personal belongings to compensate the companies; housewives organized fiestas and sold tamales and *chalupas* to pay for the oil.[27] Gradually women gained confidence in political roles, but many continued to justify their public voice in domestic terms. For example, women organized against PRI vote fraud in Buena Vista, Morelos, to guarantee communal lands for their children and grandchildren. On election day, they joined the townsmen in occupying the munici-

pal building to assure a fair count, and instead of fleeing to their homes
when the army arrived, they domesticated the soldiers by offering them
food and drink.[28]

By framing political participation in terms of the family, and by imagin-
ing the nation as a community of cooks, women tacitly acknowledged the
patriarchal structure of society. Gilberto Freyre, a Brazilian sociologist
noted for looking on the bright side of inequality, described cuisine as one
of the "expressions of patriarchal civilization" that flourished best in the
former slaveholding capital of Bahia.[29] The *marianista* ideal of domesticity
appeared in late nineteenth-century Mexico at a time when feminists in
Europe and the United States were marching to demand equal rights. But
even after the Revolution of 1910, effective suffrage for males remained
largely a dream, so the lack of female political activism seems more under-
standable. Linda Colley, in her magisterial study of British nationalism,
wrote that women invoked domestic values in large part to prove to themselves that entering politics meant not abandoning family duties, but fulfilling them.[30] Time spent in the kitchen therefore had the paradoxical effect
both of diverting women from civic participation and of helping to expand
their public roles. And middle-class women were not alone in this quest for
citizenship.

## Cuisine and Class

Nationalism and gastronomy in Western Europe share a common heritage
as cultural artifacts of the emerging middle classes. Benedict Anderson has
explained how the spread of print capitalism, particularly newspapers and
novels, first inspired the invention of national communities.[31] Moreover, as
Edmund S. Morgan has shown, politicians in eighteenth-century England
and the United States proceeded to invent the concept of popular sovereignty to justify their own power gained in resisting a sovereign king.[32]
According to Rebecca Spang, gastronomy, defined as the study, discussion,
and pursuit of good food, arose in early nineteenth-century France as an
assertion of individual taste in opposition to the spectacle of court cuisine.
The Parisian bourgeoisie, in particular, cultivated the appreciation of food
as a privileged art that helped establish their social distinction.[33] These
forms of middle-class political and cultural domination appealed greatly to
Western-educated nationalist leaders in other parts of the world as well, but
attempts to impose European models often met with sharp resistance from
indigenous cultures.

Although Chinese gastronomic literature extends back at least a thousand years, until quite recently it was the province of a bureaucratic elite concerned more with the Mandate of Heaven than with the sovereignty of people. Consideration of national consciousness and culinary sensibility therefore begins with eighteenth-century France. Rebecca Spang gave an insightful account of the emergence of Parisian restaurant culture from the moral and medical literature of the Enlightenment. She debunked the culinary legend attributing restaurants to the French Revolution of 1789, and demonstrated that professional chefs actually began catering to middle-class consumers more than three decades earlier. Moreover, instead of reproducing aristocratic cuisine, the first establishments literally served "restaurants," thick bouillons believed to "restore" health to sensitive souls with digestive troubles or weak chests. These "waterless soups," made by slowly reducing several pounds of meat without added water to a mere cup of broth, appealed to an urban elite, both noble and bourgeois, nostalgic for the simple life of an idealized countryside. And because each customer suffered from unique ailments, restaurants offered individual servings from menus listing many different bouillons, a novel idea at the time that has since become standard practice.[34]

Restaurant menus and culinary literature tore loose from their medical moorings in the first half of the nineteenth century to form a new and autonomous culture of gastronomy. Food no longer simply provided nourishment; it became a separate world of sensual pleasures waiting to be explored by inventive chefs and intrepid gourmets. The pioneers of gastronomic literature, Grimod de la Reynière and Jean Anthelme Brillat-Savarin, used literary metaphors and scientific language to translate these elusive flavors for aspiring epicures. Meanwhile, gourmet guidebooks mapped out a new geography of France in which the palace of Versailles was replaced by pheasants and the cathedral at Reims by bottles of champagne. Parisian restaurant menus likewise stood apart from the outside world; for example, chicken *Mexicaine* was not some version of *mole*, but rather a bird sautéed in butter, covered in veal gravy, and garnished with sweet peppers.[35]

The exclusivity of this gastronomic culture provided a source of social distinction for those initiated in its obscure rituals. Although restaurants were in theory democratic institutions, open to anyone who could pay the check, in practice waiters skillfully assigned customers to their social rank. Simply ordering a meal in a famous restaurant demanded a high degree of literacy in the new culinary idiom, and any lapse could lead to humiliation. Spang related the story of a provincial family that mistook the menu selection for a fixed banquet and ordered dishes in the sequence they appeared on the list. After seven different soups, they gave up before reaching the first entrée. But the savvy patron, who dueled with waiters and emerged victorious, gained admittance to a sophisticated aristocracy judged by individual taste rather than family lineage.[36]

The self-absorbed nature of this gourmet discourse led Spang to deny it any nationalist content: "In the gastronomer's world, the man of taste had to be able to 'set aside' petty national allegiances in his omnivorous pursuit of quality."[37] But the rejection of political involvement does not imply a corresponding absence of national identity. Grimod's gastronomical world was in fact a French one, to which foreign dishes gained admittance only when "adopted and above all perfected" by French chefs. The recipe for mock turtle soup, cited by Spang as overcoming national pride, concluded with praise for the chef who cooks it and thereby gives "French nationality to a dish which had up till then been advanced by the English every time they wished to exalt their cooking to the detriment of our own."[38] Nor did Brillat-Savarin miss any opportunity to assert the superiority of French civilization over all others.[39]

Numerous cultures eager to gain the political distinction of nationhood likewise asserted their claims to a sophisticated national cuisine. Arjun Appadurai and Penny Van Esterik have described the ways that middle-class Indian and Thai women blended diverse regional cooking styles into polyglot national cultures.[40] In 1929, Dionisio Pérez wrote a volume on Spanish cuisine in which he denounced the "pernicious confusion of cookbooks that mix genuine Spanish dishes with French, Italian, and even English ones, and that give the appearance of scantiness, if not inferiority, to Spanish cooking."[41] The Republic of Georgia, upon gaining independence from the Soviet Union, created a Ministry of Public Catering in part to record the country's diverse cuisines.[42] Perhaps the most zealous of all culinary nationalists have been the Basques, who positively exult in the fame won by local chefs in the foreign capitals of New York, London, Paris, and Madrid. One writer asserted that "there are few places where chefs would think about cooking in quite the same terms of idealistic pride and 'integrity' as in the Basque Country. They firmly believe that cooking is part of the heritage of a nation or region and that the ritual of eating and drinking well are an essential part of Basque idiosyncracy."[43]

Capitalist profits, not just patriotic pride, stimulated much of this interest in fomenting national cuisines. Dionisio Pérez observed in his guide to Spanish gastronomy that "when we say cuisine, we say production."[44] French culinary renown stimulated demand for the country's wine in California, cheese in Upper Volta, and asparagus in Vietnam.[45] Italian pasta,

Russian caviar, and Idaho potatoes (in McDonald's french fries) have also developed international markets. Many governments have promoted national food industries to protect against foreign encroachment. The Iron Chancellor Otto von Bismarck, for example, encouraged the consumption of "German" rye bread in order to avoid dependence on imported wheat from rival nations.[46] One of the twentieth century's largest industries, tourism, has also inspired the development of national cuisines. Pérez wrote his guide as a tour of Spanish regional cooking and published it with the National Corporation of Tourism. Mexico likewise touted local dishes as attractions for tourist pesos. Even the French succumbed to this lure, which forced them to concede that restaurants worthy of the name existed outside of Paris, though not very far outside. The early twentieth-century food critic Maurice-Edmond Sailland, known as Curnonsky, "Prince of Gourmets," promoted French regional cooking as "the ideal marriage of tourism and gastronomy."[47]

Yet no single bourgeois logic explains the intricate connections between class and nationalism. The Mexican national cuisine passed through three distinct periods reflecting different conceptions of citizenship. In the nineteenth century, elites defined the national cuisine as essentially European, excluding tamales and other corn products from respectable dinner tables, even as they denied the franchise to both rural and urban poor. Porfirian and revolutionary concern for mobilizing a national workforce led to a second period, roughly 1900 to 1946, of the tortilla discourse. During this time, a desire to indoctrinate the lower class into bourgeois standards of morality prompted a campaign to replace corn with wheat in the national diet. Finally, about 1946, once populist reform had spent its momentum and the capitalist economy had incorporated maize, the middle class appropriated tamales for themselves, transforming a basic element of popular culture into a symbol of national unity.

Nineteenth-century Mexican elites aspired to create a Mexican nation in the image of Europe. Although the examples of Benito Juárez and Ignacio Altamirano tempered their racism, elites used the seemingly primitive culture of both Native Americans and rural mestizos to disqualify them from participation in national politics. French cuisine, deliberately calculated to exclude the unsophisticated, further contributed to the apparent cultural superiority of the elite who hobnobbed at Porfirian banquets and restaurants. Nor was this snobbery limited to Mexico. Industrial barons of the Gilded Age asserted aristocratic pretensions by dining on French cuisine at Delmonico's, in the heart of supposedly democratic New York City. At the same time, Egyptian elites adopted European culture, including its cuisine, as part of an effort to catch up with the industrial powers. Yet other countries, most notably China, preserved their cuisine unaltered, even at the height of nineteenth-century modernization efforts. This form of culinary imperialism therefore seemed to affect primarily those societies already unsure of the value of their native culture.[48]

The tortilla discourse arose about 1900 from the intersection of several lines of Mexican social thought. Porfirian social reformers, like their European counterparts, sought to instill bourgeois notions of morality among the lower classes in order to mold an efficient workforce. Nutritional reform gained a high priority in Mexico because the inferiority of corn seemed to explain underdevelopment scientifically, but without resorting to the racist theories prominent in Western Europe and the United States. Similar reasoning influenced sociologist Gilberto Freyre, who attributed Brazilian backwardness to poor diet rather than to racial miscegenation or the tropical climate. Yet unlike Francisco Bulnes, Freyre applauded the contributions of Africans and Native Americans to the national culture. Therefore, rather than distinguishing between well-fed conquistadors and emaciated underlings, he admitted that even the Portuguese colonizers were malnourished. High profits from sugar production led planters to neglect food crops for the slaves, while for themselves they imported Iberian wheat, oil, wine, and even fruits, which usually went bad during the transatlantic voyage.[49]

The third stage of Mexico's national cuisine, in which the middle class appropriated popular symbols as national standards, became a more common pattern in the modern world. For example, twentieth-century Egyptian nationalists rejected the European culture so recently embraced by their nineteenth-century predecessors. In place of continental cuisine, they harkened back to the ancient *ful medames* (brown beans), once eaten by Pharaohs although more recently associated with servants and peasants.[50] Brazilians took as their national dish *feijoada*, formerly made only by slaves, of black beans, rice, and assorted animal parts including beef tongue and pigs' ears, similar to "soul food" in the United States. Peter Fry suggested that this use of ethnic food to characterize the nation converted potentially subversive symbols into tame bulwarks of an unequal society.[51] India represents a limiting case of this appropriation of popular cuisine because of the rigid dietary laws of the caste system. High castes defiled themselves by eating the foods of their social inferiors, and thus lower-class dishes, particularly meat, could not gain wide acceptance as symbols of national unity.

Many cosmopolitan Mexicans have likewise been appalled by the thought of being identified with peasant food. In 1988, one of the country's largest banks sponsored a volume paying homage to each of the major ingredients in Mexican cuisine, including spices, herbs, tomatoes, mushrooms, fish, meat, cheese, and *bread*.[52] And in 1970, thirty years after nutritional science discredited Bulnes's theories, Abel Quezada restated the tortilla discourse, writing that "when the soil was covered with corn, Mexicans were small and weak. Then Juan Garrido planted wheat . . . and they began to grow stronger and taller."[53] These three goals of efforts to forge a Mexican national cuisine — the desire to acquire social distinction, to effect nutritional reforms, and to achieve national unity — therefore represented competing ideologies rather than discrete periods.

But these elite constructions of culture do not exclude the possibility of a genuinely popular national cuisine. Antonio Gramsci and E. P. Thompson have shown that the lower classes create their own cultural spaces independent of elite centers, for example, in marketplaces rather than opera houses.[54] Fish and chips restaurants, although generally shunned by elites, were important centers of working-class culture in Britain between 1870 and 1940.[55] Mexico City restaurants provide another example of this autonomous popular culture. Already by 1920, two decades before José Inés Loredo introduced Tampico-style beef to the capital's elite, inexpensive *taquerías* and *torterías* gave working-class customers the opportunity to sample a variety of regional specialties, diverse *antojitos*, Guadalajara's *pozole*, and Veracruz seafoods.[56] Even *campesinos* who never left their native village could sample new foods prepared by traveling vendors who accompanied carnival troupes on their route from one saint's day celebration to the next.[57] The inclusion of popular dishes in national cuisine may represent not a hegemonic practice to co-opt the working classes, as Fry suggested, but rather popular participation in creating the national community.

Moreover, gastronomy itself is largely an exercise in artificial distinction between "refined" elite cuisine and "vulgar" popular cooking. Connoisseurs scorn immediate sensual pleasures available to anyone, and seek instead sublimated experiences, intellectual exercises in eating that are only open to an educated elite.[58] But while the availability of ingredients depends on economic resources, the desire for "good" food is universal in mankind, for all cultures have developed cuisines. During lobster season in Baja California, even poor fishermen prepare lobster Thermidor, a dish reserved for the elite in Paris restaurants.[59] Nevertheless, the true genius of popular-sector cooks is their skill at transforming unwanted scraps into delicious dishes.

## Culinary Imperialism

The supreme test for any expression of national culture is neither beauty nor sophistication, but authenticity. A "genuine" work of art, however humble, demonstrates a nation's cultural autonomy, and this distinctiveness in turn justifies its claims to political sovereignty. As a result, definitions of authenticity evolve to suit nationalist programs. Nineteenth-century Mexican Creoles, for example, pointed to Aztec greatness as the basis for their independence from Spanish rule, yet imported their culture largely from Europe — a contradiction illustrated by Porfirian paintings of pre-Columbian scenes executed in neoclassical style. The mural renaissance finally reclaimed Native American art as authentic in the 1920s, when revolutionary governments began claiming legitimacy as representatives of a mestizo nation. In much the same way, the search for authentic regional recipes has competed with the allure of the international "other" in creating national cuisines.[60]

Concern for authentic origins has fueled countless culinary rivalries, including the great mayonnaise polemic between the Spanish Port Mahón and the French city Bayonne, as well as Italian disputes with China over the invention of pasta and with France over the first white cream sauce.[61] Legends surrounding *mole poblano, pozole,* and *chiles en nogada* likewise sought to establish the originality of the Mexican national cuisine. Assertions of authenticity, already a standard feature of nineteenth-century Mexican culinary literature, became even more prominent in twentieth-century nostalgia cookbooks and facsimile editions. In a similar manner, Gilberto Freyre, who formulated Brazil's modern nationalism in the 1920s and 1930s based on the unique blend of three races, located Indian and African contributions to the national identity in the Native American cassava and cashews and the African blend of palm oil and malagueta pepper, which were combined in such dishes as the Bahian seafood stew *vatapá.*[62]

Nevertheless, the construction of a national cuisine inevitably reduced complex regional dialects to a few stereotyped dishes, thereby undermining the search for authenticity. Even the most comprehensive volumes, such as Josefina Velázquez de León's *Platillos regionales,* could include only a fraction of Mexico's diverse regional dishes. Moreover, she often adapted these recipes to the needs of urban cooks; for the *zacahuil,* the giant Huastecan tamal cooked in a pit and capable of feeding an entire village, she instructed readers to use a scanty three kilograms of maize and to bake it in the oven.[63] The Thai national cuisine admitted ethnic Lao food in an even more bowdlerized form. As recently as the 1960s, Bangkok residents could sample this northeastern cooking style only by visiting construction sites and boxing arenas where Lao migrant workers spent their time. Restaurants later marketed this food to middle-class audiences by adding more sugar, tempering the chile pepper bite, and deleting ingredients such as fermented fish and insects.[64] Perhaps the greatest distortions of regional styles came through the creation of French restaurant culture. A dish served *"à la Lyonnaise"* in Paris would probably contain onions, although the most characteristic dishes of Lyon are pork products such as *oreille de porc* (grilled pig's ear). The phrase Périgord style at least acknowledged local ingredients, truffles, but the cooking was still Parisian.[65]

Jean-François Revel went so far as to deny the existence of national cuisines, recognizing only regional and international cooking styles. He observed that many local specialties could not be reproduced nationwide; for example, a seafood stew from Livorno did not have the same flavor when made in Florence, a hundred kilometers inland. While acknowledging tacos, tamales, and *mole poblano* as some of the finest regional dishes found anywhere, Revel considered them products "not of art, but of ethnography." A regional cuisine comprised a fixed corpus of recipes, essentially limited to local resources. True artistry distinguished itself only at the level of international cuisine, which he defined somewhat circularly as "the great cuisine *capable* of being internationalized, because the *chefs* who understand it are men . . . capable of integrating, remodeling, rethinking, and even more, rewriting the dishes of all countries and all regions, or at least those that are susceptible to it." Some dishes — he suggested Indian curry and paella Valenciana — "once refined and improved, are better as dishes of international cuisine than as regional dishes. At other times, the transposition is practically impossible" because the foods were bound to the soil. So what was this secret knowledge, this Foucauldian discourse of kitchen power, understood only by great chefs, that made remodeling, rethinking, and rewriting possible? Revel answered simply, the techniques of French *haute cuisine*.[66]

This conclusion, that the only true cuisine was French cuisine, commands attention for all its brazen tone. The Chinese might snort derisively at Revel's rather sheepish qualification that their food was "too rich and too complete" to be improved by French fiddling.[67] But many Western cooks still genuflect toward Paris, accepting its judgment as the universal standard of culinary art. The muralist José Clemente Orozco once denounced nationalist support for folk art as an impediment to the creation of high art, explaining that "each race will be able to make and will have to make, its intellectual and emotional contributions to that universal tradition, but will *never* be able to impose on it the local and transitory modalities of the minor arts."[68] Numerous Mexican chefs have likewise begun to abandon "local and transitory modalities" of popular cooking in order to contribute to international cuisine.

*Nouvelle* Mexican cuisine, blending Old World techniques with New World ingredients, burst onto the culinary world in the 1980s like a banana flambé with tequila. Strictly speaking, its novelty was questionable, for restauranteurs had been offering *cuitlacoche crêpes* since the 1950s, and less deliberate French-Mexican combinations dated back to the nineteenth century. At least one new feature was the attention paid to diet-conscious diners by cutting down on traditional sources of fat such as lard and cheese, although as with its French counterpart, this goal was often frustrated by heavy doses of cream and butter. Arnulfo Luengas, the Oaxacan-born, French-trained chef of the Banco Nacional de México's executive dining room, set the tone for this new cuisine with a cookbook featuring dishes such as avocado mousse with shrimp, chicken supremes with *cuitlacoche*, and Beef Wellington with chiles.[69]

Meanwhile, exquisite new combinations appeared on the menus of Mexico City's most exclusive international restaurants. Carmen Ortuño's Isadora served filet mignon stuffed with *cuitlacoche* in a cheese and *epazote* sauce; Mónica Patiño's La Galvia featured *puntas de filete en caldillo* ("a kind of Mexican *boeuf bourguignon*"); and chefs at La Circunstancia added blackberries to *mole poblano*. A food critic from the United States unknowingly testified to the ability of these restaurants to create authenticity when she noted with delight *cuitlacoche* "as a stuffing for ravioli instead of for the traditional crêpes (Mexico, remember, was once ruled by France)."[70] Sophisticated Mexican food also established a place in Zarela Martínez's eponymous New York restaurant, Rick Bayless's Frontera Grill in Chicago, Miguel Rávago's Fonda San Miguel in Austin, and John Sedlar's Abiquiu in Los Angeles. Perhaps most original of all was the restaurant in Hermosillo, Sonora, opened by a Mexican of Chinese descent who traveled to Hong Kong to discover new ways of cooking chiles and *epazote*.[71]

Purists might shudder at these liberties and consider a more appropriate title for a *nouvelle* Mexican cookbook to be "Malinche's Favorite Recipes." Nevertheless, restauranteurs and cookbook authors claimed the mantle of authenticity for their new cuisine. Alicia Gironella De'Angeli described the trendy dishes at her Mexico City restaurant, El Tajín, as "the same food we serve at home. It is one of two tendencies in Mexican cooking. The other is the popular Mexican food, the kind with the grease and cheese and everything fried. It is the traditional food that we are reinterpreting." She asserted that the new, light food actually derived from pre-Columbian origins. "We did not have the lard and the grease that most people think of as Mexican in our roots. The Spaniards brought the pigs."[72] In this way, she appropriated Aztec authenticity for elite *nouvelle cuisine* and associated lower-class foods with the villainous Spanish conquistadors.

But the popular sectors would not allow her to have such international sophistication and eat it too with a nationalist flourish. They formulated their own diverse ideas of what constituted authentic Mexican food. Maize, of course, constituted the quintessential cuisine of rural Mexico. During a drought in the Huasteca, when corn shipments arrived from the United States to relieve local shortages, *campesinos* claimed that even the pigs turned up their snouts at the imported grain.[73] But authenticity meant something entirely different in the port city of Chetumal, Quintana Roo, where Mayan women bought giant round Edam cheeses duty-free and stuffed them with *picadillo* (chopped meat filling).[74] In Mexico City, Tecate was as typical a drink as *pulque*, and street vendors sold *torta tamales*, corn dumplings sandwiched between wheat bread for a high-carbohydrate breakfast on the run. Authentic Mexican dishes even jostled for space on city streets in the United States. Mexican vendors, long a fixture of San Antonio and East L.A., began selling *birria* on Twenty-second Street in Chicago and tamales from pushcarts circling Yankee Stadium. Mario Ramírez, an immigrant from Puebla who started washing dishes in New York hotels, worked his way up to *sous*-chef at the Russian Tea Room before opening the Rinconcito Mexicano on Thirty-ninth Street in Manhattan. There he sold tamales to Mexican workers in the Garment District — offering a full meal for about three dollars — and also gained a following of midtown businessmen. "When New Yorkers taste my cooking," he claimed proudly, "they know the real Mexico and they like the real Mexico and they don't want unreal Mexico anymore."[75]

The true danger in these contests of authenticity is the possible loss of unique cuisines. Cultural imperialism imposes standardization not by force, but by convincing people of the superiority of European civilization, and by causing them to abandon their own traditions. The prestige associated with European vegetables has already driven many native *quelites* out of use, as part of a campaign begun more than four hundred years ago by priests and planters who tried to make New Spain an ecological replica of the old. Nineteenth-century cookbooks tried to portray tamales and tacos as beyond the pale of civilization. Even in the modern world, people who display a knowledge of Native American herbs are often viewed with suspicion as possible witches.[76]

The Green Revolution and the predominance of large-scale capitalist agriculture also restricted the diversity of food crops. Although Norman Borlaug collected an enormous range of germ plasm for his experiments, in practice a few varieties of maize set standards for commercial production. Dozens of other strands, which once checkered the Mexican landscape, now exist only as seed specimens filed away in research laboratories. Supermarkets likewise limit the availability of produce, selecting, in the case of tomatoes, a few basic varieties primarily for the commercial qualities of sturdiness, symmetry, and color. Colonial fruit vendors used to bring more than a dozen different types of mangos up from the Tierra Caliente, but now wholesale purchasers want only the yellow Manila. Supermarkets stock a mere handful of the fifty varieties of mushrooms once displayed in Toluca municipal markets, or of the hundred different kinds of *frijoles* boasted by Atlixco.[77]

Efforts have begun to preserve this biological diversity for future generations. Mexican nutritionists urged middle-class families to rediscover formerly neglected plants and to ask for them in supermarkets.[78] *Nouvelle* restaurants likewise revived interest in exotic ingredients and organic gardening. But in some cases the result has been to drive prices beyond the reach of the lower classes who originally ate the food. *Gusanos*, once freely available to anyone who bothered to pick them off a cactus paddle, now sell in Mexico City restaurants for twenty dollars a plate. And the fajita craze in the southwestern United States caused formerly inexpensive flank steak to double in price.[79]

Popular-sector cooks nevertheless continue to innovate, redefining for themselves the meaning of Mexican food as they create delicious, economical meals. Indeed, the greatest harm one could do to a hungry cook would be to force her to adhere to a fixed standard of authenticity. The most insidious aspect of Revel's program of cultural imperialism is the insistence that regional cooking "*should* remain identical and routine, and does not progress but rather rejects every other flavor that is not its very own."[80] Such a restrictive definition of authenticity facilitates the elite goal of transforming national culture into a tool of hegemony, a method of excluding any potentially subversive popular expression. Authenticity is an ongoing contest, equally open to chile-and-pork tamales, filet mignon with *cuitlacoche*, and peanut butter and jelly *empanadas*. The process succeeds only if no side finally wins, thereby causing recipes to be lost. Brillat-Savarin believed that "the discovery of a new dish is more beneficial to humanity than the discovery of a new star."[81] By the same token, the loss of a dish makes the world a little bit darker.

## Post-National Cuisine

Capitalist agribusiness has imposed ever greater standardization on global food markets, both by limiting the availability of local fruits and vegetables and by supplying unfamiliar foods from distant lands. While Mexico City supermarkets stock fewer varieties of *frijoles*, mushrooms, and mangos, they compensate by offering Italian cheese, African couscous, and Chinese soy sauce. The botanical and ecological diversity that formerly separated regional cuisines is therefore losing relevance in the modern world. Where the Mexica once used fresh corn tortillas to distinguish themselves from barbarians, no sharp borders divide Mexican food from Tex-Mex and Cal-Mex variants. One might predict that national cuisines will one day exist only as etymological notes in a common international cookbook.

No less a figure than Octavio Paz, in a 1969 postscript to his *Labyrinth of Solitude*, described national character as yet another mask that hides humanity.[82] In the postmodern world, people may take a lesson from the pre-Columbian gods, who had the ability to change their masks at will, thereby assuming the character of other spirits. Middle-class residents of Mexico City can already choose from a variety of different ethnic and fast food restaurants, eating Chinese noodles one night and Kentucky Fried Chicken the next. But the Colonel's "original recipe" achieved a global presence at the expense of losing all ties to the Southern cooks who created it. For other ethnic and regional foods to avoid a similar fate — being reduced to chemical formulas locked away at corporate headquarters somewhere — they must be kept alive through regular use. In much the same way, the diversity of corn will be lost if strains are not planted and cooked regularly; it is not enough to preserve their mummified seeds in a research laboratory. Nor will literature alone preserve a cuisine, for even as cookbook sales boom in the United States, people cook ever fewer meals at home.[83]

Yet Mexican cuisine need not be either reduced to the monotony of a Taco Bell menu or cryogenically frozen to await the next turn on the ethnic restaurant fashion wheel. Cuisines live and grow as long as people continue to cook them, changing ingredients and techniques perhaps, but still respecting those who cooked before them. One such moment of respect for Mexican cuisine comes each year in the ritual preparation of Christmas tamales. In houses rich and poor, throughout the republic and among immigrants to the United States, women prepare tens or even hundreds of dozens of tamales to feed their networks of extended family and friends. And in doing so they commune with the spirits of Tlatelolco's market women.[84]

# Epilogue

Connections between cuisine and identity — what people eat and who they are — reach deep into Mexican history. The native inhabitants of Mesoamerica placed themselves in a cosmological food chain by offering sacrifices of human flesh to maize gods in return for vegetable crops to feed people. Europeans meanwhile took communion through the medium of wheat, the only grain acceptable for the Holy Eucharist according to Catholic doctrine. During the colonial period, corn tortillas and wheat bread became both symbols of and sustenance for two largely separate societies, the *república de los indios* and the *república de los españoles*. Although staple grains divided the inhabitants of New Spain, other foods such as chickens, chiles, pork, and beans crossed ethnic boundaries to provide the basis for a common cuisine. Even the most Hispanophile colonists acquired a taste for chile peppers, and their piquant taste came to distinguish Creole food from Spanish. Chiles now form part of the national identity, captured in the popular Mexican refrain: "*Yo soy como el chile verde, picante pero sabroso*" (I am like the green chile, hot but tasty).[1]

The national cuisine ultimately afforded equal status to wheat and corn, but only in the twentieth century, following both a social revolution that exalted mestizos as the true representatives of the Mexican nation and a dietary revolution that displaced carbohydrates as the staples of life. The first change appeared vividly in the ironic contrast between Mexico's two celebrations of the independence centennial. In 1910, to honor the peasant rebellion of Father Hidalgo, the dictator Porfirio Díaz invited government officials and foreign diplomats to a banquet of chicken Talleyrand, pheasant galatines, and truffled timbales. In 1921, to commemorate the conservative

163

coup of General Iturbide, the revolutionary Alvaro Obregón sponsored a popular fiesta of tortilla soup, Mexican rice, and *mole poblano*.[2] Revolutionary administrations clearly understood the power of food as a national symbol, even though they shared the Porfirian faith in capitalist development. And as a result of this modernization, Mexicans have increasingly substituted sugar and fats for corn and beans. Indeed, one of the modern world's great ironies is that only the wealthy can afford to eat like peasants. Expensive restaurants serve organically grown produce while the masses subsist on pesticide-laden *frijoles*.[3]

Modern changes in Mexican diets seem all the more radical when compared with the apparent conservatism of eating habits prior to the twentieth century. But the natural resilience of the national cuisine defies any simple contrast between traditional peasant cooking and industrial food processing. Mexican women have always displayed a genius for bringing out the taste, if not the nutritional value, of available foods. That these ingredients now include store-bought mayonnaise and Knorr-brand bouillon cubes may cause gourmet eyes to roll, but popular-sector chefs seem to care little for such snobbery. And although food processing machinery has largely replaced the skills of hand-patting tortillas and *metate*-grinding sauces, women are not about to surrender to the onslaught of frozen dinners and microwave ovens.

The significance of food in female identity likewise illustrates this blend of continuity and change. Mexican women at first defined their place in the national community through domestic and religious symbols such as the legendary nuns who created *mole poblano*. But as they gained confidence in their public roles they gradually overcame the need to seek legitimacy through purity and self-sacrifice. Waitresses at the Monterrey restaurant, *La Parroquia* (The Parish Church), subverted traditional standards of female respectability by serving tequila and flirting with customers while dressed as nuns.[4] Laura Esquivel's best-selling novel *Like Water for Chocolate* employed culinary themes to attack the restrictions of patriarchal society. Her sensual descriptions and obvious love of Mexican food made a persuasive feminist case for the rejection of traditional domesticity. In this way, women continue to redefine the national cuisine to fit their changing circumstances.

Street-corner food vendors, perhaps the most resilient of all cooks, have likewise survived in a changing Mexican society. Descended from the *tamaleras* of Tlatelolco, by way of the *pulque* shop cooks of New Spain, they now are likely to be found selling food on the steps of Metro stations or from the beds of pickup trucks. But however they operate, they will always have customers, for even the wealthiest Mexicans enjoy their enchiladas and tamales. These anonymous street vendors, not famous gourmet chefs, were the true authors of the national cuisine, demonstrating that at least in Mexico, the hungrier the cook, the tastier the food.

# Notes

INTRODUCTION

1. Bernardino de Sahagún, *The Florentine Codex: General History of the Things of New Spain*, trans. Arthur J. O. Anderson and Charles Dibble, 12 books in 13 vols. (Santa Fe: School of American Research, 1950–82), 2:70, 148 (page references here and hereafter indicate book rather than volume number).

2. Benedict Anderson, *Imagined Communities: Reflections on the Origin and Spread of Nationalism*, rev. ed. (London: Verso, 1991).

3. Arjun Appadurai, "How to Make a National Cuisine: Cookbooks in Contemporary India," *Comparative Studies in Society and History* 30, no. 1 (January 1988): 3–24.

4. Jack Goody, *Cooking, Cuisine, and Class: A Study in Comparative Sociology* (Cambridge: Cambridge University Press, 1982), 97–153.

5. Michael Freeman, "Sung," in *Food in Chinese Culture: Anthropological and Historical Perspectives*, ed. K. C. Chang (New Haven: Yale University Press, 1977), 143–45.

6. Jean-François Revel, *Un festín en palabras: Historia literaria de la sensibilidad gastronómica de la Antigüedad a nuestros días*, trans. Lola Gavarrón (Barcelona: Tusquets Editores, 1980), 28–32, 233.

7. Diana Kennedy, *The Cuisines of Mexico*, rev. ed. (New York: Harper and Row, 1986), xvi.

8. Laura Esquivel, *Like Water for Chocolate: A Novel in Monthly Installments, with Recipes, Romances, and Home Remedies*, trans. Carol Christensen and Thomas Christensen (New York: Doubleday, 1992).

9. In the early 1980s, the combined consumption of wheat and rice briefly surpassed that of corn in urban areas before the economic crisis restored the latter's dominance, which has always held in the countryside. See Adolfo Chávez and José Antonio Roldán, "Los alimentos de México: La alimentación de los señores y de los plebeyos," *Mexico Desconocido* 17, no. 191 (January 1993): 60–65.

ONE: THE PEOPLE OF CORN

1. For lake traffic, see Bernal Díaz del Castillo's account of the Sad Night, when the canoes carried vengeful Aztec warriors instead of chiles and tomatoes. *The Discovery and Conquest of Mexico, 1517–1521,* trans. A. P. Maudslay (London: George Routledge, 1928), 421–24. See also Charles Gibson, *The Aztecs under Spanish Rule: A History of the Indians of the Valley of Mexico, 1519–1810* (Stanford: Stanford University Press, 1964), 362–64; Ross Hassig, *Trade, Tribute, and Transportation: The Sixteenth-Century Political Economy of the Valley of Mexico* (Norman: University of Oklahoma Press, 1985), 65; Toribio de Motolinía, *Motolinía's History of the Indians of New Spain,* trans. and ed. Francis Borgia Streck (Washington, D.C.: Academy of American Franciscan History, 1951), 104–5. On population estimates, see Inga Clendinnen, *Aztecs: An Interpretation* (Cambridge: Cambridge University Press, 1991), 305.

2. Jacques Soustelle, *The Daily Life of the Aztecs on the Eve of the Spanish Conquest,* trans. Patrick O'Brian (New York: Macmillan, 1962), 10–28; William E. Doolittle, *Canal Irrigation in Prehistoric Mexico: The Sequence of Technological Change* (Austin: University of Texas Press, 1990), 125–26; Fernando Cortés, *Five Letters of Cortés to the Emperor,* trans. J. Bayard Morris (New York: W. W. Norton, 1991), 87–93; Díaz del Castillo, *Discovery and Conquest of Mexico,* 299–302; Clendinnen, *Aztecs,* 20.

3. Hassig, *Trade, Tribute, and Transportation,* 62; Cortés, *Five Letters,* 87, 93.

4. For a sixteenth-century map of Tlatelolco, see Jacqueline de Durand-Forest, "Cambios económicos y moneda entre los aztecas," *Estudios de Cultura Náhuatl* 9 (1971): 122. Charles Gibson dated this map to after the conquest, but native authorities continued to run the market in 1533, so presumably the old order would have prevailed. See *Aztecs under Spanish Rule,* 353, 569. For plant descriptions, see Sophie D. Coe, *America's First Cuisines* (Austin: University of Texas Press, 1994), 88–107; Diana Kennedy, *The Art of Mexican Cooking: Traditional Mexican Cooking for Aficionados* (New York: Bantam, 1989), 135–77; Sahagún, *Florentine Codex,* 8:67–69, 11:136–41; Cortés, *Five Letters,* 87–88; Díaz del Castillo, *Discovery and Conquest of Mexico,* 302.

5. Quoted in Raymond Sokolov, *Why We Eat What We Eat: How the Encounter Between the New World and the Old Changed the Way Everyone on the Planet Eats* (New York: Summit Books, 1991), 21.

6. Sahagún, *Florentine Codex,* 10:80; Coe, *America's First Cuisines,* 95–100.

7. Motolinía, *Motolinía's History,* 258, 280; Sahagún, *Florentine Codex,* 10:79.

8. Sahagún, *Florentine Codex,* 11:279–89.

9. This Mexican cook's phrase was quoted by Diana Kennedy, *Recipes from the Regional Cooks of Mexico* (New York: Harper and Row, 1978), 148.

10. Richard C. MacNeish, "Ancient Mesoamerican Civilization," *Science* 143 (1964): 532.

11. Kent V. Flannery, "Vertebrate Fauna and Hunting Patterns," in *Environment*

*and Subsistence*, vol. 1 of *The Prehistory of the Tehuacan Valley*, ed. Douglas S. Byers (Austin: University of Texas Press, 1967), 132–77.

12. Byers, *Environment and Subsistence*, 178–255; Barbara L. Stark, "The Rise of Sedentary Life," in *Archaeology*, vol. 1 of *Supplement to the Handbook of Middle American Indians*, ed. Jeremy A. Sabloff (Austin: University of Texas Press, 1981), 345–55.

13. Margaret Park Redfield, "Notes on the Cookery of Tepoztlan, Morelos," *American Journal of Folklore* 42, no. 164 (April-June 1929):167–96; Nathanial Whetten, *Rural Mexico* (Chicago: University of Chicago Press, 1948), 305; Oscar Lewis, *Life in a Mexican Village: Tepoztlán Revisited* (Urbana: University of Illinois Press, 1951), 72.

14. René Millon, "Teotihuacan: City, State, and Civilization," in Sabloff, *Archaeology*, 198–243; Sahagún, *Florentine Codex*, 8:69, 9:34.

15. The protein in either beans or maize alone lacks some of the eight amino acids needed by the human body. When eaten together, beans provide lysine missing from corn, and corn contains cystine lacking in beans, although rather low levels of methionine still limit the full utilization of proteins. William T. Sanders, Jeffrey R. Parsons, and Robert S. Santley, *The Basin of Mexico: Ecological Processes in the Evolution of a Civilization* (New York: Academic Press, 1979), 376; Hector Arraya, Marina Flores, and Guillermo Arroyave, "Nutritive Value of Basic Foods and Common Dishes of the Guatemalan Rural Populations: A Theoretical Approach," *Ecology of Food and Nutrition* 11 (1981): 171–76; Peter Farb and George Armelagas, *Consuming Passions: The Anthropology of Eating* (Boston: Houghton Mifflin, 1980), 174; Whetten, *Rural Mexico*, 308–12.

16. Janet Long-Solís, *Capsicum y cultura: La historia del chilli* (Mexico City: Fondo de Cultura Económica, 1986); Paul Rozin, "Human Food Selection," in *The Psychobiology of Human Food Selection*, ed. Lewis M. Barker (Westport, Conn.: Avi Publishing Company, 1982), 234, 238–39; Farb and Armelagas, *Consuming Passions*, 174.

17. Sherburne F. Cook and Woodrow Borah, "Indian Food Production and Consumption in Central Mexico Before and After the Conquest (1500–1650)," in *Essays in Population History: Mexico and California*, ed. Sherburne F. Cook and Woodrow Borah (Berkeley: University of California Press, 1979), 136.

18. See especially chapter 9.

19. Sahagún, *Florentine Codex*, 10:184, 187. For depictions of Mixtec banquets, see *The Codex Nuttall: A Picture Manuscript from Ancient Mexico*, ed. Zelia Nuttall (New York: Dover Publications, 1975), 5, 28–31. Chile taxonomy is described by Long-Solís, *Capsicum y cultura*, 70–72; Kennedy, *Art of Mexican Cooking*, 460.

20. Jeffrey R. Parsons, "The Role of Chinampa Agriculture in the Food Supply of Aztec Tenochtitlan," in *Cultural Change and Continuity: Essays in Honor of James Bennett Griffin*, ed. Charles E. Cleland (New York: Academic Press, 1975), 233–57.

21. *Codex Mendoza*, commentaries by Kurt Ross (Fribourg: Productions Liber, 1978), 62–63; Diego Durán, *The Aztecs*, trans. Fernando Horcasitas and Doris Heyden (New York: Orion Press, 1974), 116.

22. William A. Haviland, "Stature at Tikal, Guatemala: Implications for Ancient Maya Demography and Social Organization," *American Antiquity* 32, no. 3 (July 1967): 316–25.

23. Cook and Borah, "Indian Food Production," 161.

24. Diego Durán, *Book of the Gods and Rites and The Ancient Calendar*, trans. and ed. Fernando Horcasitas and Doris Heyden (Norman: University of Oklahoma Press, 1971), 154–60.

25. Guillermo Bonfil Batalla, *México profundo: Una civilización negada* (Mexico City: Editorial Grijalbo, 1990), 33–34.

26. Sahagún, *Florentine Codex*, 6:172, 10:12.

27. Clendinnen, *Aztecs*, 161.

28. Ibid., 57–68; Sahagún, *Florentine Codex*, 2:79, 4:117–24, quotes from 122.

29. Sahagún, *Florentine Codex*, 10:179–89. For comparative examples, see Emily Gowers, *The Loaded Table: Representations of Food in Roman Literature* (Oxford: Clarendon Press, 1993), 56; K. C. Chang, "Ancient China," in Chang, *Food in Chinese Culture*, 41–42.

30. Frances Karttunen and James Lockhart, *The Art of Nahuatl Speech: The Bancroft Dialogues* (Berkeley: University of California Press, 1987), 159.

31. Sahagún, *Florentine Codex*, 10:21.

32. Clendinnen, *Aztecs*, 65–66. For the famine of One Rabbit, see Durán, *Aztecs*, 144.

33. Miguel León-Portilla, *Aztec Thought and Culture: A Study of the Ancient Nahuatl Mind*, trans. Jack Emory Davis (Norman: University of Oklahoma Press, 1963), 163.

34. Sahagún, *Florentine Codex*, 2:3, 9.

35. Michael Harner, "The Ecological Basis for Aztec Sacrifice," *American Ethnologist* 4, no. 1 (February 1977): 117–35; Marvin Harris, *Good to Eat: Riddles of Food and Culture* (New York: Simon and Schuster, 1985), 232; Alamán cited in Eusebio Dávalos Hurtado, "La alimentación entre los mexicas" *Revista Mexicana de Estudios Antropológicos* (1954–1955): 177.

36. Marshall Sahlins, "Culture as Protein and Profit," *New York Review of Books*, Nov. 23, 1978, 45–53. The animal foods available at the market of Tlatelolco may not have supplied the entire Valley of Mexico, but they would have offset any deficiencies among priests and warriors who actually practiced ritual cannibalism.

37. Sahagún, *Florentine Codex*, 6:132, 171, 203.

38. Ibid., 6:91; Clendinnen, *Aztecs*, quotes from 251, 263.

39. Díaz del Castillo, *Discovery and Conquest of Mexico*, 290–91; Cortés, *Five Letters*, 97.

40. Madeleine Pelner Cosman, *Fabulous Feasts: Medieval Cookery and Ceremony* (New York: George Braziller, 1976).

41. Durán, *Aztecs*, 136; Sahagún, *Florentine Codex*, 6:124–26.

42. Louise M. Burkhart, *The Slippery Earth: Nahua-Christian Moral Dialogue in Sixteenth-Century Mexico* (Tucson: University of Arizona Press, 1989), 132–41.

43. Sahagún, *Florentine Codex*, 10:53.

44. Ibid., 8:37–40.

45. Ibid., 1:19, 7:13, 8:37–40; Kennedy, *Art of Mexican Cooking*, 41–52; Durán, *Book of the Gods*, 403–4.

46. Sahagún, *Florentine Codex*, 6:95–96; 10:53.

47. Clendinnen, *Aztecs*, 162; Durán, *Aztecs*, 131, 142.

48. Hassig, *Trade, Tribute, and Transportation*, 73; Sahagún, *Florentine Codex*, 4:20.

49. Durán, *Book of the Gods*, 275.

50. Sahagún, *Florentine Codex*, 4:124. See also Durán, *Book of the Gods*, 415–16.

51. Durán, *Book of the Gods*, 151. The calendar festivals are described in Sahagún, *Florentine Codex*, 2:79, 101, 140.

52. Mark Miller, *Coyote Cafe: Foods from the Great Southwest* (Berkeley: Ten Speed Press, 1989), 182; Penny Van Esterik, "From Marco Polo to McDonald's: Thai Cuisine in Transition," *Food and Foodways* 5, no. 2 (1992): 177–94. For a discussion of the delights—and dangers--of blending chiles, see Kennedy, *Art of Mexican Cooking*, 461.

53. Harold McGee, *On Food and Cooking: The Science and Lore of the Kitchen* (New York: Charles Scribners, 1984), 608–9.

54. James Lockhart, ed., *"We People Here": Nahuatl Accounts of the Conquest of Mexico* (Berkeley: University of California Press, 1993), 79–80.

55. Ibid., 257.

56. Miguel León-Portilla, ed., *The Broken Spears: The Aztec Account of the Conquest of Mexico*, trans. Lysander Kemp (Boston: Beacon Press, 1962), 138.

57. Ibid., 146.

### TWO: THE CONQUESTS OF WHEAT

1. The ingredients come from the first recorded *mole* recipes in *Novisimo arte de cocina — o — Escelente coleccion de las mejores recetas* (Mexico City: C. Alejandro Valdés, 1831), 34; *El cocinero mexicano o coleccion de los mejores recetas para guisar al estilo americano y de las mas selectas segun el metodo de las cocinas Española, Italiana, Francesa e Inglesa*, 3 vols. (Mexico City: Imprenta de Galvan a cargo de Mariano Arevalo, 1831), 1:172–74. For best results in the modern kitchen, follow Diana Kennedy's recipe in *Cuisines of Mexico*, 199–203.

2. For a summary of *mole* legends, see Miguel Guzmán Peredo, *Crónicas gastronómicas* (Mexico City: Fontmara, 1991), 27–29.

3. "Cookbooks and Culture in Early Latin America," paper presented at *Simposio 1492: El encuentro de dos comidas*, Puebla, Puebla, July 7, 1992.

4. José Luis Juárez, "La lenta emergencia de la comida mexicana, ambigüedades criollas 1750–1800" (Lic. thesis, Escuela Nacional de Antropología e Historia, 1993), 60–61; Rosalva Loreto López, "Prácticas alimenticias en los conventos de mujeres en la Puebla del siglo XVIII," paper presented at the *Simposio 1492: El encuentro de dos comidas*, Puebla, Puebla, July 6, 1992. See also Josefina Muriel,

*Cultura femenina novohispana* (Mexico City: Universidad Nacional Autónoma de México, 1982), 478–80.

5. Judith Friedlander, *Being Indian in Hueyapan: A Study of Forced Identity in Contemporary Mexico* (New York: St. Martin's Press, 1975), 96–98.

6. Redfield, "Note on the Cookery of Tepoztlan," 179.

7. For a discussion of the baroque aesthetic, see Irving A. Leonard, *Baroque Times in Old Mexico: Seventeenth-Century Persons, Places, and Practices* (Ann Arbor: University of Michigan Press, 1959).

8. Justo Sierra, *The Political Evolution of the Mexican People*, trans. Charles Ramsdell (Austin: University of Texas Press, 1969), 131.

9. Jaime Vicens Vives, *An Economic History of Spain*, trans. Frances M. López-Morillas (Princeton: Princeton University Press, 1969), 22–24, 48–56; Leonard A. Churchin, *Roman Spain: Conquest and Assimilation* (London: Routledge, 1991), 128.

10. Maguelonne Toussaint-Samat, *A History of Food*, trans. Anthea Bell (Cambridge, Mass.: Blackwell, 1992), 373–74; Vicens Vives, *Economic History of Spain*, 63–67.

11. Reay Tannahill, *Food in History* (New York: Crown Publishers, 1988), 77.

12. C. Anne Wilson, *Food and Drink in Britain: From the Stone Age to Recent Times* (New York: Barnes and Noble, 1974), 233.

13. Andrew M. Watson, "The Arab Agricultural Revolution and Its Diffusion, 700–1100," *Journal of Economic History* 34, no. 1 (March 1974): 8–35; Vicens Vives, *Economic History of Spain*, 108–10.

14. T. Sarah Peterson, *Acquired Taste: The French Origins of Modern Cooking* (Ithaca: Cornell University Press, 1994), 1–14, quote from 7.

15. *Traducción Española de un manuscrito anónimo del siglo XIII sobre la cocina Hispano-Magribi*, trans. Ambrosio Huici Miranda (Madrid: Ayuntamiento de Valencia, 1966), 24, 254–65; John A. Crow, *Spain: The Root and the Flower*, 3d ed. (Berkeley: University of California Press, 1985), 176.

16. Toby Peterson, "The Arab Influence on Western European Cooking," *Journal of Medieval History* 6 (September 1980): 317–40; Diego Granado, *Libro del arte de cocina* (Madrid: Sociedad de Bibliófilos Españoles, 1971 [1599]), xxxvi; Peterson, *Acquired Taste*, 2.

17. Vicens Vives, *Economic History of Spain*, 5.

18. Emmanuel Le Roy Ladurie, *Montaillou: The Promised Land of Error*, trans. Barbara Bray (New York: George Braziller, 1978), 113, quote from 134; Caroline Walker Bynum, *Holy Feast and Holy Fast: The Religious Significance of Food to Medieval Women* (Berkeley: University of California Press, 1987), 2, 113–86; John C. Super, "El concepto de la nutrición en Juan de Aviñón," *Medicina Española* 82 (May-June 1983): 167–73; Nancy Eekhof-Stork, *The World Atlas of Cheese* (Amsterdam: Spectrum International Publishing, 1976), 130.

19. Vicens Vives, *Economic History of Spain*, 304; Peter Boyd-Bowman, *Patterns of Spanish Emigration to the New World, 1493–1580* (Buffalo: Council on International Studies, SUNY, 1973).

20. For an insightful reconstruction of this meal, see Coe, *America's First Cuisines*, 241–46.

21. François Chevalier, *Land and Society in Colonial Mexico: The Great Hacienda*, ed. Lesley Byrd Simpson, trans. Alvin Eustis (Berkeley: University of California Press, 1970), 84–94; John C. Super, *Food, Conquest, and Colonization in Sixteenth-Century Spanish America* (Albuquerque: University of New Mexico Press, 1988), 26–28; Alfred W. Crosby, Jr., *The Columbian Exchange: Biological and Cultural Consequences of 1492* (Westport, Conn.: Greenwood Press, 1972), 75–79.

22. Carlo Ginzberg, *The Cheese and the Worms: The Cosmos of a Sixteenth-Century Miller*, trans. John Tedeschi and Anne Tedeschi (New York: Penguin Books, 1982), 119.

23. Cheryl English Martin, *Rural Society in Colonial Morelos* (Albuquerque: University of New Mexico Press, 1985), 12.

24. Crosby, *Columbian Exchange*, 65–74; Coe, *America's First Cuisines*, 240.

25. Even the cooks of Provence, now renowned for their use of olive oil, relied on pork fat in early modern times. Jacques Revel, "A Capital City's Privileges: Food Supplies in Early-Modern Rome," in *Food and Drink in History: Selections from the Annales Economies, Sociétés, Civilisations*, ed. Robert Forster and Orest Ranum, trans. Elborg Forster and Patricia Ranum (Baltimore: Johns Hopkins University Press, 1979), 37–49; Jean-Jacques Hémardinquer, "The Family Pig of the Ancien Régime: Myth or Fact?" in ibid., 50–72.

26. Super, *Food, Conquest, and Colonization*, 85.

27. William B. Taylor, *Drinking, Homicide, and Rebellion in Colonial Mexican Villages* (Stanford: Stanford University Press, 1979), 34–40.

28. Thomas Gage, *Thomas Gage's Travels in the New World*, ed. J. Eric S. Thompson (Westport, Conn.: Greenwood Press, 1981), 143–45.

29. Archivo General de la Nación (hereafter cited as AGN), Inquisición, vol. 435, exp. 104, fo. 139.

30. Jan Read, Maite Manjón, and Hugh Johnson, *The Wine and Food of Spain* (Boston: Little, Brown and Company, 1987), 38.

31. Quote from Super, *Food, Conquest, and Colonization*, 29; Kennedy, *Cuisines of Mexico*, 194–97.

32. Peterson, *Acquired Taste*, 183–208; Piero Camporesi, *Exotic Brew: The Art of Living in the Age of Enlightenment*, trans. Christopher Woodall (Cambridge: Polity Press, 1994), 27–35.

33. Juárez, "La lenta emergencia," 103–5.

34. Granado, *Libro del arte de cocina*, xxvii, 56, 85, 89, 148, 203.

35. John D. Bergamini, *The Spanish Bourbons: The History of a Tenacious Dynasty* (New York: G. P. Putnam's Sons, 1974), 50.

36. Because of multiple editions, cookbook citations include the date of publication. *El cocinero mexicano* (1831), 1:103; Kennedy, *Cuisines of Mexico*, 262–68.

37. *Nuevo y sencillo arte de cocina, reposteria y refrescos dispuesto por una mexicana y*

*experimentado por personas inteligentes antes de darse a la prensa* (Mexico City: Imprenta de Santiago Perez, 1836), 157–59; *El cocinero mexicano* (1831), 1:243, 257.

38. Granado, *Libro del arte de cocina*, 98. The presence of walnut sauces in Italian Renaissance cookbooks is affirmed by Giuliano Bugialli, *The Fine Art of Italian Cooking*, 2d ed. (New York: Times Books, 1989), 67.

39. Peggy K. Liss, *Mexico under Spain, 1521–1556: Society and the Origins of Nationality* (Chicago: University of Chicago Press, 1975), 96–97.

40. Sherburne F. Cook and Woodrow Borah, *The Indian Population of Central Mexico, 1531–1610* (Berkeley: University of California Press, 1960); Borah and Cook, *The Aboriginal Population of Central Mexico on the Eve of the Spanish Conquest* (Berkeley: University of California Press, 1963). Although some scholars consider their pre-Columbian population figures to be vastly inflated, their data for the post-contact demographic disaster are uncontested.

41. Gibson, *Aztecs under Spanish Rule*, Ibid., 224–26, 322–24; Chevalier, *Land and Society*, 61–62; Virginia García Acosta, *Los precios del trigo en la historia colonial de México* (Mexico City: Centro de Investigaciones y Estudios Superiores en Antropología Social, 1988).

42. William B. Taylor, *Landlord and Peasant in Colonial Oaxaca* (Stanford: Stanford University Press, 1972), 48, 71.

43. Quoted in Burkhart, *Slippery Earth*, 166.

44. Oliver Ross, "Wheat Growing in Northern New Spain," *North Dakota Quarterly* 45, no. 3 (Summer 1977): 61–69.

45. Durán, *Book of the Gods*, 414.

46. Ortiz de Montellano, *Aztec Medicine, Health, and Nutrition*, (New Brunswick: Rutgers University Press) 107–8.

47. This practice continued into the nineteenth century. Fanny Chambers [Iglehart] Gooch, *Face to Face with the Mexicans* (New York: Fords, Howard, and Hulbert, 1887), 437.

48. Redfield, "Notes on the Cookery of Tepoztlan," 168; Ellen Messer, "Zapotec Food Plants: The Transformation of Two Cultures," paper presented at *Simposio 1492: El encuentro de dos comidas*, Puebla, Puebla, July 7, 1992.

49. James Lockhart, ed., *"We People Here": Nahuatl Accounts of the Conquest of Mexico* (Berkeley: University of California Press, 1993), 80.

50. Quoted in Sonia Corcuera, *Entre gula y templanza: Un aspecto de la historia mexicana* (Mexico City: Universidad Nacional Autónoma de México, 1981), 69.

51. Fernand Braudel, *The Structures of Everyday Life: The Limits of the Possible*, vol. 1 of *Civilization and Capitalism, 15th-18th Century*, trans. Siân Reynolds (New York: Harper and Row, 1979), 120.

52. Cook and Borah, "Indian Food Production," 169.

53. Enrique Florescano, *Precios del maíz y crisis agrícolas en México (1708–1810)* (Mexico City: El Colegio de México, 1969), 89–91; Alejandra Moreno Toscano, "Tres problemas en la geografía del maíz, 1600–1624," *Historia Mexicana* 14, no. 4 (1965): 635; Ross, "Wheat Growing," 65.

54. Chevalier, *Land and Society*, 93; Gibson, *Aztecs under Spanish Rule*, 346; Charles Gibson, *Tlaxcala in the Sixteenth Century* (New Haven: Yale University Press, 1952), 151–53; Nancy Farriss, *Maya Society under Colonial Rule: The Collective Enterprise of Survival* (Princeton: Princeton University Press, 1984), 182.

55. Coe, *America's First Cuisines*, 234.

56. James Lockhart, *The Nahuas after the Conquest: A Social and Cultural History of the Indians of Central Mexico, Sixteenth through Eighteenth Centuries* (Stanford: Stanford University Press, 1992), 278.

57. María de los Angeles Romero Frizzi, "La agricultura en la época colonial," in *La agricultura en tierras mexicanas desde sus origines hasta nuestros días*, ed. Teresa Rojas (Mexico City: Editorial Grijalba, 1991), 159; Gibson, *Aztecs under Spanish Rule*, 320; Messer, "Zapotec Food Plants," 4–5; René Acuña, ed., *Relaciones geográficas del siglo XVI: Antequera*, 2 vols. (Mexico City: Universidad Nacional Autónoma de México, 1984), 1:356.

58. Lockhart, *Nahuas after the Conquest*, 188; Taylor, *Landlord and Peasant*, 20–21.

59. Virginia García Acosta, *Las panaderías, sus dueños y trabajadores. Ciudad de México, siglo XVIII* (Mexico City: Centro de Investigaciones y Estudios Superiores de Antropología Social, 1989), 53, 73–81.

60. Sergio Rivera Ayala, "Lewd Songs and Dances from the Streets of Eighteenth-Century New Spain," in *Rituals of Rule, Rituals of Resistance: Public Celebrations and Popular Culture in Mexico*, ed. William H. Beezley, Cheryl English Martin, and William E. French (Wilmington, Del.: Scholarly Resources, 1994), 40–41.

61. Alicia María González, "'Guess How Doughnuts Are Made': Verbal and Nonverbal Aspects of the *Panadero* and His Stereotype," in *"And Other Neighborly Names": Social Process and Cultural Images in Texas Folklore*, ed. Richard Bauman and Roger D. Abrahams (Austin: University of Texas Press, 1981), 104–21.

62. Taylor, *Landlord and Peasant*, 13–17; Alexander von Humboldt, *Ensayo político sobre el reino de la Nueva España* (Mexico City: Editorial Porrúa, 1966), 156; Ronald Spores, *The Mixtecs in Ancient and Colonial Times* (Norman: University of Oklahoma Press, 1984), 124.

63. Romero Frizzi, "La agricultura," 164.

64. Acuña, *Relaciones geográficas*, 1:332, 36.

65. Gage, *Thomas Gage's Travels*, 141.

66. On keeping up appearances in New Spain, see Linda A. Curcio-Nagy, "Giants and Gypsies: Corpus Christi in Colonial Mexico City," in Beezley, Martin, and French, *Rituals of Rule, Rituals of Resistance*, 1–26; Charles Gibson, *Spain in America* (New York: Harper and Row, 1966), 133.

67. Richard S. Dunn, *Sugar and Slaves: The Rise of the Planter Class in the English West Indies, 1624–1713* (Chapel Hill: University of North Carolina Press, 1972), 263–64.

68. Claudio Lomnitz Adler, *Exits from the Labyrinth: Culture and Ideology in the Mexican National Space* (Berkeley: University of California Press, 1992), 264.

69. Magnus Mörner, *Race Mixture in the History of Latin America* (Boston: Little

Brown and Company, 1967); John K. Chance, *Race and Class in Colonial Oaxaca* (Stanford: Stanford University Press, 1978).

70. R. Douglas Cope, *The Limits of Racial Domination: Plebeian Society in Colonial Mexico City, 1660–1720* (Madison: University of Wisconsin Press, 1994), 23, 55.

71. Mörner, *Race Mixture*, 59.

72. María Concepción García Sáiz, *Las castas mexicanas: Un género pictórico americano* (Milan: Olivetti, 1990), 86, 98.

73. María José Rodilla, "Un quevedo en Nueva España satiriza las castas," *Artes de México: Nueva Epoca* 8 (Summer 1990): 41–49, author's translations.

74. Gibson, *Aztecs under Spanish Rule*, 155, 323; Messer, "Zapotec Food Plants," 20.

75. Quoted in Juárez, "La lenta emergencia," 107–8.

76. Quoted in Cope, *Limits of Racial Domination*, 129.

77. Quoted in Crosby, *Columbian Exchange*, 65.

78. For medieval dishes, see Peterson, *Acquired Taste*, 1–14; Cosman, *Fabulous Feasts*, 42–49, 176, 181.

79. See the *pulpería* inventories in AGN, Ramo Civil, leg. 15, exp. 10; leg. 53, no. 93; leg. 103, no. 67. I thank Linda Arnold for sharing her catalog of Inventarios y Aprecios de Bienes.

THREE: MANY CHEFS IN THE NATIONAL KITCHEN

1. Preface and 1:177.

2. *Nuevo cocinero mejicano* (1868), x.

3. *Nuevo y sencillo arte* (1836), iv. See also *Libro de cocina: Arreglado a los usos y costumbres nacionales* (Mexico City: Imp. de I. Guerrero, n.d.).

4. Narciso Bassols, *La cocinero poblana y el libro de las familias. Novisimo manual práctico de cocina española, francesa, inglesa, y mexicana*, 2 vols. (Puebla: Narciso Bassols, 1877), 1:3.

5. Vicenta Torres de Rubio, *Cocina michoacana* (Zamora, Michoacán: Imprenta Moderna, 1896), iii–iv.

6. *Recetas prácticas para la señora de casa sobre cocina, repostería, pasteles, nevería, etc.* (Guadalajara: Imp. del Orfanatorio del Sagrado Corazón de Jesús, 1892), 3.

7. *Nuevo y sencillo* (1836).

8. *Nuevo cocinero mejicano* (1868), 879, quoted in Diana Kennedy, *The Tortilla Book* (New York: Harper and Row, 1975), 98.

9. Mariano Galván Rivera, *Diccionario de cocina o el nuevo cocinero mexicano en forma de diccionario* (Mexico City: Imprenta Ignacio Cumplido, 1845), quoted in Kennedy, *Art of Mexican Cooking*, 84.

10. D. A. Brading, *The First America: The Spanish Monarchy, Creole Patriots, and the Liberal State, 1492–1867* (Cambridge: Cambridge University Press, 1991), 580–84, 667.

11. Jean Franco, *Plotting Women: Gender and Representation in Mexico* (New York:

Columbia University Press, 1989), 79–101; Silvia Marina Arrom, *The Women of Mexico City, 1790–1857* (Stanford: Stanford University Press, 1985), 14–52. Carmen Ramos Escandón, "Señoritas porfirianas: mujer e ideología en el México progrerista, 1880–1910," in *Presencia y transparencia: la mujer en la historia de México* (Mexico City: El Colegio de México, 1987).

12. See, for instance, *Semanario de las Señoritas Mejicanas* (1841), 353; *El Correo de las Señoras,* Mar. 2, 1884; *La Lira Michoacana* (1894), 47–48.

13. Arrom, *Women of Mexico City,* 63–65.

14. María Antonia Gutiérrez, *El ama de casa* (Mexico City: Librería de la Vda. de Ch. Bouret, 1899), 1.

15. Jacinto Anduiza, *El libro del hogar* (Pachuco, Hidalgo: Imprenta "La Europea," 1893), 6.

16. *Nuevo cocinero mejicano,* 62, 158, 264; *La cocinera poblana,* 1:37; Torres, *Cocina michoacana,* 28, 36, 224, 409. Donato Guerra, a hero of the French Intervention, may have tasted his namesake cod, but Moctezuma never ate the dessert named in his honor, which was made of candied sugar, ground almonds, and bread rolls.

17. Guillermo Prieto, *Memorias de mis tiempos, 1828 á 1840* (Mexico City: Librería de la Vda. de C. Bouret, 1906), 287; *Nuevo cocinero mejicano* (1868), 940; *Diario del Hogar,* Feb. 9, 1886.

18. *La Patria,* Dec. 2, 1898; *El Imparcial,* Mar. 23, 1910; *Nuevo cocinero mejicano* (1868), preface.

19. Miguel Angel Peral, *Diccionario biográfico mexicano* (Mexico City: Editorial PAC, 1944), 292; *Diccionario Porrúa de historia, biografía y geografía de México,* 3d ed., 2 vols. (Mexico City: Editorial Porrúa, 1970), 1:833, 2:1434, 1593.

20. For a comprehensive listing of cookbooks published in Mexico since 1821, see the appendix in Jeffrey M. Pilcher, "¡Vivan Tamales! The Creation of a Mexican National Cuisine" (Ph.D. diss., Texas Christian University, 1993).

21. Gooch, *Face to Face,* 494.

22. With access to a limited number of manuscript cookbooks for comparative analysis, I drew a few tentative conclusions in "Recipes for *Patria*: Cuisine, Gender, and Nation in Nineteenth-Century Mexico," in *Recipes for Reading: Community Cookbooks and Their Stories,* ed. Anne L. Bower (Amherst: University of Massachusetts Press, 1997.

23. See the recipes for *chiles fritos, sopa de bolitas, lomo frito,* and *lengua rellena* in José L. Cossío, ed., *Recetario de cocina mexicana escrito por Doña María Luisa Soto Murguindo de Cossio* (Mexico City: Vargas Rea, 1968), 24, 25, 49; and *Recetas prácticas* (1892), 144, 13, 32, 55.

24. *Manual del cocinero* (1856), 175.

25. Prieto, *Memorias de mis tiempos, 1840 á 1853,* 83.

26. *Nuevo cocinero mejicano* (1868), 879; Torres, *Cocina michoacana* (1896), 340–50.

27. *El cocinero mexicano* (1831), 1:270; *Nuevo cocinero mejicano* (1868), 334.

28. Manuel Gamio, *Forjando patria,* 2d ed. (Mexico City: Editorial Porrúa, 1960), 12.

29. *El cocinero mejicano* (1834), 1:391.

30. Jesús Ruvalcaba Mercado, *Vida cotidiana y consumo de maíz en la huasteca veracruzana* (Mexico City: Centro de Investigaciones y Estudios Superiores en Antropología Social, 1987), 65–66; Dolores Avila Hernández, "Región centro norte," in *Atlas cultural de México: Gastronomía*, ed. Dolores Avila Hernández et al. (Mexico City: Grupo Editorial Planeta, 1988), 67–78. This discussion draws on insights from Lomnitz-Adler, *Exits from the Labyrinth*, 51–56.

31. Ana Graciela Bedolla and Juan E. Vanegas, *La comida en el medio lacustre: Culhuacán* (Mexico City: Instituto Nacional de Antropología e Historia, 1990).

32. John G. Bourke, "The Folk-Foods of the Rio Grande Valley and of Northern Mexico," *Journal of American Folk-Lore* (1895): 41–71; William Bullock, *Six Months Residence and Travels in Mexico* (Port Washington, N.Y.: Kennikat Press, 1971 [1824]), 431; Gooch, *Face to Face*, 62–64; Ignacio González-Polo, ed., *Reflexiones y apuntes sobre la ciudad de México (fines de la colonia)* (Mexico City: Deparamento del Distrito Federal, 1981): 61.

33. Prieto, *Memorias de mis tiempos, 1828 á 1840*, 106, 115, 121.

34. Although *carnitas* have come to be considered a regional specialty of Michoacán, in the nineteenth century the term referred to any bit of fried meat. See Archivo Histórico de la Ciudad de México (hereafter cited as AHCM), vol. 3775, exp. 583; *Boletín del Consejo Superior de Gobierno*, May 17, 1904.

35. Prieto, *Memorias de mis tiempos*, 1828 á 1840, 57–60, 82–83; John E. Kicza, *Colonial Entrepreneurs: Families and Business in Bourbon Mexico City* (Albuquerque: University of New Mexico Press), 127–29.

36. Juan Pedro Viqueira Albán, *¿Relajados o reprimidos? Diversiones públicas y vida social en la ciudad de México durante el Siglo de las Luces* (Mexico City: Fondo de Cultura Económica, 1987), 160–62; Fanny Calderón de la Barca, *Life in Mexico: The Letters of Fanny Calderón de la Barca*, ed. Howard T. Fisher and Marion Hall Fisher (Garden City, N.Y.: Doubleday, 1966), 541–42; Gooch, *Face to Face*, 285, 438.

37. Calderón de la Barca, *Life in Mexico*, 194–99; Martín González de la Vara, *La historia del helado en México* (Mexico City: Maas y Asociados, 1989), 41.

38. Manuel Rivera Cambas, *Viaje através del Estado de México (1880–1883)* (Mexico City: Biblioteca Enciclopédica del Estado de México, 1972), 247–48; Prieto, *Memorias de mis tiempos, 1828 á 1840*, 104–5, 117.

39. Prieto, *Memorias de mis tiempos, 1828 á 1840*, 15; Gooch, *Face to Face*, 495–96.

40. Prieto, *Memorias de mis tiempos, 1828 á 1840*, 52.

41. Edward Tayloe, *Mexico, 1825–1828: The Journal and Correspondence of Edward Thornton Tayloe*, ed. C. Harvey Gardiner (Chapel Hill: University of North Carolina Press, 1959), 19; Olive Percival, *Mexico City: An Idler's Note-Book* (Chicago: Herbert S. Stone and Co., 1901), 131–32.

42. This everyday routine left only the vaguest archival traces such as a shopping list with a cryptic, unsigned note that may have been to a literate cook named Pasecita. Instituto Nacional de Antropología e Historia (hereafter cited as INAH), VI–101, vol. 66.

43. *Nuevo cocinero mejicano* (1868), 951.

44. *El Mundo*, Mar. 28, 1890; Virginia Rodríguez Rivera, *La comida en el México antiguo y moderno* (Mexico City: Editorial Promaca, 1965), 120–42; Torres, *Cocina michoacana* (1896), 193.

45. Redfield, "Notes on the Cookery of Tepoztlan," 178; Rodríguez Rivera, *La comida*, 131, 143; Gisela Salinas Sánchez, "Región centro," in Avila Hernández et al., *Atlas cultural*, 105. For a fuller description of Judas burnings, see William H. Beezley, *Judas at the Jockey Club and Other Episodes of Porfirian Mexico* (Lincoln: University of Nebraska Press, 1987), 89–124.

46. *El cocinero mexicano* (1831), 108–9.

47. Rodríguez Rivera, *La comida*, 146; Kennedy, *Art of Mexican Cooking*, 194–95.

48. See also *La cocinera poblana* (1877), 2:64.

49. *Nuevo cocinero mejicano* (1868), 940.

50. Prieto, *Memorias de mis tiempos, 1828 á 1840*, 286–87.

51. Prieto, *Memorias, 1840 á 1853*, 137; Antonio García Cubas, *El libro de mis recuerdos* (Mexico City: Secretaría de Educación Pública, 1946), 40; Gooch, *Face to Face*, 291. Although in the twentieth century *chongos* refer to a specific dish of cooked milk curds, in the nineteenth this term covered a wide variety of desserts made of bread, cheese, and syrup. See Ireneo Paz, ed., *Diccionario del hogar*, 2 vols. (Mexico City: Imprenta de I. Paz, 1901), 1:439.

52. AGN, Tierras, vol. 2920, exp. 2, fo. 195–230.

53. Mary Barton, *Impressions of Mexico with Brush and Pen* (London: Meuthen and Co., 1911), 16.

54. García Cubas, *El libro de mis recuerdos*, 12; Rivera Cambas, *Viaje através*, 152, 195; *Monterey News*, May 25, 1905; Redfield, "Notes on the Cookery of Tepoztlan," 177.

55. Viqueira Albán, *¿Relajadas o reprimidos?*, 164–69; *El Comercio de Morelia*, July 22, 1899. The transformation of Judas burnings on Holy Saturday into birthday piñatas likewise illustrates this trivialization of popular festival. See Beezley, *Judas at the Jockey Club*, 118.

56. Carlos González Peña, *La fuga de la quimera* (Mexico City: Editorial Stylo, 1949), 16–17.

57. Ruvalcaba Mercado, *Vida cotidiana*, 5; John M. Ingham, *Mary, Michael, and Lucifer: Folk Catholicism in Central Mexico* (Austin: University of Texas Press, 1986), 119.

58. *Mexicanos pintados por si mismos: Obra escrita por una sociedad de literatos* (Mexico City: Símbolo, 1946 [1855]), 232; *El maíz, fundamento de la cultura popular mexicana* (Mexico: Museo Nacional de Culturas Populares, 1982), 30; J. Frank Dobie, *The Mexico I Like* (Dallas: Southern Methodist University Press, 1942), 106.

59. *La Guacamayo*, Dec. 28, 1905.

60. *El Pinche*, June 9, 1904; *El Hijo del Ahuizote*, Feb. 12, 1899.

61. Ruth Behar, "Sexual Witchcraft, Colonialism, and Women's Powers: Views from the Mexican Inquisition," in *Sexuality and Marriage in Colonial Latin America*, ed. Asunción Lavrín (Lincoln: University of Nebraska Press, 1989), 178–206.

62. Oscar Lewis, *Five Families: Mexican Case Studies in the Culture of Poverty* (New York: Basic Books, 1959), 270.

63. Archivo Histórico de la Secretaría de Salud (hereafter cited as AHSS), Inspección de Alimentos y Bebidas, box 1, exp. 1; AHCM, vol. 3668, exp. 58; vol. 3669, exp. 81. See also José Félix Alonso Gutiérrez, *Guía del Fondo Salubridad Pública*, 4 vols. (Mexico City: Imprenta de la Secretaría de Salud, 1991), 1:1.

64. AHSS, Inspección, box 1, exp. 9. See also Percival, *Mexico City*, 41.

65. Prieto, *Memorias de mis tiempos, 1828 á 1840*, 90.

66. AHSS, Inspección, box 1, exp. 4.

67. *El cocinero mexicano* (1831), 1:214; *El Siglo XIX*, Sept. 3, 1870; *La Opinión Nacional*, Sept. 5, 1870.

68. AHCM, vol. 3668, exp. 93.

69. María del Carmen Anquérez y Bolanos, *La medicina tradicional en México: proceso histórico, sincretismos y conflictos* (Mexico City: Universidad Nacional Autónoma de México, 1983).

70. *El Monitor Republicano*, June 24, 1870.

71. *Memoria que el Oficial Mayor encargado de la Secretaría de Estado y del Despacho de Gobernación presenta al Séptimo Congreso Constitucional* (Mexico City: Imprenta del Gobierno, 1874), 108–10.

72. William E. French, "Prostitutes and Guardian Angels: Women, Work and the Family in Porfirian Mexico," *Hispanic American Historical Review* 72, no. 4 (November 1992): 545.

73. Ibid., 546–53; William E. French, "*Progreso Forzado*: Workers and the Inculcation of the Capitalist Work Ethic in the Parral Mining District," in Beezley, Martin, and French, *Rituals of Rule, Rituals of Resistance*, 191–212.

74. *Violetas del Anáhuac*, Oct. 7, 1888; Anduiza, *El libro del hogar* (1893), 6.

75. *El Imparcial*, July 2, 1898.

76. Ibid., July 1, 1898; *La Mujer*, June 8, 1880, Nov. 22, 1881.

77. *El Imparcial*, Jan. 13, Aug. 26, 1899.

78. See editorials in the school's paper *La mujer*, Apr. 15, 1881; *El Imparcial*, July 2, Nov. 30, Dec. 2, 1898.

79. Quoted in Mary Kay Vaughan, *State, Education, and Social Class in Mexico, 1880–1928* (DeKalb: Northern Illinois University Press, 1982), 36.

80. Calderón de la Barca, *Life in Mexico*, 55, 129, 170, 614.

81. Stephen Mennell, *All Manners of Food: Eating and Taste in England and France from the Middle Ages to the Present* (Oxford: Basil Blackwell, 1985); Rebecca Lee Spang, "A Confusion of Appetites: The Emergence of Paris Restaurant Culture, 1740–1848" (Ph.D. diss., Cornell University, 1993); Camporesi, *Exotic Brew*, 27–35.

82. William H. Beezley, "The Porfirian Smart Set Anticipates Thorstein Veblen in Guadalajara," in Beezley, Martin, and French, *Rituals of Rule, Rituals of Resistance*, 178. The fact that the Ritz Carlton was in London demonstrates the hegemony of French cuisine throughout Europe.

83. *El cocinero mexicano* (1831), 1:2, 262, 2:77. See also Alexandre Dumas, *Dictionary of Cuisine*, trans. Louis Colman (New York: Avon Books, 1958), 48.

84. *Manual del cocinero y cocinera, tomada del periodico literario La Risa* (Puebla: Imprenta de José María Macías, 1849), 66–75, 307; *Novísimo arte de cocina* (1831), 30; Gutiérrez, *El ama de casa* 352–54; Anduiza, *El libro del hogar*, 283; *Nuevo cocinero mejicano* (1868), 795; Torres, *Cocina michoacana* (1896), 45, 446, 695; Paz, *Diccionario del hogar*, 1:474, 606, 2:1320–38.

85. See, for example, *Semana de las Señoritas* (1851), 1:75; *Diario del Hogar*, Feb.5, 1882; *El Correo de las Señoras*, Feb. 24, 1884; *El Comercio de Morelia*, Oct. 5, 1894; *La Semana en el Hogar*, Aug. 12, 1895; *El Heraldo del Hogar*, July 20, 1910.

86. Jean Anthelme Brillat-Savarin, *Fisiología del gusto*, trans. Eufemio Romero (Mexico City: Imprenta de Juan R. Navarro, 1852); *El libro de cocina de Jules Gouffé, antiguo jefe de cocina del Jockey Club de Paris*, 2 vols. (Mexico City: Ed. Rodríguez y Co., 1893).

87. Torres, *Cocina michoacana* (1896), 340–50.

88. AHSS, Inspección, box 1, exp. 5; Brigitte Boehm de Lameiras, *Comer y vivir en Guadalajara. Divertimiento historico-culinario* (Zamora: El Colegio de Michoacán, 1996).

89. García Cubas, *El libro de mis recuerdos*, 50–53; Luis González y González, Emma Cosío Villegas, and Guadalupe Monroy, *La República Resturada: La vida social*, vol. 3 of *Historia moderna de México*, ed. Daniel Cosío Villegas (Mexico City: Editorial Hermes, 1956), 492–93.

90. *El Imparcial*, June 3, 1898; *Monterey News*, Sept. 18, 1903; *The Mexican Herald*, Jan. 19, Apr. 26, 1908.

91. Salvador Novo, *Cocina mexicana: Historia gastronómica de la Ciudad de México* (Mexico City: Editorial Porrúa, 1993), 125–35.

92. Ibid., 135–37; *Recuerdo gastronómico del centenario, 1810–1910* (Mexico: N.p., 1910); Beezley, "Porfirian Smart Set," 180; *Monterey News*, Sept. 18, 1903; Brigitte Boehm de Lamerias, "Cambio y tradición en la cultura alimenticia de Guadalajara," in *Herencia española en la cultura material de las regiones de México. Casa, vestido y sustento*, ed. Rafael Diego Fernández (Zamora: El Colegio de Michocacán, 1993), 529–37; Harvey A. Levenstein, *Revolution at the Table: The Transformation of the American Diet* (New York: Oxford University Press, 1988), 96.

93. García Cubas, *El libro de mis recuerdos*, 52–53.

94. *El cocinero mexicano* (1831), 1:178; Camporesi, *Exotic Brew*, 49.

95. See, for example, *El cocinero mexicano* (1831), vol. 2; *Manual del cocinero y cocinera* (1849), 80–312; *Nuevo y sencillo arte* (1836), 32–134, 162–72, 195–217.

96. Gooch, *Face to Face*, 498.

97. Calderón de la Barca, *Life in Mexico*, 55, 156.

98. Bullock, *Six Months Residence in Mexico*, 253.

99. *Nuevo y sencillo arte* (1836), iv; *Manual del cocinero y cocinera* (1849), 92; Hortensia Rendón de García, *Antiguo manual de cocina yucateca; fórmulas para condimentar los*

*platos más usuales en la península*, 7th ed., 3 vols. (Mérida: Librería Burrel, 1938 [1st ed., 1898]), 55.

100. Cossío, *Recetario de cocina mexicana*, 7, 46–47; cf. *Recetas prácticas*, 95–97. Marianita Vázquez, "Cuaderno de cosina," attributed dessert recipes to Mariana and Jesús María; and Carmen Cabrera cooked artichokes using Pachita's recipe. See Eugenio del Hoyo Cabrera, ed., *La cocina jerezana en tiempos de López Velarde* (Mexico City: Fondo de Cultura Económica 1988), 48. See also Patricia Preciado Martin, *Songs My Mother Sang to Me: An Oral History of Mexican American Women* (Tucson: University of Arizona Press, 1992), 56.

101. *Recetas prácticas* (1892), 3; *Recetas selectas de cocina* (Mexico City: Tip. de Manuel León Sánchez, 1911), 5; *Nuestro libro* (1912).

102. Torres, *Cocina michoacana* (1896), 39, 58, 74, 102.

103. Ibid., 62; *Recetas prácticas* (1892), 103; *Recetas de cocina* (1911), quoted by Kennedy, *Regional Cooks of Mexico*, 138.

104. Torres, *Cocina michoacana* (1896), 193, 340–50, 752. On Guadalupine devotion, see Jacques Lafaye, *Quetzalcoatl and Guadalupe: The Formation of Mexican National Consciousness* (Chicago: University of Chicago Press, 1982). For a description of the 1895 crowning ceremony, see Beezley, "Porfirian Smart Set," 181–82.

105. *La Libertad*, Dec. 23, 1883; *Excelsior*, Dec. 11, 1926.

106. *Recetas prácticas* (1892), 172; *Nuestro libro* (1912), 40–44.

107. Torres, *Cocina michoacana* (1896), v.

108. *El Imparcial*, Aug. 29, 1897.

109. Calderón de la Barca, *Life in Mexico*, 20.

110. Payno quoted in Novo, *Cocina mexicana*, 312.

111. *El cocinero mexicano* (1831), 1:306.

112. *El cocinero mejicano* (1834), 1:3.

113. *Nuevo cocinero mejicano* (1868), 879. See also Kennedy, *Art of Mexican Cooking*, 84.

114. Concepción Lombardo de Miramón, *Memorias* (Mexico City: Editorial Porrúa, 1980), 473; INAH, box 34, 4th series, leg. 109, doc. 16F, "*Almuerzo del 12 de Dic. 1865*," "*Dinér du 14 Jauvier.*" Although Maximilian allowed *almuerzo* menus to be printed in Spanish and to include *mole*, the imperial dinner remained strictly French in language and content.

115. *Calendario del cocinero, para el año de 1865* (Mexico City: Imprenta Literaria, 1865), 51; *Calendario del cocinero, para el año de 1866* (Mexico City: Imprenta Literaria, 1866), 37–41. Linda Curcio-Nagy kindly pointed out these volumes in the rare book collection of the Biblioteca Nacional de Antropología e Historia.

### FOUR: THE TORTILLA DISCOURSE

1. Francisco Bulnes, *El porvenir de las naciones Hispano-Americanas ante las conquistas recientes de Europa y los Estados Unidos* (Mexico City: Imprenta de Mariano

Nava, 1899), 6, 19. On the Juárez polemic, see Charles A. Weeks, *The Juárez Myth in Mexico* (Tuscaloosa: University of Alabama Press, 1987), 54–70.

2. Daniel Cosío Villegas, "The Young Researcher," in *Research in Mexican History: Topics, Methodology, Sources,* ed. Richard E. Greenleaf and Michael C. Meyer (Lincoln: University of Nebraska Press, 1973), 5; AGN, Francisco Bulnes, vol. 11, exp. 7.

3. Rockefeller Foundation Archives (hereafter cited as RFA), group 1.1, series 323, box 1, folder 2; Manuel Gamio, *Algunas consideraciones sobre la salubridad y la demografía en México* (Mexico City: Talleres Gráficos de la Nación, 1939), 30–31; David A. Brading, "Manuel Gamio and Official Indigenismo in Mexico," *Bulletin of Latin American Research* 7, no. 1 (1988): 75–89.

4. Ignacio M. Altamirano, *El Zarco y La Navidad en las montañas,* 19th ed. (Mexico City: Editorial Porrúa, 1992). See also Doris Sommer, *Foundational Fictions: The National Romances of Latin America* (Berkeley: University of California Press, 1991).

5. Quoted in Agustín Basave Benítez, *México mestizo: Análisis del nacionalismo mexicano en torno a la mestiofilia de Andrés Molina Enríquez* (Mexico City: Fondo de Cultura Económica, 1991), 26.

6. Henry C. Schmidt, *The Roots of Lo Mexicano: Self and Society in Mexican Thought, 1900–1934* (College Station: Texas A & M University Press, 1978), 53.

7. Bulnes, *El porvenir,* 30.

8. French, *"Progreso Forzado,"* 193; Vaughan, *State, Education, and Social Class,* 29; Stephen Haber, *Industry and Underdevelopment: The Industrialization of Mexico, 1890–1940* (Stanford: Stanford University Press, 1989), 35.

9. *Informes y documentos relativos a comercio interior y exterior, agricultura, minería é industrias* (Mexico City: Oficina Tip. de la Secretaría de Fomento, 1888), 3.

10. Ibid., 213–22; Herbert Spencer, *The Study of Sociology* (New York: Appleton, 1889), 192–96, 368–69; Roberto Moreno, "Mexico," in *The Comparative Reception of Darwinism,* ed. Thomas F. Glick (Chicago: University of Chicago Press, 1988), 366–68.

11. Esteban Maqueo Castellanos, *Algunos problemas nacionales* (Mexico City: Eusebio Gómez de la Puente, 1910), 83.

12. Charles A. Hale, *The Transformation of Liberalism in Late Nineteenth-Century Mexico* (Princeton: Princeton University Press, 1989), 235–40, 253; Colin M. MacLachlan and William H. Beezley, *El Gran Pueblo: A History of Greater Mexico* (Englewood Cliffs, N.J.: Prentice Hall, 1994), 88.

13. Vaughan, *State, Education, and Social Class,* 22–23; Hale, *Transformation of Liberalism,* 228–34; Martin S. Stabb, "Indigenism and Racism in Mexican Thought, 1857–1911," *Journal of Inter-American Studies* 1 (1959): 413–14.

14. Stabb, "Indigenism and Racism," 411–15, Schmidt, *Roots of Lo Mexicano,* 50–53, Hale, *Transformation of Liberalism,* 221, 229.

15. Stephen Nissenbaum, *Sex, Diet, and Debility in Jacksonian America: Sylvester Graham and Health Reform* (Chicago: Dorsey Press, 1980), 39–52; Joachim Kühnau, "Food Cultism and Nutrition Quackery in Germany," in *Food Cultism and Nutrition*

184 *Notes to Pages 82–85*

*Quackery*, ed. Gunnar Blix (Uppsala, Sweden: Swedish Nutritional Foundation, Almqvist and Wiksells, 1970), 59–68.

16. Nancy Ray Gilmore, "The Condition of the Poor in Mexico, 1834," *Hispanic American Historical Review* 37, no. 2 (May 1957): 213–26. Gilmore notes that the charitable institutions were supported by wheat farms, but this alone does not explain feeding bread to the poor when prices of corn were lower than those of wheat. See also articles 34 through 36 of the prison code quoted in José Enrique Ampudía, ed., *Boletín del Archivo General de la Nación* 5, no. 4 (October-December 1981) and 6, no. 1 (January-March 1982), 106.

17. *La Libertad*, Dec. 23, 1883; *El Universal*, Oct. 11, 1893; Justo Sierra, *Obras completas*, 14 vols. (Mexico City: Universidad Nacional Autónoma de México, 1977) 9:126–28; Samuel Morales Pereira, *Puebla: Su higiene, sus enfermedades* (Mexico City: Oficina Tip. de la Secretaría de Fomento, 1888), 40–45.

18. Bulnes, *El porvenir*, 10–11, 17.

19. Ibid., 5–7, 17.

20. Luis Mesa, "Impresiones de la lectura de la obra que publicó el señor Ingeniero Don Francisco Bulnes, titulada *El porvenir de las naciones Hispano-Americanas ante las recientes conquistas de Europa y los Estados Unidos*," *Revista Positiva* 2 (March 1902): 92–99; *El Imparcial*, Aug. 23, 1899.

21. For a fascinating look at the origins of nutritional science, see Hillel Schwartz, *Never Satisfied: A Cultural History of Diets, Fantasies, and Fat* (New York: The Free Press, 1986).

22. Maqueo Castellanos, *Algunos problemas nacionales*, 83; Flores quoted in Moisés González Navarro, *El Porfiriato: La vida social*, vol. 4 of *Historia moderna de México*, ed. Daniel Cosío Villegas (Mexico City: Editorial Hermes, 1956), 152.

23. Archivo Histórico de la Secretaría de Educación Pública (hereafter cited as AHSEP), box 135, exp. 63; box 136, exp. 5; box 468, exp. 4.

24. Julio Guerrero, *El génesis del crimen en México: Estudio de psiquiatría social* (Mexico City: Librería de la Vda. de Ch. Bouret, 1901), 148–49; Francisco Bulnes, *El Pulque* (Mexico City: Imprenta de Murguía, 1909); González Navarro, *La vida social*, 74–79; *El Imparcial*, Mar. 14, 1902.

25. On the limits of deterministic scientific explanations, see Nancy Leys Stepan, *"The Hour of Eugenics": Race, Gender, and Nation in Latin America* (Ithaca: Cornell University Press, 1991), 73. On *científico* racial thought, see William D. Raat, "Los intelectuales, el positivismo y la cuestión indígena," *Historia Mexicana* 20, no. 3 (1971): 412–27; Moisés González Navarro, "Las ideas raciales de los científicos, 1890–1910," *Historia Mexicana* 37, no. 4 (1988): 565–83. William Beezley coined the term *Porfirian Persuasion* in his *Judas at the Jockey Club*, 13.

26. *El Monitor Republicano*, Mar. 2, 1877. See also Vaughan, *State, Education, and Social Class*, 145; Alan R. Sandstrom, *Corn Is Our Blood: Culture and Ethnic Identity in a Contemporary Indian Village* (Norman: University of Oklahoma Press, 1991), 345.

27. On education, see Vaughan, *State, Education, and Social Class*, 22–23; Hale, *Transformation of Liberalism*, 227–33; José Manuel Puig Casauranc, "Como son y

por que son así nuestras escuelas rurales," *Publicación de la Secretaría de Educación Pública* 13, no. 17 (1927): 5. Railroads and development are discussed by John Coatsworth, *Growth against Development: The Economic Impact of Railroads in Porfirian Mexico* (DeKalb: Northern Illinois University Press, 1981).

28. Joseph Cotter, "Before the Green Revolution: Mexican Agricultural Science Policy, 1920–1949" (Ph.D. diss., University of California at Santa Barbara, 1993). For wheat production, see John Coatsworth, "Anotaciones sobre la producción de alimentos durante el Porfiriato," *Historia Mexicana* 26, no. 2 (1976): 167–87. On rural bakeries, see Luis González y González, *San José de Gracia: Mexican Village in Transition*, trans. John Upton (Austin: University of Texas Press, 1972), 68.

29. *El Imparcial*, Sept. 8, 1898, July 23, 1899, Feb. 14, 1906; *El Colono*, Nov. 10, 1895; *El Economista Mexicano*, Aug. 21, 1909.

30. *Cocina michoacana* (1896), 758.

31. *Monterey News*, Feb. 14, 1903.

32. French, *"Progreso Forzado,"* 199–207. See also Haber, *Industry and Underdevelopment*, 54.

33. Jesús Flores y Escalante, *Brevísima historia de la cocina mexicana* (Mexico City: Asociación Mexicana de Estudios Fonográficos, 1994), 209–15; José Vasconcelos, *Ulises Criollo*, 8th ed. (Mexico City: Ediciones Botas, 1937), 251.

34. *El Imparcial*, July 9, 1902.

35. Quoted in Tony Morgan, "Proletarians, Politicos, and Patriarchs: The Use and Abuse of Cultural Customs in the Early Industrialization of Mexico City, 1880–1910," in Beezley, Martin, and French, *Rituals of Rule, Rituals of Resistance*, 165.

36. María del Carmen Reyna, "Las condiciones del trabajo en las panaderías de la Ciudad de México durante la segunda mitad del siglo XIX," *Historia Mexicana* 31, no. 3 (1982): 431–48.

37. Andrés Molina Enríquez, *Los grandes problemas nacionales* (Mexico City: Editorial Era, 1978 [1909]), 279.

38. Ibid., 349–51. See also Basave Benítez, *México mestizo*, 111.

39. Frederick C. Turner, *The Dynamic of Mexican Nationalism* (Chapel Hill: University of North Carolina Press, 1968).

40. Adrian A. Bantjes, "Burning Saints, Molding Minds: Iconoclasm, Civic Ritual, and the Failed Cultural Revolution," in Beezley, Martin, and French, *Rituals of Rule, Rituals of Resistance*, 261–94.

41. Friedrich Schuler, "Cardenismo Revisited: The International Dimensions of the Post-Reform Cárdenas Era, 1937–1940" (Ph.D. diss., University of Chicago, 1990).

42. Jean Meyer, *The Cristero Rebellion: The Mexican People Between Church and State* (Cambridge: Cambridge University Press, 1976); Bantjes, "Burning Saints, Molding Minds," 276–78; Marjorie Becker, "Torching la Purísima, Dancing at the Altar: The Construction of Revolutionary Hegemony in Michoacán," in *Everyday Forms of State Formation: Revolution and Negotiation of Rule in Modern Mexico*, ed. Gilbert M. Joseph and Daniel Nugent (Durham: Duke University Press, 1994).

43. Gamio, *Forjando patria*, 183; Alan Knight, "Racism, Revolution, and *Indigenismo*: Mexico, 1910–1940," in *The Idea of Race in Latin America, 1870–1940*, ed. Richard Graham (Austin: University of Texas Press, 1990), 71–113; Jean Charlot, *The Mexican Mural Renaissance, 1920–1925* (New Haven: Yale University Press, 1967).

44. James W. Wilkie, *The Mexican Revolution: Federal Expenditure and Social Change since 1910* (Berkeley: University of California Press, 1967), 208–13.

45. AHSEP, box 156, exp. 39; box 157, exp. 22.

46. Vaughan, *State, Education, and Social Class*, 127–164; Victoria Lerner, *La educación socialista*, vol. 17 of *Historia de la Revolución mexicana*, ed. Luis González y González (Mexico City: El Colegio de México, 1979); Ramón Eduardo Ruiz, *Mexico: The Challenge of Poverty and Illiteracy* (San Marino, Calif: The Huntington Library, 1963).

47. Gamio, *Algunas consideraciones*, 29–31; *El Universal*, July 14, 1931, June 6, 1934; *Excelsior*, Apr. 3, 1933.

48. Quoted by Leonel Durán, "Pluralidad y homogeneidad cultural," in *Política cultural para un país multiétnico*, ed. Rodolfo Stavenhagen and Margarita Nolasco (Mexico City: Secretaría de Educación Pública, 1988), 42; José Vasconcelos, *El tormento* (Mexico City: Ediciones Botas, 1938), 331; José N. Iturriaga, *De tacos, tamales, y tortas* (Mexico City: Editorial Diana, 1987), 17.

49. Felipe Hernández Gómez, "El maestro rural en las comunidades indígenas," *Los maestros y la cultura nacional, 1920–1952*, 5 vols. (Mexico City: Secretaría de Educación Pública, 1987) 2:30–32; Frank Tannenbaum, *Mexico: The Struggle for Peace and Bread* (New York: Alfred A. Knopf, 1950), 159; Wilfrid Hardy Callcott, *Liberalism in Mexico, 1857–1929* (Stanford: Stanford University Press, 1931), 296.

50. Clementina Cerrilla, "Seis menus de poco costo (Transmitido por radio)," *Publicaciones de la Secretaría de Educación Pública* 13, no. 1 (1927); AHSEP, box 9473, exp. 17; *El esfuerzo educativo en México*, 2 vols. (Mexico City: Secretaría de Educación Pública, 1928), 2:538–40; Whetten, *Rural Mexico*, 301.

51. AHSEP, box 155, exp. 21; box 156, exp. 34; box 402, exp. 91, 95; box 776, exp. 43.

52. Joseph Cotter, "The Origins of the Green Revolution in Mexico: Continuity or Change?" in *Latin America in the 1940s: War and Postwar Transitions*, ed. David Rock (Berkeley: University of California Press, 1994), 235–36; *El Nacional*, May 15, 1937.

53. AHSEP, box 798, exp. 11; Whetten, *Rural Mexico*, 291–92, 302–17; Beezley, *Judas at the Jockey Club*, 85–87.

54. Wilkie, *Mexican Revolution*, 208–13.

55. *Necesidades esenciales en México: Situación actual y perspectivas al año 2000*, vol. 1, *Alimentación* (Mexico City: Siglo XXI, 1982), 34; Oscar Lewis, *Tepoztlán Village in Mexico* (New York: Holt, Rinehart and Winston, 1960), 11.

56. Levenstein, *Revolution at the Table*, 44–59, 102–5, quote from 105.

57. Ibid., 87–89, 112–20; Harvey A. Levenstein, *Paradox of Plenty: A Social History of Eating in America* (New York: Oxford University Press, 1993), 64–100.

58. Alfredo Ramos Espinosa, *La alimentación en México* (Mexico City: N.p., 1939).

59. Enrique Cárdenas de la Peña, *Enlace SZ-INN: Crónica de un Instituto* (Mexico City: Instituto Nacional de Nutrición, 1991), 43–46; RFA, group 1.1, series 323, box 12, folders 80, 81.

60. RFA, group 1.1, series 323, box 12, folders 81, 82, 83. See also Daphne A. Roe, *A Plague of Corn: A Social History of Pellagra* (Ithaca: Cornell University Press, 1973).

61. Cárdenas de la Peña, *Enlace SZ-INN*, 35–37, 55, 209; José Alvarez Amezquita, *Historia de la Salubridad en México*, 3 vols. (Mexico City: Secretaría de Salubridad y Asistencia, 1955), 3:733.

62. Francisco de P. Miranda, *El maíz: Contribución al estudio de los alimentos mexicanos* (Mexico City: N.p., 1948), 6, 20–25; RFA, group 1.1, series 323, box 12, folder 81, Payne report, 1943.

63. Juan Ventosa Roig, "La alimentación popular," *Biblioteca Enciclopédica Popular* 2d época, no. 173 (1947): 86.

64. RFA, group 1.1, series 323, box 12, folders 80, 81; Carlos Pérez Hidalgo, ed., *Estudios de 1963 a 1974*, vol. 2 of *Encuestras nutricionales en México* (Mexico City: Instituto Nacional de Nutrición, 1976), 236–45; Guillermo Bonfil Batalla, *Diagnóstico sobre el hambre en Sudzal, Yuc. (Un ensayo de antropología aplicada)* (Mexico City: Instituto Nacional de Antropología e Historia, 1962), 129; Ramos Espinosa, *La alimentación en México*, 121.

65. Gilbert M. Joseph, *Revolution from Without: Yucatán, Mexico, and the United States, 1880–1924* (Durham: Duke University Press, 1980), 24; John Kenneth Turner, *Barbarous Mexico* (Austin: University of Texas Press, 1969).

66. RFA, group 1.1, series 323, box 12, folders 81, 82. Caribbean sugar plantation slaves likewise consumed a more nutritious diet when allowed to grow their own subsistence crops than when fed exclusively on rations. See Kenneth F. Kiple, *The Caribbean Slave: A Biological History* (Cambridge: Cambridge University Press, 1984).

FIVE: REPLACING THE AZTEC BLENDER

1. AGN, Ramo Presidentes, Lázaro Cárdenas, exp. 604.11/83.

2. Quoted in *El Imparcial*, Aug. 20, 1902.

3. Redfield, "Notes on the Cookery of Tepoztlan," 167–96; Whetten, *Rural Mexico*, 305; Lewis, *Life in a Mexican Village*, 72.

4. Kennedy, *Cuisines of Mexico*, 61–63.

5. Arnold J. Bauer, "Millers and Grinders: Technology and Household Economy in Meso-America," *Agricultural History* 64, no. 1 (Winter 1990), 1–10.

6. AGN, Patentes, box 5, exp. 375; box 8, exp. 489.

7. Ramón Sánchez Flores, *Historia de la tecnología y la invención en México* (Mexico City: Fomento Cultural Banamex, 1980), 389–94; *El Mundo*, Sept. 5, 1901, *El Imparcial*, July 6, 1902.

8. AHCM, vol 2414, exp. 1A, 1C, 1G; vol. 3211, exp. 1. See also Dawn Keremitsis, "Del metate al molino: La mujer mexicana de 1910 a 1940," *Historia Mexicana* 33 (October-December 1983): 286–88.

9. AGN, Patentes, box 5, exp. 375; box 24, exp. 1113; Fomento, Patentes y Marcas, leg. 150, exp. 4, 33, 86.

10. AGN, Luis Romero, sec. X, no. 17.

11. AGN, Luis Romero, sec. X, no. 4; *El Imparcial*, Sept. 2, 1902; *Excelsior*, Apr. 9, 1972.

12. AGN, Fomento, Patentes y Marcas, leg. 150, exp. 17, 22.

13. AGN, Fomento, Patentes y Marcas, leg. 150, exp. 38; *El Imparcial*, July 18, 1906.

14. AGN, Fomento, Patentes y Marcas, leg. 150, exp. 13, 54. See also Jaime Aboites A., *Breve historia de un invento olvidado: Las máquinas tortilladoras en México* (Mexico City: Universidad Autónoma Metropolitana, 1989), 57.

15. Aboites, *Breve historia de un invento*, 36–37, 64–71; AGN, Fomento, Patentes y Marcas, leg. 150, exp. 9, 75.

16. Aboites, *Breve historia de un invento*, 39, 47; Miranda, *El maíz*, 82; AGN, Luis Romero, sec. X, no. 17.

17. AGN, Patentes, leg. 150, exp. 58; Luis Romero, sec. XVII, no. 53; Luis Romero R. "Estudio y analisís de las harinas de masa de maíz: Su importancia en la República mexicana" (Tesis profesional de Químico, UNAM, 1932).

18. Nacional Financiera, *La industria de la harina de maíz* (Mexico City: NAFINSA, 1982), 13–14; *La industria de maíz* (Mexico City: Primsa Editorial, 1989), 108–14; Adriana Cópil, "La guerra de las tortillas," *Contenido* (July 1992), 42–47; Aboites, *Breve historia de un invento*, 50–51; *Forbes*, July 15, 1996.

19. Karl Kaerger, quoted in Bauer, "Millers and Grinders," 13.

20. Wendy Waters, "Roads, the Carnivalesque, and the Mexican Revolution: Transforming Modernity in Tepoztlán, 1928–1943" (Master's thesis, Texas Christian University, 1994), 165–70.

21. Quote from Redfield, "Notes on the Cookery of Tepoztlan," 182; Miranda, *El maíz*, 82.

22. Quoted in Bauer, "Millers and Grinders," 16.

23. Waters, "Roads, the Carnivalesque, and the Mexican Revolution," 167, 173.

24. Ibid., 164; Lewis, *Life in a Mexican Village*, 99, 108; Manuel Avila, *Tradition and Growth: A Study of Four Mexican Villages* (Chicago: University of Chicago Press, 1969), 53.

25. AGN, Cárdenas, exp. 604.11/21, 604.11/149, 604.11/155; Michael Belshaw, *A Village Economy: Land and People of Huecorio* (New York: Columbia University Press, 1967), 219–20.

26. *El Universal*, Nov. 11, 1933.

27. AGN, Cárdenas, exp. 604.11/67, 604.11/91, 604.11/92.

28. AGN, Cárdenas, exp. 604.11/121; Keremetsis, "Del metate al molino," 297.

29. Mary Kay Vaughan, "The Educational Project of the Mexican Revolution:

The Response of Local Societies (1934–1940)," in *Molding the Hearts and Minds: Education, Communications, Social Change in Latin America*, ed. John A. Britton (Wilmington, Del.: SR Books, 1994), 105–27; idem, "Rural Women's Literacy and Education during the Mexican Revolution: Subverting a Patriarchal Event?," in *Creating Spaces, Shaping Transitions: Women of the Mexican Countryside, 1850–1990*, ed. Heather Fowler-Salamini and Mary Kay Vaughan (Tucson: University of Arizona Press, 1994), 109–15.

30. Waters, "Roads, the Carnivalesque, and the Mexican Revolution," 168, 172.

31. RFA, group 1.1, series 323, box 1, folder 2; box 4, folder 25. The statement actually referred to substitute tortillas made with sorghum. See also Wilbur J. Granberg, *The Otomi Indians of Mexico* (New York: Praeger, 1970), 10.

32. RFA, group 6.13, series 1.1, box 57, folder 652.

33. RFA, group 6.13, series 1.1, box 57, folder 652.

34. Hermann Bausinger, *Folk Culture in a World of Technology*, trans. Elke Dettmer (Bloomington: Indiana University Press, 1990).

35. Robert V. Kemper, *Migration and Adaptation: Tzintzuntzan Peasants in Mexico City* (Beverly Hills: Sage Publications, 1977), 29, 152; Maria da Glória Marroni de Velázquez, "Changes in Rural Society and Domestic Labor in Atlixco, Puebla, 1940–1990," in Fowler-Salamini and Vaughan, *Creating Spaces, Shaping Transitions*, 223.

36. Quoted in Marroni de Velázquez, "Changes in Rural Society," 221.

37. Stephen R. Niblo, *War, Diplomacy, and Development: The United States and Mexico, 1938–1948* (Wilmington, Del.: Scholarly Resources, 1995), 127–39; Clark W. Reynolds, *The Mexican Economy: Twentieth-Century Structure and Growth* (New Haven: Yale University Press, 1970), 153.

38. Rodolfo Stavenhagen, "Collective Agriculture and Capitalism in Mexico: A Way Out or a Dead End?," in *Modern Mexico: State, Economy, and Social Conflict*, ed. Nora Hamilton and Timothy F. Harding (Beverly Hills: Sage Publications, 1986), 262–85.

39. Steven E. Sanderson, *The Transformation of Mexican Agriculture: International Structure and the Politics of Rural Change* (Princeton: Princeton University Press, 1986); Alain de Janvry, *The Agrarian Question and Reformism in Latin America* (Baltimore: Johns Hopkins University Press, 1981).

40. The State Food Agency has passed through a number of different permutations, including the Comité Regulador del Mercado de Trigo (established 1937), Comité Regulador del Mercado de las Subsistencias (1938), Nacional Distribuidora y Reguladora, S.A. de C.V. (1941), Compañía Exportadora e Importadora Mexicana, S.A. (1949), Compañía Nacional de Subsistencias Populares, S.A. (1961), and Sistema Alimenticia Mexicana (1980). It was finally dismantled in the early 1990s. See Enrique C. Ochoa, "The Politics of Feeding Mexico: The State and the Marketplace since 1934" (Ph.D. diss., University of California, Los Angeles, 1993), 23, 80–97, 311.

41. On the origins of the Green Revolution, see E. C. Stakman, Richard Bradfield, and Paul Manglesdorf, *Campaigns against Hunger* (Cambridge, Mass.: Belknap

Press, 1967). For a critical evaluation of this project, see Cynthia Hewitt de Al-cántara, *Modernizing Mexican Agriculture: Socioeconomic Implications of Technological Change, 1940–1970* (Geneva: United Nations Research Institute for Social Development, 1976). On early Mexican research, see Joseph Cotter, "The Rockefeller Foundation's Mexican Agricultural Project: A Cross-Cultural Encounter, 1943–1949," in *Missionaries of Science: The Rockefeller Foundation in Latin America*, ed. Marcos Cueto (Bloomington: Indiana University Press, 1994), 97–125.

42. Archivo Ramón Fernández y Fernández, El Colegio de Michoacán, Zamora, Michoacán, box 123, exp. 54, fol. 276–78.

43. Deborah Fitzgerald, "Exporting American Agriculture: The Rockefeller Foundation in Mexico, 1943–1953," in Cueto, *Missionaries of Science*, 72–96.

44. Hewitt, *Modernizing Mexican Agriculture*, 118–20, 173–75; Paul Lamartine Yates, *Mexico's Agricultural Dilemma* (Tucson: University of Arizona Press, 1981), 68–87; Wilkie, *Mexican Revolution*, 130–36.

45. Hewitt, *Modernizing Mexican Agriculture*, 176–80; Aida Mostkoff and Enrique C. Ochoa, "Complexities of Measuring the Food Situation in Mexico: Supply versus Self-Sufficiency of Basic Grains, 1925–82," in *Society and Economy in Mexico*, ed. James W. Wilkie (Los Angeles: UCLA Latin American Center Publications, 1990), 117–46.

46. Judith Adler Hellman, *Mexico in Crisis* (New York: Holmes and Meier Publishers, 1978), 56; Roger D. Hansen, *The Politics of Mexican Development* (Baltimore: Johns Hopkins University Press, 1971), 72–95; Harry E. Cross and James A. Sandos, *Across the Border: Rural Development in Mexico and Recent Migration to the United States* (Berkeley: Institute of Governmental Studies, University of California, Berkeley, 1981).

47. For rural grocery stores, see Ochoa, "Politics of Feeding Mexico," 257–64. On the urban bias, see Sanderson, *Transformation of Mexican Agriculture*, 260.

48. Matt Moffett, "Mexicans Convert as a Matter of Politics," *Wall Street Journal*, June 1, 1988.

49. Leticia Serrano Andrade, "El consumo de alimentos industrializados en una comunidad rural de la Zona Norte del Estado de Veracruz" (Thesis, Escuela de Salud Pública de México, 1984), 5; Matt Moffett, "A Mexican War Heats Up for Cola Giants," *Wall Street Journal*, Apr. 26, 1993.

50. *El Imparcial*, May 17, 1901; Monterey News, Feb. 4, 1903; Bárbara Hibino, "Cervecería Cuauhtémoc: A Case Study of Technological and Industrial Development in Mexico," *Mexico Studies/Estudios Mexicanos* 8, no. 1 (Winter 1992): 12–43; Haber, *Industry and Underdevelopment*, 52–54; Diego López Rosado, *El abasto de productos alimenticios en la ciudad de México* (Mexico City: Fondo de Cultura Económica, 1988), 188; J. C. Louis and Harvey Z. Yazijian, *The Cola Wars* (New York: Everest House, 1980), 46. I will examine the Porfirian meat-packing industry in a forthcoming work.

51. Haber, *Industry and Underdevelopment*, 132–38, 150–56; López Rosado, *El*

*abasto de productos alimenticios*, 358, 376; Niblo, *War, Diplomacy, and Development*, 127–39.

52. Waters, "Roads, the Carnivalesque, and the Mexican Revolution," 78; Louis and Yazijian, *Cola Wars*, 60.

53. José Antonio Roldán Amaro, *Hambre y riqueza en la historia contemporanea de México*, anexo 1 of *Historia del hambre en México*, ed. Pablo González Casanova (Mexico City: Instituto Nacional de Nutrición, 1986), 40; Carol Meyers de Ortiz, *Pequeño comercio de alimentos en colonias populares de Ciudad Nezahuacóyotl: Análisis de su papel en la estructura socioeconómica urbana* (Guadalajara: Editorial Universidad de Guadalajara, 1990), 33; Moffett, "Mexican War Heats Up for Cola Giants," B1, 6; Louis and Yazijian, *Cola Wars*, 133.

54. Ochoa, "Politics of Feeding Mexico," 273.

55. Quote from "La entrevista: Dr. Adolfo Chávez Villasana," *Cuadernos de Nutrición* 6, no. 9 (July-September 1983): 12–16; Clara Jusidman, "El maíz en los procesos de globalización y modernización," *Cuadernos de Nutrición* 16, no. 1 (January-February 1993): 41–42; *La industria de maíz*, 128–30; Cópil, "La guerra de las tortillas," 43–47.

56. Esther Casanueva, "La ayuda alimentaria directa," *Cuadernos de Nutrición* 10, no. 6 (November 1987): 35.

57. Nacional Financiera, *La industria de la harina de maíz*, (Mexico City: NAFINSA, 1982): 51; Naranjo, *Informe de programas*, 225–26; Cárdenas de la Peña, *Enlace SZ-INN*, 352, 537–39, 550–58; Ochoa, "Politics of Feeding Mexico," 245.

58. David Márquez Ayala, "Las empresas transnacionales y sus efectos en el consumo alimentario," in *Transnacionales, agricultura, y alimentación*, ed. Rodolfo Echeverría Zuno (Mexico City: Editorial Nueva Imagen, 1982), 218; Naranjo, *Informe de programas*, 228–34.

59. Chávez and Roldán, "Los alimentos de México," 65.

60. Quote from Beverly Chiñas, "Viajeras zapotecas," in *Mercados de Oaxaca*, ed. Martin Diskin and Scott Cook, trans. Antonieta S. M. de Hope (Mexico City: Dirección General de Publicaciones del Consejo Nacional para la Cultura y las Artes, 1989), 211.

61. RFA, group 1.1, series 323, box 2, folder 9; Whetten, *Rural Mexico*, 295.

62. Adolfo Chávez et al., *La nutrición en México y la transición epidemiológica* (Mexico City: Instituto Nacional de Nutrición, 1993), 33, 78; Gilberto Balam, "La alimentación de los campesinos mayas del estado de Yucatán (Primera parte)," *Cuadernos de Nutrición* 16, no. 6 (November-December 1993): 41; Ruvalcaba Mercado, *Vida cotidiana*, 31, 39; Messer, "Zapotec Food Plants," 8.

63. Messer, "Zapotec Food Plants," 9; Ruvalcaba Mercado, *Vida cotidiana*, 31–34, 39–44; Bonfil Batalla, *Diagnóstico sobre el hambre*, 65.

64. K. M. DeWalt, P. B. Kelly, and G. H. Pelto, "Nutritional Correlates of Economic Microdifferentiation in a Highland Mexican Community," in *Nutritional Anthropology: Contemporary Approaches to Diet and Culture*, ed. Norge W. Jerome, Randy

F. Kandel, Gretel H. Pelto (Pleasantville, N.Y.: Redgrave Publishing, 1980), 213; Serrano Andrade, "El consumo de alimentos industrializados," 29; Chávez et al., *La nutrición en México*, 28; Balam, "La alimentación de los campesinos mayas," 43.

65. Chávez et al., *La nutrición en México*, 47–78.

66. Sidney Mintz, *Sweetness and Power: The Place of Sugar in Modern History* (New York: Viking, 1985).

67. Aboites, *Breve historia de un invento*, 16.

### SIX: APOSTLES OF THE ENCHILADA

1. She published the book herself under the trade name Ediciones J. Velázquez de León. Unless otherwise noted, all her works were published in Mexico City under this rubric and citations will include only the date of publication.

2. Hellman, *Mexico in Crisis*, 56; Roderic A. Camp, *The Making of a Government: Political Leaders in Modern Mexico* (Tucson: University of Arizona Press, 1984); James W. Wilkie and Paul D. Wilkins, "Quantifying the Class Structure of Mexico, 1895–1970," in *Statistical Abstracts of Latin America*, vol. 21, ed. James W. Wilkie and Stephen Haber (Los Angeles: UCLA Latin American Center Publications, 1981), 577–90; Frank R. Brandenburg, *The Making of Modern Mexico* (Englewood Cliffs, N.J.: Prentice-Hall, 1964).

3. See, for example, Velázquez de León, *Platillos regionales*, 11–15.

4. Octavio Paz, *The Labyrinth of Solitude*, trans. Lysander Kemp (New York: Grove Press, 1961), 86–88.

5. Franco, *Plotting Women*, 131.

6. Larissa Adler Lomnitz and Marisol Pérez-Lizaur, *A Mexican Elite Family, 1820–1980: Kinship, Class, and Culture*, trans. Cinna Lomnitz (Princeton: Princeton University Press, 1987), 231–33.

7. Larissa Adler Lomnitz, *Networks and Marginality: Life in a Mexican Shantytown*, trans. Cinna Lomnitz (New York: Academic Press, 1977); idem, "Horizontal and Vertical Relations and the Social Structure of Urban Mexico," *Latin American Research Review* 17, no. 2 (1982): 51–74.

8. For calavera chauffeurs, see *Mignon: La revista de la mujer* (Puebla), October 1960. Migration is examined by Kemper, *Migration and Adaptation*. On women's rights, see Ward M. Morton, *Woman Suffrage in Mexico* (Gainesville: University of Florida Press, 1962).

9. Wilkie, *Mexican Revolution*, 208; Meyer and Sherman, *Course of Mexican History*, 4th ed. (New York: Oxford University Press, 1991), 683.

10. Josefina Velázquez de León, *Cocina popular: 30 menús económicos* (n.d.); idem, *Cómo cocinar en tiempos de carestía* (n.d.).

11. In slightly modified order: José Quintín Olascoaga, *Cocina dietética mexicana* (Mexico City: Secretaría de Educación Pública, 1961); Margarita del Valle, *Cocina vegetariana*, 2d ed. (Mexico City: Olimpo, 1956); Alfonso G. Alarcón, *La cocina de la infancia*, 3d ed. (Mexico City: Gema, 1954); Josefina Velázquez de León, *Cómo*

*improvisar fiestas* (n.d.); idem, *Carnes; recetas prácticas de platillos de carnes de res, ternera, cerdo, carnero y animales de caza,* 2d ed. (1956); idem, *Cocina para enfermos* (1968); María Enriqueta Bruixola, *Cocinando con microondas* (Mexico City: Diana, 1984); Marcela Meyer, *Cocina vegetariana afrodisiaca* (Mexico City: Editorial Posada, 1991).

12. Brandenburg, *Making of Modern Mexico,* 312; Asociación Nacional de Fabricantes de Aparatos Domésticos, *La industria manufacturera de aparatos domésticos en México: Memoria que pública la A.N.F.A.D., 1947–1957* (Mexico City: N.p., 1958).

13. Ochoa, "Politics of Feeding Mexico," 44–45.

14. Herbert Cerwin, *These Are the Mexicans* (New York: Reynal and Hitchcock, 1947), 267; Carmen Bueno, *Preparación y venta de comida fuera del hogar: Un estudio cualitativo de la ciudad de México* (Mexico City: El Colegio de México/Centro de Estudios Sociológicos, 1988); *Restaurante,* November 1969.

15. Elizabeth Borton de Treviño, *Where the Heart Is* (Garden City, N.Y.: Doubleday, 1962), 66.

16. Janice F. Fisher, "The Social Life of the Upper Sector Girl in a Mexican City" (Master's thesis, California State University, Long Beach, 1973), 77–80, 91.

17. David Lorey, *The Rise of the Professions in Twentieth-Century Mexico: University Graduates and Occupational Change since 1929* (Los Angeles: UCLA Latin American Center Publications, 1992), 199–203.

18. Borton de Treviño, *Where the Heart Is,* 257.

19. Ruth Schwartz Cowan, *More Work for Mother: The Ironies of Household Technology from the Open Hearth to the Microwave* (New York: Basic Books, 1983).

20. Levenstein, *Paradox of Plenty,* 33.

21. Adela Mena de Castro, *Cocina campechana: Un libro para el hogar,* 2d ed. (Mexico City: La Impresora, 1936), 6, 27.

22. Faustina Lavalle, *La exquisita cocina de Campeche: 400 recetas experimentadas* (Mexico City: Imprenta "Londres," 1939), 19.

23. Personal interview with Juan Luis Mutizaval Velázquez de León, Mexico City, June 30, 1994.

24. Andrew H. Whiteford, *Two Cities of Latin America: A Comparative Description of Social Classes* (Garden City, N.Y.: Doubleday, 1964), 110–11.

25. For a mouth-watering description of this Sonoran tradition, see Ernesto Camou Healy, "La nostalgia del rancho: Notas sobre la cultura urbana y la carne asada," in *Sociedad, Economía y Cultura Alimentaria,* ed. Shoko Doode and Emma Paulina Pérez (Hermosillo, Sonora: Centro de Investigación en Alimentación y Desarrollo/Centro de Investigaciones y Estudios Superiores en Antropología Social, 1994), 421–29.

26. Lomnitz and Pérez-Lizaur, *A Mexican Elite Family,* 89–91, 97, 180, 187.

27. Ibid., 223.

28. Guadalupe Rivera and Marie-Pierre Colle, *Frida's Fiestas: Recipes and Reminiscences of Life with Frida Kahlo* (New York: Clarkson Potter, 1994), 47–49; Patricia Quintana with Carol Haralson, *Mexico's Feasts of Life* (Tulsa, Okla.: Council Oaks

Books, 1989), 129; C. Gandia de Fernández, *Cocina mexicana* (Mexico City: Libro-Mex Editores, 1980), 44, 86. That these were invented traditions is supported by the absence of Independence Day festival foods in the collection of Rodríguez Rivera, *La cocina*, 120–59.

29. *Excelsior*, Feb. 4, 1947.

30. Ibid., June 5, 1946.

31. Rivera and Colle, *Frida's Fiestas*, 23, 30, 159.

32. María Aguilar de Carbia, *Marichu va a la cocina y recibe con distinción* (Mexico City: Editorial Epoca, 1971 [originally published c. 1933]); idem, *Mexico through my kitchen window* (Mexico City: A. Mijares, 1938). See also the selection in the *Catálogo general de la Librería Andrés Botas e hijo, Sucr.* (Mexico City: Botas, 1928).

33. *Mignon*, December 1938; December 1939; March, October 1940; June, October 1943; January 1948.

34. Carlos de Gante, "Santa Rosa de Lima y el Mole de Guajolote," *Excelsior*, Dec. 12, 1926. See also Rafael Heliodoro Valle, "Anales del mole de guajolote," in *La cultura popular vista por las élites (Antología de artículos publicados entre 1920 y 1952)*, ed. Irene Vázquez Valle (Mexico City: Universidad Nacional Autónoma de México, 1989), 421–33.

35. Eugenio Gómez, "La cocina vernacula," *Ethnos* 1, no. 1 (November 1922 – January 1923): 81–85.

36. Rodríguez Rivera, *La comida*, iv–v. See also her bibliographical work, *Mujeres folkloristas* (Mexico City: Instituto de Investigaciones Estéticas, Universidad Nacional Autónoma de México, 1967), 202–19.

37. Agustín Aragón Leyva published a regular series in *Restaurante* throughout the 1950s. See also the studies of Xochimilco published in the same magazine from January through May 1961.

38. Interview with Juan Luis Mutizaval Velázquez de León.

39. Josefina Velázquez de León, *Cocina de Guanajuato* (n.d.), 38; idem, *Antojitos mexicanos* (1946); idem, *Tamales y atoles*, 2d ed. (1956); Rita Molinar, *Antojitos y cocina mexicana* (Mexico City: Editorial Pax-Mexico, 1969).

40. *Comida familiar en el Estado de Jalisco* (Mexico City: Banrural, 1988), 13.

41. Melitón Salazar Monroy, *La típica cocina poblana y los guisos de sus religiosas* (Puebla: N.p., 1945), 8.

42. Artemio del Valle-Arizpe, "El mole de guajolote," quoted in Enrique Cordero y Torres, *Leyendas de la Puebla de los Angeles* (Mexico City: N.p., 1972), 187–95.

43. *El Universal*, July 1, 1964; *Restaurante*, June 1952.

44. *Diario de Puebla*, Jan. 19, 1952.

45. *Restaurante*, August 1963.

46. The fungus was described as *"comestible entre la gente del campo,"* by Leovigildo Islas Escarcega, *Vocabulario campesino nacional* (Mexico City: Editorial Beatriz de Silva, 1945), 31. The one exception to elite disdain appeared in a nineteenth-century recipe from the ever-adventurous Catalan gourmet, Narciso Bassols, *Cocina*

*poblana*, 2:66. Virginia Rodríguez Rivera collected a recipe from Puebla, but did not specify the informant in her *La cocina*, 62.

47. Kennedy, *Art of Mexican Cooking*, 171.

48. Susanna Palazuelos and Marilyn Tausend, *México: The Beautiful Cookbook: Authentic Recipes from the Regions of Mexico* (San Francisco: Collins Publishers, 1991), 75.

49. Wendy Waters, "Calles at the Crossroads of Mexican History: New Roads, Old Directions" (Senior honors thesis, University of British Columbia, 1992).

50. Interview with Juan Luis Mutizaval Velázquez de León.

51. Francisco J. Santamaría, *Americanismo y barbarismo: Entretenimientos lexicográficos y filológicos* (Mexico City: Consejo Editorial del Gobierno del Estado de Tabasco, 1980), 73.

52. Manuel Toussaint, *Oaxaca* (Mexico City: Editorial "Cultura," 1926), 93.

53. Novo, *Cocina mexicana*, 146.

54. Lavalle, *La exquisita cocina de Campeche*, 11, 15.

55. Velázquez de León, *Platillos regionales*, 14.

56. *Recetario del pescador y otras recetas populares* (Mexico City: Museo Nacional de Culturas Populares, 1984), 8; *Restaurante*, May 1955.

57. *Excelsior*, Aug. 10, 1947.

58. Rosa, Marquesa de Castellar, *My Stove Is My Castle* (Mexico City: Edit. Intercontinental, 1956), 14–16, 31, 44.

59. Sebastián Verti, *Tradiciones mexicanas* (Mexico City: Editorial Diana, 1991), 396–98.

60. *Comer como dios manda* (Mexico City: Ediciones Culturales, 1977), 72, 98, 150.

61. *Excelsior*, Apr. 16, 1945; Dec. 6, 1947.

62. Carmen Toscano de Moreno Sánchez, *Las senadoras suelen guisar* (Mexico City: Instituto Nacional de Protección a la Infancia, 1964).

63. Márquez Ayala, "Las empresas transnacionales," 216–19.

64. *Comer como dios manda*, 60–64; *Excelsior*, Aug. 1, 1945; Jan. 6, 1947.

65. *Excelsior*, Feb. 9, 1945; Lewis, *Five Families*, 306.

66. Josefina Velázquez de León, *Cocina de Sonora* (1958), 16; Mena de Castro, *Cocina campechana*, 71; Concepción Hernández de Rodríguez, *Cocina y repostería práctica*, 3d ed. (Mérida: Cia. Tip. Yucateca, n.d.), 15; *Mujer* (Morelia), July 15, 1967.

67. *Excelsior*, Apr. 15, July 14, Sept. 1, Dec. 16, 1945; June 2, 1947.

68. *Mignon: La revista de la mujer* (Puebla), January 1956, March 1962.

69. Palazuelos and Tausend, *México*, 127–28.

70. *Restaurante*, July 1971.

71. Personal interview with Brigitte Boehm de Lameiras, Zamora, Michoacán, July 17, 1995.

72. Liah Greenfeld, *Nationalism: Five Roads to Modernity* (Cambridge, Mass.: Harvard University Press, 1992), 373.

73. *Excelsior*, Mar. 15, 1945; Aug. 1, 1946; July 8, 1947.

74. The rise of Mexican American restaurants is described by Donna Gabaccia, *We Are What We Eat* (Cambridge, Mass.: Harvard University Press, forthcoming).

75. *El Heraldo del Hogar*, Sept. 15, Oct. 16, 1913; *El Hogar*, Feb. 15, 1914.

76. Ilene V. O'Malley, *The Myth of the Revolution: Hero Cults and the Institutionalization of the Mexican State, 1920–1940* (New York: Greenwood Press, 1986), 63–70.

77. John W. Sherman, *The Mexican Right and the End of Revolutionary Reform, 1929–1940* (New York: Praeger, 1997).

78. Adela Fernández, *La tradicional cocina mexicana y sus mejores recetas/Traditional Mexican Cooking and Its Best Recipes* (Mexico City: Panorama Editorial, 1985), 11–37; María Elena Sodi de Pallares, *Ensayo sobre las excelencias de la cocina mexicana* (Mexico City: N.p., 1958); Salvador Novo, *Cocina mexicana o Historia Gastronómica de la Ciudad de México* (Mexico City: Porrúa, 1967); Amando Farga, *Historia de la comida en México* (Mexico City: Costa Amic, 1968).

79. Sodi de Pallares, *Ensayo sobre las excelencias de la cocina mexicana*, 15; Farga, *Historia de la comida*, 20–25; Guzmán Peredo, *Crónicas gastronómicas*, 7; *Restaurante*, January 1970.

80. Novo, *Cocina mexicana*, 29; Farga, *Historia de la comida*, 82.

81. *Restaurante*, October 1952; Sodi de Pallares, *Ensayo sobre las excelencias de la cocina mexicana*, 35–36.

82. Compare this vision with Jaime del Arenal Fenochio, "El nacionalismo conservador mexicano del siglo XX," in *El nacionalismo en México*, ed. Cecilia Noriega Elio (Zamora: El Colegio de Michoacán, 1992), 329–54; Lomnitz and Pérez-Lizaur, *A Mexican Elite Family*, 195–99.

83. See his "Introduction: Inventing Traditions," in *The Invention of Tradition*, ed. Eric Hobsbawm and Terence Ranger (Cambridge: Cambridge University Press, 1983), 1–14.

84. *Excelsior*, Aug. 13, 1947.

85. Josefina Velázquez de León, *Como cocinar en los aparatos modernos* (1950), 117, 272, 284, 319.

86. See the magazines *Mujeres: Expresión Feminina*, Jan. 31, 1967; *Restaurante*, July 1953. Facsimiles of nineteenth-century cookbooks include *Manual del cocinero, dedicado a las señoritas mexicanas: Edición facsimilar 1856* (Mexico City: Joaquín Porrúa, 1983); *Manual del cocinero y cocinera tomado del periódico literario La Risa* (Mexico City: Gobierno del Estado de Puebla, 1992). For other nostalgic visions of Mexican cuisine, see Melitón Salazar Monroy, *La típica cocina poblana y los guisos de sus relígiosas* (Puebla: N.p., 1945); *Cuaderno de guisados caseros. El Parador de José Luis* (Mexico City: Impulsora Turística, 1979); Dolores Sánchez de Pineda, *Comida traditional de San Cristobal de las Casas* (Mexico City: Private printing, 1988); María Luisa Montes de Oca de Castro, *Ayer y hoy en la cocina yucateca: recopilación de antiguas y auténticas recetas regionales* (Mérida: N.p., 1990).

87. José L. Cossío, ed., *Recetas de biscochos de desayuno, galletas, dulces y otros escrito por Doña Guadalupe Cossío y Soto* (Mexico City: Vargas Rea, 1969); idem, *Recetario de cocina mexicana*; Del Hoyo, *La cocina jerezana*.

88. Palazuelos and Tausend, *México*, 88.

89. *Excelsior*, Oct. 8, 1947.

90. Meyer and Sherman, *Course of Mexican History*, 665–71; MacLachlan and Beezley, *El Gran Pueblo*, 369–70.

91. Roderic A. Camp, "Political Modernization in Mexico: Through a Looking Glass," in *The Evolution of the Mexican Political System*, ed. Jaime E. Rodríguez O. (Wilmington, Del.: Scholarly Resources, 1993), 247.

92. Alan Riding, *Distant Neighbors: A Portrait of the Mexicans* (New York: Vintage, 1986), 147–49, 159–62; Jeffry A. Frieden, *Debt, Development and Democracy: Modern Political Economy and Latin America, 1965–1985* (Princeton: Princeton University Press, 1991), 190–98.

93. Interview with Juan Luis Mutizaval Velázquez de León.

94. Josefina Velázquez de León *Cómo cocinar en tiempos de carestía* (Mexico City: Editorial Diana, 1987); idem, *Cómo aprovechar los sobrantes de la comida* (Mexico City: Editorial Universo, 1987).

95. *Personalidades en la cocina: Las recetas favoritas de artistas, de gente famosa y de restaurantes* (Mexico City: Solo Por Ayudar — Editorial Diana, 1985).

SEVEN: RECIPES FOR *PATRIA*

1. Lin Yutang, *My Country and My People*, 2d ed. (New York: Reynal and Hitchcock, 1937 [1935]), 337, 339.

2. Ramón López Velarde, *Poesías completas y el minutero*, 4th ed. (Mexico City: Editorial Porrúa, 1968), 265; Fernando González Gortázar, "By Way of Introduction," in *Mexican Monuments: Strange Encounters*, ed. Helen Escobedo (New York: Abbeville Press, 1989), 12.

3. George L. Mosse, *The Nationalization of the Masses: Political Symbolism and Mass Movements in German from the Napoleonic Wars through the Third Reich* (Ithaca: Cornell University Press, 1991), 2, 16.

4. Anderson, *Imagined Communities*, 12–22.

5. French inclinations toward ethnic nationalism culminated in the Vichy regime. See Herman Lebovics, *True France: The Wars over Cultural Identity, 1900–1945* (Ithaca: Cornell University Press, 1992). See also Craig Calhoun, "Nationalism and Ethnicity," *Annual Review of Sociology* 19 (1993): 211–39.

6. Ernest Gellner, *Nations and Nationalism* (Ithaca: Cornell University Press, 1983).

7. Guy P. C. Thomson, "Popular Aspects of Liberalism in Mexico, 1848–1888," *Bulletin of Latin American Research* 10, no. 3 (1991): 265–92; Florencia Mallon, *Peasant and Nation: The Making of Post Colonial Mexico and Peru* (Berkeley: University of California Press, 1995). See also John A. Hall, "Nationalism: Classified and Explained," *Daedalus* 122, no. 3 (Summer 1993): 1–28; Joy Elizabeth Hayes, "Radio Broadcasting and Nation Building in Mexico and the United States, 1925–1945" (Ph.D. diss., University of California, San Diego, 1994), 11–18.

8. For comparative perspectives on gender and nationalism, see Donna J. Guy, *Sex and Danger in Buenos Aires: Prostitution, Family, and Nation in Argentina* (Lincoln: University of Nebraska Press, 1991); George L. Mosse, *Nationalism and Sexuality: Respectability and Abnormal Sexuality in Modern Europe* (New York: Howard Fertig, 1985), 5, 18; Anderson, *Imagined Communities*, 143–44.

9. Cynthia Enloe, *Does Khaki Become You? The Militarisation of Women's Lives* (London: Pluto Press, 1983), 7, 15, 211–12.

10. Gerda Lerner, *The Creation of Patriarchy* (New York: Oxford University Press, 1986), chapters 7 and 9.

11. K. C. Chang, "Introduction," in Chang, *Food in Chinese Culture*, 11, 18–19; Freeman, "Sung," 165–66.

12. Goody, *Cooking, Cuisine, and Class*, 101–2, 131.

13. Ibid., 102–5, 192–93. Exceptions to this generalization of male control over court cuisine included Mesoamerica and Thailand. See Van Esterik, "From Marco Polo to McDonald's" 185.

14. Chang, "Introduction," 11; Revel, *Un festín en palabras*, 237, 241.

15. Quoted in Goody, *Cooking, Cuisine, and Class*, 148.

16. Paul Bertolli with Alice Waters, *Chez Panisse Cooking* (New York: Random House, 1988), xiii. See also Paul Stoller, *The Taste of Ethnographic Things: The Senses in Anthropology* (Philadelphia: University of Pennsylvania Press, 1989), chapter 1.

17. This line of thought was inspired by Donna Gabaccia's forthcoming book, *We Are What We Eat.*

18. Appadurai, "How to Make a National Cuisine," 15–22.

19. Van Esterik, "From Marco Polo to McDonald's" 188–90.

20. Martha Chapa and Martha Ortiz, *Cocina de Querétaro: Sabor a Independencia* (Mexico City: Gobierno del Estado de Querétaro, 1990), 11–29.

21. Appadurai, "How to Make a National Cuisine," 20.

22. Eric J. Hobsbawm, *Nations and Nationalism since 1780: Programme, Myth, Reality*, 2d ed. (Cambridge: Cambridge University Press, 1992), 142.

23. Bynum, *Holy Feast and Holy Fast*, 275.

24. Sor Juana Inés de la Cruz, *Obras completas*, 4 vols. (Mexico City: Fondo de Cultura Económica, 1951), 4:450.

25. Deborah Silverman, "The 'New Woman,' Feminism, and the Decorative Arts in Fin-de-Siècle France," in *Eroticism and the Body Politic*, ed. Lynn Hunt (Baltimore: Johns Hopkins University Press, 1991), 148; Beth Barton, "Mothers, Morality, and Nationalism in Pre-1919 Egypt," in *The Origins of Arab Nationalism*, ed. Rashid Khalidi et al. (New York: Columbia University Press, 1991), 271–88.

26. O'Malley, *Myth of the Revolution*, 113–44.

27. MacLachlan and Beezley, *El Gran Pueblo*, 324.

28. JoAnn Martin, "Antagonisms of Gender and Class in Morelos," in Fowler-Salamini and Vaughan, *Creating Spaces, Shaping Transitions*, 225–26.

29. Gilberto Freyre, *The Masters and the Slaves: A Study in the Development of*

*Brazilian Civilization*, trans. Samuel Putnam (New York: Alfred A. Knopf, 1946), xix.

30. Linda Colley, *Britons: Forging the Nation, 1707–1837* (New Haven: Yale University Press, 1992), 277.

31. Anderson, *Imagined Communities*, 22–36.

32. Edmund S. Morgan, *Inventing the People: The Rise of Popular Sovereignty in England and America* (New York: W. W. Norton and Co., 1988).

33. Spang, "Confusion of Appetites," 16–17, 173, 183, 266–68.

34. Ibid., 32, 77–83, 93–94, 168–71, 265.

35. Ibid., 188–94, 260–63. For the Mexican chicken recipe, see Auguste Escoffier, *The Escoffier Cook Book: A Guide to the Fine Art of Cookery* (New York: Crown Publishers, 1969), 519.

36. Spang, "Confusion of Appetites," 258–68. See also Jean Anthelme Brillat-Savarin, *The Physiology of Taste, or Meditations on Transcendental Gastronomy* (New York: Dover, 1960), 119–39.

37. Spang, "Confusion of Appetites," 215.

38. Quoted in Giles MacDonogh, *A Palate in Revolution: Grimod de La Reynière and the Almanach des Gourmands* (London: Robin Cook, 1987), 121, 180.

39. Brillat-Savarin, *Physiology of Taste*, 53, 113, 219, 258.

40. Appadurai, "How to Make a National Cuisine," 5; Van Esterik, "From Marco Polo to McDonald's," 188.

41. Dionisio Pérez, *Guía del buen comer español* (Madrid: Patronato Nacional del Turismo, 1929), 10.

42. Darra Goldstein, *The Georgian Feast: The Vibrant Culture and Savory Food of the Republic of Georgia* (New York: HarperCollins, 1993), 40.

43. María José Sevilla, *Life and Food in the Basque Country* (New York: New Amsterdam Books, 1990), 147.

44. Pérez, *Guía del buen comer español*, 12.

45. Goody, *Cooking, Cuisine, and Class*, 184; Binh Duong and Marcia Kiesel, *Simple Art of Vietnamese Cooking* (New York: Prentice Hall, 1991), 88.

46. I thank Ron Shearer for this information.

47. Maurice-Edmond Sailland, *Traditional Recipes of the Provinces of France, selected by Curnonsky*, trans. and ed. Edwin Lavin (Garden City, N.Y.: Doubleday, 1961), 13–15.

48. On adoption of French cuisine, see Claudia Roden, *A New Book of Middle Eastern Food* (New York: Penguin, 1985), 43; Levenstein, *Revolution at the Table*, chapter 2. For Chinese rejection, see Jonathan Spence, "Ch'ing," in Chang, *Food in Chinese Culture*, 286; Lin, *My Country and My People*, 340–41.

49. Freyre, *Masters and the Slaves*, 44–60.

50. See the nationalist cookbook by Basima Zaki Ibrahim quoted by Goody, *Cooking, Cuisine, and Class*, 131. On popular Egyptian cuisine, see Roden, *New Book of Middle Eastern Food*, 13, 161, 324.

51. Peter Fry, "Feijoada e soul food: Notas sobre a manipulaçao de símbolos étnicos e nacionais," *Ensaios de Opinião* 2, no. 2 (1977): 44–47.

52. Maria Stoopen, *El universo de la cocina mexicana* (Mexico City: Fomento Cultural Banamex,1988), 67–96.

53. *Excelsior*, Nov. 17, 1970.

54. Antonio Gramsci, *Selections from the Prison Notebooks*, ed. Quintin Hoare and Geoffrey Nowell Smith (New York: International Publishers, 1971); E. P. Thompson, "Eighteenth-century English Society: Class Struggle without Class?" *Social History* 3, no. 2 (May 1978): 133–65.

55. John K. Walton, *Fish and Chips and the British Working Class, 1870–1940* (Leicester: Leicester University Press, 1992), 13–15.

56. AHCM, vol. 2405, exp. 3, 4, 9, 12, 19.

57. The largest *molcajete* I have ever seen belonged to a traveling food vendor from Puebla, who was serving breakfast at the celebration of the Virgin of Carmen (July 15, 1994) in Catemaco, Veracruz. Such carnival troupes date back at least to the nineteenth century.

58. See Pierre Bourdieu, *Distinction*, trans. Richard Nice (Cambridge: Harvard University Press, 1986), postscript.

59. *Recetario del pescador*, 13.

60. JoAnn Martin, "Contesting Authenticity: Battles over the Representation of History in Morelos, Mexico," *Ethnohistory* 40, no. 3 (Summer 1993): 438–65; Hayes, "Radio Broadcasting and Nation Building," 32–41. For Porfirian art, see Jean Charlot, *Mexican Art and the Academy of San Carlos, 1785–1915* (Austin: University of Texas Press, 1962), 134, 147. Other representative works can be seen at the Museo Nacional de Bellas Artes, Mexico City.

61. Pérez, *Guía del buen comer español*, 34; MacDonogh, *Palate in Revolution*, 136; Bugialli, *Fine Art of Italian Cooking*.

62. Gilberto Freyre, *Manifesto Regionalista* (Recife: Instituto Joaquim Nabuco de Pesquisas Sociais, 1967 [1926]), 45–63; idem, *Masters and the Slaves*, 51–64, 125–32, 459–70.

63. Josefina Velázquez de León, *Cocina de San Luis Potosí* (1957), 111–12.

64. Van Esterik, "From Marco Polo to McDonald's," 182–83.

65. Len Deighton, *ABC of French Food* (New York: Bantam Books, 1990), 33, 124–25.

66. Revel, *Un festín en palabras*, 32–33, 207–8.

67. Ibid., 258.

68. Quoted in Brading, "Manuel Gamio and Official Indigenismo," 87.

69. *El universo de la cocina mexicana: Recetario* (Mexico City: Fomento Cultural Banamex, 1988), 18, 40, 48.

70. Patricia Sharpe, "Mix Masters," *Texas Monthly* 19, no. 6 (June 1991): 44.

71. Interview with Brigitte Boehm.

72. Quoted in Florence Fabricant, "Mexican Chefs Embrace a Lighter Cuisine of Old," *The New York Times*, May 3, 1995.

73. Ruvalcaba Mercado, *Vida cotidiana*, 85.

74. Palazuelos and Tausend, *México*, 132.

75. Molly O'Neill, "Mexicans Show New York Their Real Food," *The New York Times*, Aug. 25, 1993.

76. Ana Naranja B. et al., *Informe de programas y proyectos de doce años, 1976–1987* (Mexico City: Instituto Nacional de Nutrición, 1987), 202; Messer, "Zapotec Food Plants," 4–5, 17.

77. Personal interview with Adolfo Chávez Villasana, Mexico City, June 29, 1995.

78. Ana Bertha Pérez, "De la cocina rural a la dieta urbana," *Cuadernos de Nutrición* 10, no. 6 (November 1987): 42–47.

79. Personal interview with Edward Gámez, Fort Worth, Texas, March 26, 1992.

80. Revel, *Un festín en palabras*, 210.

81. Brillat-Savarin, *Physiology of Taste*, xxxiv.

82. See Linda B. Hall, "Masks and Mirrors: Octavio Paz's Search for National Identity," *Southwest Review* (Spring 1972): 95.

83. Eben Shapiro, "Thousands of Cookbooks in Search of Some Cooks," *Wall Street Journal*, Mar. 2, 1994.

84. Brett Williams, "Why Migrant Women Feed Their Husbands Tamales: Foodways as a Basis for a Revisionist View of Tejano Family Life," in *Ethnic and Regional Foodways in the United States: The Performance of Group Identity*, ed. Linda Keller Brown and Kay Mussell (Knoxville: University of Tennessee Press, 1984), 113–26; Beverly Bundy, "The Tamale Tradition," *Fort Worth Star-Telegram*, Dec. 18, 1991; Mary Sánchez, "Gift-wrapped for the Holidays," *Kansas City Star*, Dec. 6, 1995.

EPILOGUE

1. Herón Pérez Martínez, *Refrán viejo nunca miente: Refranero mexicano* (Zamora: El Colegio de Michoacán, 1993), 129.

2. Elaine C. Lacey, "Meaning, Memory, and National Identity: The Centennial Celebration of Mexican Independence, 1921," paper presented at the Calcott Symposium on Latin America, Columbia, S.C., Feb. 17, 1996; *Recuerdo gastronómico del centenario*.

3. For a discussion of food purchasing by Mexico City restaurants, see Bueno, *Preparación y venta de comida*, 33.

4. Robb Walsh, "The Taco Nuns of Monterrey," *Chile Pepper* 8, no. 4 (July-August 1994): 45.

# Glossary

Adobo    paste of vinegar, herbs, and chiles, originally used to pickle meat.

Aguardiente    "burning water," potent alcohol distilled from maguey or sugar cane.

Aguas frescas    soft drinks flavored with fruits, seeds, flowers, and melon.

Almuerzo    brunch, informal family meal taken about ten o'clock in the morning.

Antojito    "little whimsy," corn-based snack food such as a *gordita*, *chalupa*, or tamal, typically eaten on the street.

Atole    corn *masa* gruel.

Axolotl    larval salamander (*Ambystoma mexicanum*) eaten by Native Americans.

Birria    steamed or barbecued meat, often goat, a regional dish of Jalisco.

Bolillo    small, enlongated wheat bread roll.

Buñuelo    fritter.

Cabrito al pastor    barbecued kid, a regional specialty of Monterrey.

Cacique    regional political boss, in colonial times a Native American.

Campesino    peasant; agrarian worker.

Capirotada    bread pudding.

Carne asada    grilled meat, a common dish of northern Mexico. A renowned version, *carne asada a la tampiqueña*, was created by restauranteur José Inés Loredo.

Carnero    mutton.

Carnitas    bits of fried meat.

Cazuela    earthenware cooking pot.

Cena    dinner, an informal meal often eaten out as late as ten o'clock at night.

Chalupa    "canoe," oval-shaped corn *masa* snack eaten in the states of Mexico and Puebla.

Chayote    vegetable pear, oblong green-skinned fruit (*Sechium edule*) that is boiled, steamed, or fried in a variety of ways. The seed is considered a great delicacy.

Chilaquiles   dish of chile pepper sauce and leftover tortillas.

Chiles rellenos   stuffed chile peppers, often poblanos, filled with cheese or *picadillo* and fried with egg batter.

Chiles en nogada   poblano peppers stuffed with *picadillo*, bathed in a pure sauce of ground walnuts, then sprinkled with pomegranate seeds. The combination of green chiles, white sauce, and red seeds, evocative of the Mexican flag, has made it a national dish.

Chinampa   "floating" gardens, enormously productive raised fields cultivated in pre-Columbian times in the freshwater swamps of Lake Chalco-Xochimilco.

Chongos   dessert formerly made of bread, cheese, and syrup. In the twentieth century this term has come to denote cooked milk curds, a specialty of Zamora, Michoacán.

Chorizo   sausage spiced with chile peppers; the most renowned come from Toluca.

Científico   "technocrat," member of the Porfirian governing elite.

Cocolli   twisted chains of tortillas, made from special bundles of maize that were ritually hung from the ceiling, and eaten on the pre-Columbian festival of Tlacaxipehualiztli (probably March 5).

Cochinita pibil   pit-barbecued pig, a specialty of Yucatán.

Comal   earthenware griddle.

Comida   main meal of the day, typically eaten about two o'clock.

Cuitlacoche   "excrement of the gods," a black fungus (*Ustilago maydis*) that grows on ears of maize. Long used by street corner cooks as a stuffing for *quesadillas*, it has recently become a staple of nouvelle Mexican cuisine, usually served in crêpes with white sauce.

Desayuno   breakfast, a light meal of bread rolls and coffee or hot chocolate.

Epazote   an herb (*Chenopodium ambrosioides*) often cooked with beans.

Etzalli   pre-Columbian stew made of corn and beans seasoned with chile sauce, traditionally eaten on Etzalqualiztli (probably May 24), a feast dedicated to the rain god Tlaloc.

Flauta   "flute," snack made of a tortilla rolled tightly around a filling then fried.

Fonda   restaurant.

Gordita   "little fatty," fried corn masa snack resembling a small round pita bread that is filled with meat and other stuffings. In the town of Guadalupe Hidalgo, the term refers to sweet, silver-dollar-sized corn griddle cakes.

Guaje   a tree (*Acacia angustisima*) with faintly garlic-tasting seeds eaten by Native Americans.

Guava   white, yellow, or pink-fleshed fruit of an evergreen tree (*Psidium guajava*).

Gusano   larval worm that feeds on maguey leaves, either white (*Aegiale hesperiaris*) or red (*Cossos redtenbachi*). Once eaten only by *campesinos*, it is now considered a great delicacy in Mexico City restaurants.

Hoja santa   anise-scented herb (*Piper sanctum*) used extensively in the cooking of Oaxaca.

Huauzontle   an herb (*Chenopodium spp*) often cooked like chiles rellenos and served in a tomato broth.

Indigenismo   revolutionary nationalist ideology recognizing Native American contributions to Mexican culture.

Jícama   a tuber of the vine (*Pachyrrhizus erosus*) with brown skin and potato-like flesh that is sliced thinly and eaten in salads.

Maguey   century plant (*Agave sp.*) with thick, lance-shaped leaves that provided Native Americans with fibres to make cloth and rope and needle spines for sewing and surgery. Juice from the underground heart of the plant was fermented to make a thick alcoholic beverage called *pulque*.

Mamey   a salmon-colored fruit (*Calocarmum sapota*) with an almondlike flavor.

Mancha-mantel   "table-cloth stainer," a sweet and sour dish of meat, fruit, and chile peppers.

Masa   a dough of *nixtamal* ground on a metate and used to make tortillas and *antojitos*. *Masa harina*, or "*masa* flour," is an industrial dehydrated version.

Merienda   afternoon snack, typically of sweets and hot chocolate.

Metate   three-legged grinding stone, often made of basalt, with a muller called a *mano* or *metlapitl*, used in preparing corn and chile sauces.

Molcajete   three-legged basalt mortar with a pestle called a *tejolote* used for grinding and serving chile sauces.

Mole   chile pepper sauce or stew often made with a variety of ground nuts and spices.

Nixtamal   corn cooked in a mineral lime (CaO) solution, used to prepare tortillas and *antojitos*.

Nopal   a cactus (*Opuntia sp.*) with dark green, oval shaped paddles that are grilled and eaten. Its fruit, a prickly pear, is also considered a delicacy.

Olla podrida   "rotted pottage," a Spanish stew.

Papadzules   "food of the lords," Maya enchiladas made with two sauces, one of pumpkin seeds and epazote, the other of tomato and habanero peppers, and stuffed with hard boiled eggs.

Picadillo   chopped meat stuffing made with candied fruits and used for *chiles en nogada*.

Pipían   pumpkin seed and chile pepper sauce often served with poultry.

Polkanes   "snake's heads," Maya *antojitos* made of *masa* stuffed with beans.

Pozole   hominy stew with pork, served throughout the Pacific coast region.

Puchero   Spanish stew.

Pulque   a thick, white alcoholic beverage fermented by Native Americans from the sap of the maguey plant.

Quelites   generic Spanish term for a variety of green plants gathered by Native Americans and eaten in salads, soups, *moles*, and tamales.

Quesadilla   *antojito* of corn *masa* shaped like a corn tortilla, folded around a stuffing such as mushrooms, squash flowers, or *cuitlacoche*, and then deep-fried or cooked on a *comal*.

Romeritos    bitter herbs resembling rosemary that are cooked with dried shrimp
   fritters and served during Lent.
Tamal    cake made of corn *masa* stuffed with meats, vegetables, or chiles, wrapped
   in a corn husk or banana leaf, and steamed.
Tamalada    picnic featuring tamales.
Tecuitlatl    a blue-green algae (*Spirulina geitlerii*) that grew profusely in pre-
   Columbian times on the surface of Lake Texcoco and was harvested and eaten by
   the residents of Tenochtitlán.
Tlacoyo    oval-shaped *masa antojito*, stuffed with beans and topped with salsa and
   cheese, a specialty of Mexico state.
Tlatoani    "he who speaks," Native American ruler.
Torta compuesta    sandwich made with cold cuts or hot pork or chicken along
   with beans, cheese, avocado, and pickled chiles, on a *bolillo*.
Tortilla    griddlecake made of corn *masa*, the staple food of Mesoamerican civil-
   izations.
Zacahuil    meter-long tamal wrapped in banana leaves eaten as a festival food
   by indigenous communities in the Huasteca region of Veracruz and San Luis
   Potosí.
Zapote    a tropical fruit (*Diospyros ebenaster*) with green skin, brown flesh, and a
   delicate sweet flavor.

# Select Bibliography

For a complete bibliography of cookbooks published in Mexico, see the appendix to my dissertation, "¡Vivan Tamales! The Creation of a Mexican National Cuisine," completed at Texas Christian University in 1993.

## ARCHIVES

Archivo General de la Nacion (AGN), Mexico City.
    Fomento, Patentes y Marcas
    Francisco Bulnes
    Inquisición
    Luis Romero
    Patentes
    Ramo Civil
    Ramo Presidentes, Lázaro Cárdenas
    Tierras
Archivo Histórico de la Ciudad de México (AHCM), Mexico City.
Archivo Histórico de la Secretaría de Educación Pública (AHSEP), Mexico City.
Archivo Histórico de la Secretaría de Salubridad (AHSS), Mexico City.
    Higiene Vetrinaria
    Inspección de Bebidas y Alimentos
    Laboritorio
Archivo Ramón Fernández y Fernández, Zamora, Michoacán.
Instituto Nacional de Antropología e Historia (INAH), Mexico City.
Rockefeller Foundation Archives (RFA), North Tarrytown, New York.

## Newspapers

*Boletín del Consejo Superior de Gobierno.*
*El Colono.*
*El Comercio de Morelia.*
*Contenido.*
*El Correo de las Señoras.*
*Cuadernos de Nutrición.*
*Diario de Puebla.*
*Diario del Hogar.*
*El Economista Mexicano.*
*Excelsior.*
*Forbes* (New York).
*Fort Worth Star-Telegram.*
*La Guacamayo.*
*El Heraldo del Hogar.*
*El Hijo del Ahuizote.*
*El Hogar.*
*El Imparcial.*
*Kansas City Star.*
*La Libertad.*
*La Lira Michoacana.*
*The Mexican Herald.*
*Mignon: La revista de la mujer* (Puebla).
*El Monitor Republicano.*
*Monterey News.*
*La Mujer.*
*Mujeres: Expresión Feminina.*
*El Mundo.*
*El Nacional.*
*New York Times.*
*La Opinión Nacional.*
*La Patria.*
*El Pinche.*
*Restaurante.*
*Revista Positiva.*
*Semana de las Señoritas.*
*La Semana en el Hogar.*
*Semanario de las Señoritas Mejicanas.*
*El Siglo XIX.*
*El Universal.*
*Violetas del Anáhuac.*
*Wall Street Journal* (New York).

## PERSONAL INTERVIEWS

Adolfo Chávez Villasana, Mexico City, June 29, 1995.
Edward Gámez, Fort Worth, Texas, March 26, 1992.
Juan Luis Mutizaval Velázquez de León, Mexico City, June 30, 1994.
Brigitte Boehm de Lameiras, Zamora, Michoacán, July 17, 1995.

## BOOKS AND ARTICLES

Aboites A., Jaime. *Breve historia de un invento olvidado: Las máquinas tortilladoras en México*. Mexico City: Universidad Autónoma Metropolitana, 1989.
Acuña, René, ed. *Relaciones geográficas del siglo XVI: Antequera*. 2 vols. Mexico City: Universidad Nacional Autónoma de México, 1984.
Altamirano, Ignacio M. *El Zarco y La Navidad en las montañas*. 19th ed. Mexico City: Editorial Porrúa, 1992.
Alvarez Amezquita, José. *Historia de la Salubridad en México*. 3 vols. Mexico City: Secretaría de Salubridad y Asistencia, 1955.
Anderson, Benedict. *Imagined Communities: Reflections on the Origin and Spread of Nationalism*. Rev. ed. London: Verso, 1991.
Appadurai, Arjun. "How to Make a National Cuisine: Cookbooks in Contemporary India." *Comparative Studies in Society and History* 30, no. 1 (January 1988): 3–24.
Arenal Fenochio, Jaime del. "El nacionalismo conservador mexicano del siglo XX." In *El nacionalismo en México*, edited by Cecilia Noriega Elio. Zamora: El Colegio de Michoacán, 1992.
Arraya, Hector, Marina Flores, and Guillermo Arroyave. "Nutritive Value of Basic Foods and Common Dishes of the Guatemalan Rural Populations: A Theoretical Approach." *Ecology of Food and Nutrition* 11 (1981): 171–76.
Arrom, Silvia Marina. *The Women of Mexico City, 1790–1857*. Stanford: Stanford University Press, 1985.
Avila, Manuel. *Tradition and Growth: A Study of Four Mexican Villages*. Chicago: University of Chicago Press, 1969.
Avila Hernández, Dolores. "Región centro norte." In *Atlas cultural de México: Gastronomía*, edited by Dolores Avila Hernández et al. Mexico City: Grupo Editorial Planeta, 1988.
Bantjes, Adrian A. "Burning Saints, Molding Minds: Iconoclasm, Civic Ritual, and the Failed Cultural Revolution." In *Rituals of Rule, Rituals of Resistance: Public Celebrations and Popular Culture in Mexico*, edited by William H. Beezley, Cheryl English Martin, and William E. French. Wilmington, Del.: Scholarly Resources, 1994.
Barton, Beth. "Mothers, Morality, and Nationalism in Pre-1919 Egypt." In *The Origins of Arab Nationalism*, edited by Rashid Khalidi et al. New York: Columbia University Press, 1991.

Barton, Mary. *Impressions of Mexico with Brush and Pen*. London: Meuthen and Co., 1911.

Basave Benítez, Agustín. *México mestizo: Análisis del nacionalismo mexicano en torno a la mestiofilia de Andrés Molina Enríquez*. Mexico City: Fondo de Cultura Económica, 1991.

Bauer, Arnold J. "Millers and Grinders: Technology and Household Economy in Meso-America." *Agricultural History* 64, no. 1 (Winter 1990): 1–17.

Bausinger, Hermann. *Folk Culture in a World of Technology*. Translated by Elke Dettmer. Bloomington: Indiana University Press, 1990.

Beezley, William H. *Judas at the Jockey Club and Other Episodes of Porfirian Mexico*. Lincoln: University of Nebraska Press, 1987.

——— "The Porfirian Smart Set Anticipates Thorstein Veblen in Guadalajara." In *Rituals of Rule, Rituals of Resistance: Public Celebrations and Popular Culture in Mexico*, edited by William H. Beezley, Cheryl English Martin, and William E. French. Wilmington, Del.: Scholarly Resources, 1994.

Behar, Ruth. "Sexual Witchcraft, Colonialism, and Women's Powers: Views from the Mexican Inquisition." In *Sexuality and Marriage in Colonial Latin America*, edited by Asunción Lavrín. Lincoln: University of Nebraska Press, 1989.

Belshaw, Michael. *A Village Economy: Land and People of Huecorio*. New York: Columbia University Press, 1967.

Bergamini, John D. *The Spanish Bourbons: The History of a Tenacious Dynasty*. New York: G. P. Putnam's Sons, 1974.

Boehm de Lameiras, Brigitte. "Cambio y tradición en la cultura alimenticia de Guadalajara." In *Herencia española en la cultura material de las regiones de México. Casa, vestido y sustento*, edited by Rafael Diego Fernández. Zamora: El Colegio de Michoacán, 1993.

———.*Comer y vivir en Guadalajara. Divertimiento histórico-culinario*. Zamora: El Colegio de Michoacán, 1996.

Bonfil Batalla, Guillermo. *Diagnóstico sobre el hambre en Sudzal, Yuc. (Un ensayo de antropología aplicada)*. Mexico City: Instituto Nacional de Antropología e Historia, 1962.

———. *México profundo: Una civilización negada*. Mexico City: Editorial Grijalbo, 1990.

Borton de Treviño, Elizabeth. *Where the Heart Is*. Garden City, N.Y.: Doubleday, 1962.

Bourdieu, Pierre. *Distinction*. Translated by Richard Nice. Cambridge: Harvard University Press, 1986.

Bourke, John G. "The Folk-Foods of the Rio Grande Valley and of Northern Mexico." *Journal of American Folk-Lore* (1895): 41–71.

Brading, D. A. *The First America: The Spanish Monarchy, Creole Patriots, and the Liberal State, 1492–1867*. Cambridge: Cambridge University Press, 1991.

Brading, David A. "Manuel Gamio and Official Indigenismo in Mexico." *Bulletin of Latin American Research* 7, no. 1 (1988): 75–89.

Brandenburg, Frank R. *The Making of Modern Mexico*. Englewood Cliffs, N.J.: Prentice-Hall, 1964.

Braudel, Fernand. *The Structures of Everyday Life: The Limits of the Possible*. Vol. 1 of *Civilization and Capitalism, 15th-18th Century*. Translated by Siân Reynolds. New York: Harper and Row, 1979.

Brillat-Savarin, Jean Anthelme. *The Physiology of Taste, or Meditations on Transcendental Gastronomy*. New York: Dover, 1960.

Brillat-Savarin, Jean Anthelme. *Fisiología del gusto*. Translated by Eufemio Romero. Mexico City: Imprenta de Juan R. Navarro, 1952.

Bueno, Carmen. *Preparación y venta de comida fuera del hogar: Un estudio cualitativo de la ciudad de México*. Mexico City: El Colegio de México/Centro de Estudios Sociológicos, 1988.

Bullock, William. *Six Months Residence and Travels in Mexico*. Port Washington, N.Y.: Kennikat Press, 1971 [1824].

Bulnes, Francisco. *El porvenir de las naciones Hispano-Americanas ante las conquistas recientes de Europa y los Estados Unidos*. Mexico City: Imprenta de Mariano Nava, 1899.

Burkhart, Louise M. *The Slippery Earth: Nahua-Christian Moral Dialogue in Sixteenth-Century Mexico*. Tucson: University of Arizona Press, 1989.

Bynum, Caroline Walker. *Holy Feast and Holy Fast: The Religious Significance of Food to Medieval Women*. Berkeley: University of California Press, 1987.

Calderón de la Barca, Fanny. *Life in Mexico: The Letters of Fanny Calderón de la Barca*. Edited by Howard T. Fisher and Marion Hall Fisher. Garden City, N.Y.: Doubleday, 1966.

Calhoun, Craig. "Nationalism and Ethnicity." *Annual Review of Sociology* 19 (1993): 211–39.

Camou Healy, Ernesto. "La nostalgia del rancho: Notas sobre la cultura urbana y la carne asada." In *Sociedad, Economía y Cultura Alimentaria*, edited by Shoko Doode and Emma Paulina Pérez. Hermosillo, Sonora: Centro de Investigación en Alimentación y Desarrollo/Centro de Investigaciones y Estudios Superiores en Antropología Social, 1994.

Camp, Roderic A. "Political Modernization in Mexico: Through a Looking Glass." In *The Evolution of the Mexican Political System*, edited by Jaime E. Rodríguez O. Wilmington, Del.: Scholarly Resources, 1993.

———. *The Making of a Government: Political Leaders in Modern Mexico*. Tucson: University of Arizona Press, 1984.

Camporesi, Piero. *Exotic Brew: The Art of Living in the Age of Enlightenment*. Translated by Christopher Woodall. Cambridge: Polity Press, 1994.

Chance, John K. *Race and Class in Colonial Oaxaca*. Stanford: Stanford University Press, 1978.

Chang, K. C., ed. *Food in Chinese Culture: Anthropological and Historical Perspectives*. New Haven: Yale University Press, 1977.

Chang, K. C. "Ancient China." In *Food in Chinese Culture: Anthropological and His-*

*torical Perspectives*, edited by K. C. Chang. New Haven: Yale University Press, 1977.

Chávez, Adolfo, and José Antonio Roldán. "Los alimentos de México: La alimentación de los señores y de los plebeyos." *Mexico Desconocido* 17, no. 191 (January 1993): 60–65.

Chávez, Adolfo, et al. *La nutrición en México y la transición epidemiológica*. Mexico City: Instituto Nacional de Nutrición, 1993.

Chevalier, François. *Land and Society in Colonial Mexico: The Great Hacienda*. Edited by Lesley Byrd Simpson, translated by Alvin Eustis. Berkeley: University of California Press, 1970.

Clendinnen, Inga. *Aztecs: An Interpretation*. Cambridge: Cambridge University Press, 1991.

Coatsworth, John. "Anotaciones sobre la producción de alimentos durante el Porfiriato." *Historia Mexicana* 26, no. 2 (1976): 167–87.

Coe, Sophie D. *America's First Cuisines*. Austin: University of Texas Press, 1994.

Colley, Linda. *Britons: Forging the Nation, 1707–1837*. New Haven: Yale University Press, 1992.

Cook, Sherburne F., and Woodrow Borah. "Indian Food Production and Consumption in Central Mexico Before and After the Conquest (1500–1650)." In *Essays in Population History: Mexico and California*, edited by Sherburne F. Cook and Woodrow Borah. Berkeley: University of California Press, 1979.

Cope, R. Douglas. *The Limits of Racial Domination: Plebeian Society in Colonial Mexico City, 1660–1720*. Madison: University of Wisconsin Press, 1994.

Corcuera, Sonia. *Entre gula y templanza: Un aspecto de la historia mexicana*. Mexico City: Universidad Nacional Autónoma de México, 1981.

Cortés, Fernando. *Five Letters of Cortés to the Emperor*. Translated by J. Bayard Morris. New York: W. W. Norton, 1991.

Cosío Villegas, Daniel. "The Young Researcher." In *Research in Mexican History: Topics, Methodology, Sources*, edited by Richard E. Greenleaf and Michael C. Meyer. Lincoln: University of Nebraska Press, 1973.

Cosman, Madeleine Pelner. *Fabulous Feasts: Medieval Cookery and Ceremony*. New York: George Braziller, 1976.

Cotter, Joseph. "The Origins of the Green Revolution in Mexico: Continuity or Change?" In *Latin America in the 1940s: War and Postwar Transitions*, edited by David Rock. Berkeley: University of California Press, 1994.

———. "The Rockefeller Foundation's Mexican Agricultural Project: A Cross-Cultural Encounter, 1943–1949." In *Missionaries of Science: The Rockefeller Foundation in Latin America*, edited by Marcos Cueto. Bloomington: Indiana University Press, 1994.

Cowan, Ruth Schwartz. *More Work for Mother: The Ironies of Household Technology from the Open Hearth to the Microwave*. New York: Basic Books, 1983.

Crosby, Alfred W., Jr. *The Columbian Exchange: Biological and Cultural Consequences of 1492*. Westport, Conn.: Greenwood Press, 1972.

Cross, Harry E., and James A. Sandos. *Across the Border: Rural Development in Mexico and Recent Migration to the United States.* Berkeley: Institute of Governmental Studies, University of California, Berkeley, 1981.

Crow, John A. *Spain: The Root and the Flower.* 3d ed. Berkeley: University of California Press, 1985.

Curcio-Nagy, Linda A. "Giants and Gypsies: Corpus Christi in Colonial Mexico City." In *Rituals of Rule, Rituals of Resistance: Public Celebrations and Popular Culture in Mexico,* edited by William H. Beezley, Cheryl English Martin, and William E. French. Wilmington, Del.: Scholarly Resources, 1994.

Dávalos Hurtado, Eusebio. "La alimentación entre los mexicas." *Revista Mexicana de Estudios Antropológicos* (1954–1955): 177.

DeWalt, K. M., P. B. Kelly, and G. H. Pelto. "Nutritional Correlates of Economic Microdifferentiation in a Highland Mexican Community." In *Nutritional Anthropology: Contemporary Approaches to Diet and Culture,* edited by Norge W. Jerome, Randy F. Kandel, Gretel H. Pelto. Pleasantville, N.Y.: Redgrave Publishing, 1980.

Díaz del Castillo, Bernal. *The Discovery and Conquest of Mexico, 1517–1521.* Translated by A. P. Maudslay. London: George Routledge, 1928.

Doolittle, William E. *Canal Irrigation in Prehistoric Mexico: The Sequence of Technological Change.* Austin: University of Texas Press, 1990.

Dunn, Richard S. *Sugar and Slaves: The Rise of the Planter Class in the English West Indies, 1624–1713.* Chapel Hill: University of North Carolina Press, 1972.

Durán, Diego. *Book of the Gods and Rites and The Ancient Calendar.* Edited and translated by Fernando Horcasitas and Doris Heyden. Norman: University of Oklahoma Press, 1971.

———. *The Aztecs.* Translated by Fernando Horcasitas and Doris Heyden. New York: Orion Press, 1964.

Durand-Forest, Jacqueline de. "Cambios económicos y moneda entre los aztecas." *Estudios de Cultura Náhuatl* 9 (1971): 105–24.

*El maíz, fundamento de la cultura popular mexicana.* Mexico: Museo Nacional de Culturas Populares, 1982.

Enloe, Cynthia. *Does Khaki Become You? The Militarisation of Women's Lives.* London: Pluto Press, 1983.

Esquivel, Laura. *Like Water for Chocolate: A Novel in Monthly Installments, with Recipes, Romances, and Home Remedies.* Translated by Carol Christensen and Thomas Christensen. New York: Doubleday, 1992.

Farb, Peter, and George Armelagas. *Consuming Passions: The Anthropology of Eating.* Boston: Houghton Mifflin, 1980.

Farga, Amando. *Historia de la comida en México.* Mexico City: Costa Amic, 1968.

Farriss, Nancy. *Maya Society under Colonial Rule: The Collective Enterprise of Survival.* Princeton: Princeton University Press, 1984.

Fitzgerald, Deborah. "Exporting American Agriculture: The Rockefeller Foundation in Mexico, 1943–1953." In *Missionaries of Science: The Rockefeller Founda-*

*tion in Latin America*, edited by Marcos Cueto. Bloomington: Indiana University Press, 1994.

Flannery, Kent V. "Vertebrate Fauna and Hunting Patterns." In *Environment and Subsistence*. Vol. 1 of *The Prehistory of the Tehuacan Valley*, edited by Douglas S. Byers. Austin: University of Texas Press, 1967.

Flores y Escalante, Jesús. *Brevísima historia de la cocina mexicana*. Mexico City: Asociación Mexicana de Estudios Fonográficos, 1994.

Florescano, Enrique. *Precios del maíz y crisis agrícolas en México (1708–1810)*. Mexico City: El Colegio de México, 1969.

Franco, Jean. *Plotting Women: Gender and Representation in Mexico*. New York: Columbia University Press, 1989.

Freeman, Michael. "Sung." In *Food in Chinese Culture: Anthropological and Historical Perspectives*, edited by K. C. Chang. New Haven: Yale University Press, 1977.

French, William E. "*Progreso Forzado*: Workers and the Inculcation of the Capitalist Work Ethic in the Parral Mining District." In *Rituals of Rule, Rituals of Resistance: Public Celebrations and Popular Culture in Mexico*, edited by William H. Beezley, Cheryl English Martin, and William E. French. Wilmington, Del.: Scholarly Resources, 1994.

———. "Prostitutes and Guardian Angels: Women, Work and the Family in Porfirian Mexico." *Hispanic American Historical Review* 72, no. 4 (November 1992): 529–53.

Freyre, Gilberto. *Manifesto Regionalista*. Recife: Instituto Joaquim Nabuco de Pesquisas Sociais, 1967 [1926].

———. *The Masters and the Slaves: A Study in the Development of Brazilian Civilization*. Translated by Samuel Putnam. New York: Alfred A. Knopf, 1946.

Friedlander, Judith. *Being Indian in Hueyapan: A Study of Forced Identity in Contemporary Mexico*. New York: St. Martin's Press, 1975.

Fry, Peter. "Feijoada e soul food: Notas sobre a manipulaçao de símbolos étnicos e nacionais." *Ensaios de Opinião* 2, no. 2 (1977): 44–47.

Gabaccia, Donna. *We Are What We Eat*. Cambridge, Mass.: Harvard University Press, forthcoming.

Gage, Thomas. *Thomas Gage's Travels in the New World*. Edited by J. Eric S. Thompson. Westport, Conn.: Greenwood Press, 1981.

Gamio, Manuel. *Algunas consideraciones sobre la salubridad y la demografía en México*. Mexico City: Talleres Gráficos de la Nación, 1939.

———. *Forjando patria*. 2d ed. Mexico City: Editorial Porrúa, 1960.

García Acosta, Virginia. *Las panaderías, sus dueños y trabajadores. Ciudad de México, siglo XVIII*. Mexico City: Centro de Investigaciones y Estudios Superiores de Antropología Social, 1989.

———. *Los precios del trigo en la historia colonial de México*. Mexico City: Centro de Investigaciones y Estudios Superiores en Antropología Social, 1988.

García Cubas, Antonio. *El libro de mis recuerdos*. Mexico City: Secretaría de Educación Pública, 1946.

García Sáiz, María Concepción. *Las castas mexicanas: Un género pictórico americano*. Milan: Olivetti, 1990.

Gellner, Ernest. *Nations and Nationalism*. Ithaca: Cornell University Press, 1983.

Gibson, Charles. *Spain in America*. New York: Harper and Row, 1966.

———. *The Aztecs under Spanish Rule: A History of the Indians of the Valley of Mexico, 1519–1810*. Stanford: Stanford University Press, 1964.

———. *Tlaxcala in the Sixteenth Century*. New Haven: Yale University Press, 1952.

Gilmore, Nancy Ray. "The Condition of the Poor in Mexico, 1834." *Hispanic American Historical Review* 37, no. 2 (May 1957): 213–26.

Ginzberg, Carlo. *The Cheese and the Worms: The Cosmos of a Sixteenth-Century Miller*. Translated by John Tedeschi and Anne Tedeschi. New York: Penguin Books, 1982.

González, Alicia María. " 'Guess How Doughnuts Are Made': Verbal and Nonverbal Aspects of the *Panadero* and His Stereotype." In *"And Other Neighborly Names": Social Process and Cultural Images in Texas Folklore*, edited by Richard Bauman and Roger D. Abrahams. Austin: University of Texas Press, 1981.

González Casanova, Pablo, ed. *Historia del hambre en México*. Mexico City: Instituto Nacional de Nutrición, 1986.

González de la Vara, Martín. *La historia del helado en México*. Mexico City: Maas y Asociados, 1989.

González Gortázar, Fernando. "By Way of Introduction." In *Mexican Monuments: Strange Encounters*, edited by Helen Escobedo. New York: Abbeville Press, 1989.

González Navarro, Moisés. *El Porfiriato: La vida social*. Vol. 4 of *Historia moderna de México*, edited by Daniel Cosío Villegas. Mexico City: Editorial Hermes, 1956.

———. "Las ideas raciales de los científicos, 1890–1910." *Historia Mexicana* 37, no. 4 (1988): 565–83.

González Peña, Carlos. *La fuga de la quimera*. Mexico City: Editorial Stylo, 1949.

González y González, Luis. *San José de Gracia: Mexican Village in Transition*. Translated by John Upton. Austin: University of Texas Press, 1972.

González y González, Luis, Emma Cosío Villegas, and Guadalupe Monroy. *La República Resturada: La vida social*. Vol. 3 of *Historia moderna de México*, edited by Daniel Cosío Villegas. Mexico City: Editorial Hermes, 1956.

Gooch, Fanny Chambers [Iglehart]. *Face to Face with the Mexicans*. New York: Fords, Howard, and Hulbert, 1887.

Goody, Jack. *Cooking, Cuisine, and Class: A Study in Comparative Sociology*. Cambridge: Cambridge University Press, 1982.

Gowers, Emily. *The Loaded Table: Representations of Food in Roman Literature*. Oxford: Clarendon Press, 1993.

Graham, Sandra Lauderdale. *House and Street: The Domestic World of Servants and Masters in Nineteenth-Century Rio de Janeiro*. Cambridge: Cambridge University Press, 1988.

Gramsci, Antonio. *Selections from the Prison Notebooks*. Edited by Quintin Hoare and Geoffrey Nowell Smith. New York: International Publishers, 1971.

Greenfeld, Liah. *Nationalism: Five Roads to Modernity*. Cambridge, Mass.: Harvard University Press, 1992.

Guerrero, Julio. *El génesis del crimen en México: Estudio de psiquiatría social*. Mexico City: Librería de la Vda. de Ch. Bouret, 1901.

Guy, Donna J. *Sex and Danger in Buenos Aires: Prostitution, Family, and Nation in Argentina*. Lincoln: University of Nebraska Press, 1991.

Haber, Stephen H. *Industry and Underdevelopment: The Industrialization of Mexico, 1890–1940*. Stanford: Stanford University Press, 1989.

Hale, Charles A. *The Transformation of Liberalism in Late Nineteenth-Century Mexico*. Princeton: Princeton University Press, 1989.

Hall, John A. "Nationalism: Classified and Explained." *Daedalus* 122, no. 3 (Summer 1993): 1–28.

Hansen, Roger D. *The Politics of Mexican Development*. Baltimore: Johns Hopkins University Press, 1971.

Harner, Michael. "The Ecological Basis for Aztec Sacrifice." *American Ethnologist* 4, no. 1 (February 1977): 117–35.

Harris, Marvin. *Good to Eat: Riddles of Food and Culture*. New York: Simon and Schuster, 1985.

Hassig, Ross. *Trade, Tribute, and Transportation: The Sixteenth-Century Political Economy of the Valley of Mexico*. Norman: University of Oklahoma Press, 1985.

Haviland, William A. "Stature at Tikal, Guatemala: Implications for Ancient Maya Demography and Social Organization." *American Antiquity* 32, no. 3 (July 1967): 316–5.

Hayes, Joy Elizabeth. "Radio Broadcasting and Nation Building in Mexico and the United States, 1925–1945." Ph.D. diss., University of California, San Diego, 1994.

Heliodoro Valle, Rafael. "Anales del mole de guajolote." In *La cultura popular vista por las élites (Antología de artículos publicados entre 1920 y 1952)*, edited by Irene Vázquez Valle. Mexico City: Universidad Nacional Autónoma de México, 1989.

Hellman, Judith Adler. *Mexico in Crisis*. New York: Holmes and Meier Publishers, 1978.

Hémardinquer, Jean-Jacques. "The Family Pig of the Ancien Régime: Myth or Fact?" In *Food and Drink in History: Selections from the Annales Economies, Sociétés, Civilisations*, edited by Robert Forster and Orest Ranum, translated by Elborg Forster and Patricia Ranum. Baltimore: Johns Hopkins University Press, 1979.

Hewitt de Alcántara, Cynthia. *Modernizing Mexican Agriculture: Socioeconomic Implications of Technological Change, 1940–1970*. Geneva: United Nations Research Institute for Social Development, 1976.

Hobsbawm, Eric. "Introduction: Inventing Traditions." In *The Invention of Tradition*, edited by Eric Hobsbawm and Terence Ranger. Cambridge: Cambridge University Press, 1983.

———. *Nations and Nationalism since 1780: Programme, Myth, Reality*. 2d ed. Cambridge: Cambridge University Press, 1992.

*Informes y documentos relativos a comercio interior y exterior, agricultura, minería é industrias*. Mexico City: Oficina Tip. de la Secretaría de Fomento, 1888.

Iturriaga, José N. *De tacos, tamales, y tortas*. Mexico City: Editorial Diana, 1987.

Juárez, José Luis. "La lenta emergencia de la comida mexicana, ambigüedades criollas 1750–1800." Licenciado thesis, Escuela Nacional de Antropología e Historia, 1993.

Karttunen, Frances, and James Lockhart. *The Art of Nahuatl Speech: The Bancroft Dialogues*. Berkeley: University of California Press, 1987.

Kemper, Robert V. *Migration and Adaptation: Tzintzuntzan Peasants in Mexico City*. Beverly Hills: Sage Publications, 1977.

Keremitsis, Dawn. "Del metate al molino: La mujer mexicana de 1910 a 1940." *Historia Mexicana* 33 (October–December 1983): 285–302.

Kicza, John E. *Colonial Entrepreneurs: Families and Business in Bourbon Mexico City*. Albuquerque: University of New Mexico Press, 1983.

Kiple, Kenneth F. *The Caribbean Slave: A Biological History*. Cambridge: Cambridge University Press, 1984.

Knight, Alan. "Racism, Revolution, and *Indigenismo*: Mexico, 1910–1940." In *The Idea of Race in Latin America, 1870–1940*, edited by Richard Graham. Austin: University of Texas Press, 1990.

*La industria de maíz*. Mexico City: Primsa Editorial, 1989.

Lacey, Elaine C. "Meaning, Memory, and National Identity: The Centennial Celebration of Mexican Independence, 1921." Paper presented at the Calcott Symposium on Latin America, Columbia, S.C., Feb. 17, 1996.

Lafaye, Jacques. *Quetzalcoatl and Guadalupe: The Formation of Mexican National Consciousness*. Chicago: University of Chicago Press, 1982.

Le Roy Ladurie, Emmanuel. *Montaillou: The Promised Land of Error*. Translated by Barbara Bray. New York: George Braziller, 1978.

Lebovics, Herman. *True France: The Wars over Cultural Identity, 1900–1945*. Ithaca: Cornell University Press, 1992.

León-Portilla, Miguel. *Aztec Thought and Culture: A Study of the Ancient Nahuatl Mind*. Translated by Jack Emory Davis. Norman: University of Oklahoma Press, 1963.

León-Portilla, Miguel, ed. *The Broken Spears: The Aztec Account of the Conquest of Mexico*. Translated by Lysander Kemp. Boston: Beacon Press, 1962.

Leonard, Irving A. *Baroque Times in Old Mexico: Seventeenth-Century Persons, Places, and Practices*. Ann Arbor: University of Michigan Press, 1959.

Lerner, Gerda. *The Creation of Patriarchy*. New York: Oxford University Press, 1986.

Levenstein, Harvey A. *Paradox of Plenty: A Social History of Eating in America.* New York: Oxford University Press, 1993.

———. *Revolution at the Table: The Transformation of the American Diet.* New York: Oxford University Press, 1988.

Lewis, Oscar. *Five Families: Mexican Case Studies in the Culture of Poverty.* New York: Basic Books, 1959.

———. *Life in a Mexican Village: Tepoztlán Revisited.* Urbana: University of Illinois Press, 1951.

———. *Tepoztlán Village in Mexico.* New York: Holt, Rinehart and Winston, 1960.

Lin Yutang. *My Country and My People.* 2d ed. New York: Reynal and Hitchcock, 1937 [1935].

Liss, Peggy K. *Mexico under Spain, 1521–1556: Society and the Origins of Nationality.* Chicago: University of Chicago Press, 1975.

Lockhart, James. *The Nahuas after the Conquest: A Social and Cultural History of the Indians of Central Mexico, Sixteenth through Eighteenth Centuries.* Stanford: Stanford University Press, 1992.

Lockhart, James, ed. "We People Here": Nahuatl Accounts of the Conquest of Mexico. Berkeley: University of California Press, 1993.

Lombardo de Miramón, Concepción. *Memorias.* Mexico City: Editorial Porrúa, 1980.

Lomnitz, Larissa Adler. "Horizontal and Vertical Relations and the Social Structure of Urban Mexico." *Latin American Research Review* 17, no. 2 (1982): 51–74.

———. *Networks and Marginality: Life in a Mexican Shantytown.* Translated by Cinna Lomnitz. New York: Academic Press, 1977.

Lomnitz, Larissa Adler, and Marisol Pérez-Lizaur. *A Mexican Elite Family, 1820–1980: Kinship, Class, and Culture.* Translated by Cinna Lomnitz. Princeton: Princeton University Press, 1987.

Lomnitz Adler, Claudio. *Exits from the Labyrinth: Culture and Ideology in the Mexican National Space.* Berkeley: University of California Press, 1992.

Long-Solís, Janet. *Capsicum y cultura: La historia del chilli.* Mexico City: Fondo de Cultura Económica, 1986.

López Rosado, Diego. *El abasto de productos alimenticios en la ciudad de México.* Mexico City: Fondo de Cultura Económica, 1988.

López Velarde, Ramón. *Poesías completas y el minutero.* 4th ed. Mexico City: Editorial Porrúa, 1968.

Loreto López, Rosalva. "Prácticas alimenticias en los conventos de mujeres en la Puebla del siglo XVIII." Paper presented at the Simposio 1492: El encuentro de dos comidas, Puebla, Puebla, July 6, 1992.

Lorey, David. *The Rise of the Professions in Twentieth-Century Mexico: University Graduates and Occupational Change since 1929.* Los Angeles: UCLA Latin American Center Publications, 1992.

*Los mexicanos pintados por sí mismos: Obra escrita por una sociedad de literatos.* Mexico City: Símbolo, 1946 [1855].

Louis, J. C., and Harvey Z. Yazijian. *The Cola Wars.* New York: Everest House, 1980.

MacLachlan, Colin M., and William H. Beezley. *El Gran Pueblo: A History of Greater Mexico.* Englewood Cliffs, N.J.: Prentice Hall, 1994.

MacNeish, Richard C. "Ancient Mesoamerican Civilization." *Science* 143 (1964): 532.

Mallon, Florencia. *Peasant and Nation: The Making of Post Colonial Mexico and Peru.* Berkeley: University of California Press, 1995.

Maqueo Castellanos, Esteban. *Algunos problemas nacionales.* Mexico City: Eusebio Gómez de la Puente, 1910.

Márquez Ayala, David. "Las empresas transnacionales y sus efectos en el consumo alimentario." In *Transnacionales, agricultura, y alimentación,* edited by Rodolfo Echeverría Zuno. Mexico City: Editorial Nueva Imagen, 1982.

Marroni de Velázquez, Maria da Glória. "Changes in Rural Society and Domestic Labor in Atlixco, Puebla, 1940–1990." In *Creating Spaces, Shaping Transitions: Women of the Mexican Countryside, 1850–1990,* edited by Heather Fowler-Salamini and Mary Kay Vaughan. Tucson: University of Arizona Press, 1994.

Martin, Cheryl English. *Rural Society in Colonial Morelos.* Albuquerque: University of New Mexico Press, 1985.

Martin, JoAnn. "Antagonisms of Gender and Class in Morelos." In *Creating Spaces, Shaping Transitions: Women of the Mexican Countryside, 1850–1990,* edited by Heather Fowler-Salamini and Mary Kay Vaughan. Tucson: University of Arizona Press, 1994.

———. "Contesting Authenticity: Battles over the Representation of History in Morelos, Mexico." *Ethnohistory* 40, no. 3 (Summer 1993): 438–65.

Martin, Patricia Preciado. *Songs My Mother Sang to Me: An Oral History of Mexican American Women.* Tucson: University of Arizona Press, 1992.

McGee, Harold. *On Food and Cooking: The Science and Lore of the Kitchen.* New York: Charles Scribners, 1984.

*Memoria que el Oficial Mayor encargado de la Secretaría de Estado y del Despacho de Gobernación presenta al Séptimo Congreso Constitucional.* Mexico City: Imprenta del Gobierno, 1874.

Mennell, Stephen. *All Manners of Food: Eating and Taste in England and France from the Middle Ages to the Present.* Oxford: Basil Blackwell, 1985.

Messer, Ellen. "Zapotec Food Plants: The Transformation of Two Cultures." Paper presented at Simposio 1492: El encuentro de dos comidas. Puebla, Puebla, July 7, 1992.

Meyers de Ortiz, Carol. *Pequeño comercio de alimentos en colonias populares de Ciudad Nezahuacóyotl: Análisis de su papel en la estructura socioeconómica urbana.* Guadalajara: Editorial Universidad de Guadalajara, 1990.

Mintz, Sidney. *Sweetness and Power: The Place of Sugar in Modern History*. New York: Viking, 1985.

Miranda, Francisco de P. *El maíz: Contribución al estudio de los alimentos mexicanos*. Mexico City: N.p., 1948.

Molina Enríquez, Andrés. *Los grandes problemas nacionales*. Mexico City: Editorial Era, 1978 [1909].

Morales Pereira, Samuel. *Puebla: Su higiene, sus enfermedades*. Mexico City: Oficina Tip. de la Secretaría de Fomento, 1888.

Moreno, Roberto. "Mexico." In *The Comparative Reception of Darwinism*, edited by Thomas F. Glick. Chicago: University of Chicago Press, 1988.

Moreno Toscano, Alejandra. "Tres problemas en la geografía del maíz, 1600–1624." *Historia Mexicana* 14, no. 4 (1965): 635.

Morgan, Edmund S. *Inventing the People: The Rise of Popular Sovereignty in England and America*. New York: W. W. Norton and Co., 1988.

Morgan, Tony. "Proletarians, Politicos, and Patriarchs: The Use and Abuse of Cultural Customs in the Early Industrialization of Mexico City, 1880–1910." In *Rituals of Rule, Rituals of Resistance: Public Celebrations and Popular Culture in Mexico*, edited by William H. Beezley, Cheryl English Martin, and William E. French. Wilmington, Del.: Scholarly Resources, 1994.

Mörner, Magnus. *Race Mixture in the History of Latin America*. Boston: Little Brown and Company, 1967.

Mosse, George L. *Nationalism and Sexuality: Respectability and Abnormal Sexuality in Modern Europe*. New York: Howard Fertig, 1985.

———. *The Nationalization of the Masses: Political Symbolism and Mass Movements in German from the Napoleonic Wars through the Third Reich*. Ithaca: Cornell University Press, 1991.

Mostkoff, Aida, and Enrique C. Ochoa. "Complexities of Measuring the Food Situation in Mexico: Supply versus Self-Sufficiency of Basic Grains, 1925–82." In *Society and Economy in Mexico*, edited by James W. Wilkie. Los Angeles: UCLA Latin American Center Publications, 1990.

Motolinía, Toribio de. *Motolinía's History of the Indians of New Spain*. Edited and translated by Francis Borgia Streck. Washington, D.C.: Academy of American Franciscan History, 1951.

Nacional Financiera. *La industria de la harina de maíz*. Mexico City: NAFINSA, 1982.

Niblo, Stephen R. *War, Diplomacy, and Development: The United States and Mexico, 1938–1948*. Wilmington, Del.: Scholarly Resources, 1995.

Nissenbaum, Stephen. *Sex, Diet, and Debility in Jacksonian America: Sylvester Graham and Health Reform*. Chicago: Dorsey Press, 1980.

Novo, Salvador. *Cocina mexicana: Historia gastronómica de la Ciudad de México*. Mexico City: Editorial Porrúa, 1993.

O'Malley, Ilene V. *The Myth of the Revolution: Hero Cults and the Institutionalization of the Mexican State, 1920–1940*. New York: Greenwood Press, 1986.

Ochoa, Enrique C. "The Politics of Feeding Mexico: The State and the Marketplace since 1934." Ph.D. diss., University of California, Los Angeles, 1993.

Parsons, Jeffrey R. "The Role of Chinampa Agriculture in the Food Supply of Aztec Tenochtitlan." In *Cultural Change and Continuity: Essays in Honor of James Bennett Griffin*, edited by Charles E. Cleland. New York: Academic Press, 1975.

Paz, Octavio. *The Labyrinth of Solitude*. Translated by Lysander Kemp. New York: Grove Press, 1961.

Percival, Olive. *Mexico City: An Idler's Note-Book*. Chicago: Herbert S. Stone and Co., 1901.

Pérez Hidalgo, Carlos, ed. *Estudios de 1963 a 1974*. Vol. 2 of *Encuestras nutricionales en México*. Mexico City: Instituto Nacional de Nutrición, 1976.

Pérez Martínez, Herón. *Refrán viejo nunca miente: Refranero mexicano*. Zamora: El Colegio de Michoacán, 1993.

Peterson, T. Sarah. *Acquired Taste: The French Origins of Modern Cooking*. Ithaca: Cornell University Press, 1994.

Peterson, Toby. "The Arab Influence on Western European Cooking." *Journal of Medieval History* 6 (September 1980): 317–40.

Pilcher, Jeffrey M. "Recipes for *Patria*: Cuisine, Gender, and Nation in Nineteenth-Century Mexico." In *Recipes for Reading: Community Cookbooks and Their Stories*, edited by Anne L. Bower. Amherst: University of Massachusetts Press, 1997.

Prieto, Guillermo. *Memorias de mis tiempos, 1828 á 1840*. Mexico City: Librería de la Vda. de C. Bouret, 1906.

———. *Memorias de mis tiempos, 1840 á 1853*. Mexico City: Librería de la Vda. de C. Bouret, 1906.

Raat, William D. "Los intelectuales, el positivismo y la cuestión indígena." *Historia Mexicana* 20, no. 3 (1971): 412–27.

*Recuerdo gastronómico del centenario, 1810–1910*. Mexico City: N.p., 1910.

Redfield, Margaret Park. "Notes on the Cookery of Tepoztlan, Morelos." *American Journal of Folklore* 42, no. 164 (April-June 1929): 167–96.

Revel, Jacques. "A Capital City's Privileges: Food Supplies in Early-Modern Rome." In *Food and Drink in History: Selections from the Annales Economies, Sociétés, Civilisations*, edited by Robert Forster and Orest Ranum, translated by Elborg Forster and Patricia Ranum. Baltimore: Johns Hopkins University Press, 1979.

Revel, Jean-François. *Un festín en palabras: Historia literaria de la sensibilidad gastronómica de la Antigüedad a nuestros días*. Translated by Lola Gavarrón. Barcelona: Tusquets Editores, 1980.

Reyna, María del Carmen. "Las condiciones del trabajo en las panaderías de la Ciudad de México durante la segunda mitad del siglo XIX." *Historia Mexicana* 31, no. 3 (1982): 431–48.

Reynolds, Clark W. *The Mexican Economy: Twentieth-Century Structure and Growth*. New Haven: Yale University Press, 1970.

Riding, Alan. *Distant Neighbors: A Portrait of the Mexicans*. New York: Vintage, 1986.

Rivera Ayala, Sergio. "Lewd Songs and Dances from the Streets of Eighteenth-Century New Spain." In *Rituals of Rule, Rituals of Resistance: Public Celebrations and Popular Culture in Mexico*, edited by William H. Beezley, Cheryl English Martin, and William E. French. Wilmington, Del.: Scholarly Resources, 1994.

Rivera Cambas, Manuel. *Viaje através del Estado de México (1880–1883)*. Mexico City: Biblioteca Enciclopédica del Estado de México, 1972.

Rodilla, María José. "Un quevedo en Nueva España satiriza las castas." *Artes de México: Nueva Epoca* 8 (Summer 1990): 41–49.

Rodríguez Rivera, Virginia. *La comida en el México antiguo y moderno*. Mexico City: Editorial Promaca, 1965.

Romero Frizzi, María de los Angeles. "La agricultura en la época colonial." In *La agricultura en tierras mexicanas desde sus origines hasta nuestros días*, edited by Teresa Rojas. Mexico City: Editorial Grijalba, 1991.

Ross, Oliver. "Wheat Growing in Northern New Spain." *North Dakota Quarterly* 45, no. 3 (Summer 1977): 61–69.

Rozin, Paul. "Human Food Selection." In *The Psychobiology of Human Food Selection*, edited by Lewis M. Barker. Westport, Conn.: Avi Publishing Company, 1982.

Ruvalcaba Mercado, Jesús. *Vida cotidiana y consumo de maíz en la huasteca veracruzana*. Mexico City: Centro de Investigaciones y Estudios Superiores en Antropología Social, 1987.

Sahagún, Bernardino de. *The Florentine Codex: General History of the Things of New Spain*. Translated by Arthur J. O. Anderson and Charles Dibble. 12 books in 13 vols. Santa Fe: School of American Research, 1950–82.

Sahlins, Marshall. "Culture as Protein and Profit." *New York Review of Books*, Nov. 23, 1978, 45–53.

Salinas Sánchez, Gisela. "Región centro." In *Atlas cultural de México: Gastronomía*, edited by Dolores Avila Hernández, et al. Mexico City: Grupo Editorial Planeta, 1988.

Sánchez Flores, Ramón. *Historia de la tecnología y la invención en México*. Mexico City: Fomento Cultural Banamex, 1980.

Sanders, William T., Jeffrey R. Parsons, and Robert S. Santley. *The Basin of Mexico: Ecological Processes in the Evolution of a Civilization*. New York: Academic Press, 1979.

Sanderson, Steven E. *The Transformation of Mexican Agriculture: International Structure and the Politics of Rural Change*. Princeton: Princeton University Press, 1986.

Sandstrom, Alan R. *Corn Is Our Blood: Culture and Ethnic Identity in a Contemporary Indian Village*. Norman: University of Oklahoma Press, 1991.

*en la ciudad de México durante el Siglo de las Luces*. Mexico City: Fondo de Cultura Económica, 1987.

Walsh, Robb. "The Taco Nuns of Monterrey." *Chile Pepper* 8, no. 4 (July-August 1994): 45.

Walton, John K. *Fish and Chips and the British Working Class, 1870–1940*. Leicester: Leicester University Press, 1992.

Waters, Wendy. "Calles at the Crossroads of Mexican History: New Roads, Old Directions." Senior honors thesis, University of British Columbia, 1992.

———. "Roads, the Carnivalesque, and the Mexican Revolution: Transforming Modernity in Tepoztlán, 1928–1943." Master's thesis, Texas Christian University, 1994.

Watson, Andrew M. "The Arab Agricultural Revolution and Its Diffusion, 700–1100." *Journal of Economic History* 34, no. 1 (March 1974): 8–35.

Whetten, Nathanial. *Rural Mexico*. Chicago: University of Chicago Press, 1948.

Whiteford, Andrew H. *Two Cities of Latin America: A Comparative Description of Social Classes*. Garden City, N.Y.: Doubleday, 1964.

Wilkie, James W. *The Mexican Revolution: Federal Expenditure and Social Change since 1910*. Berkeley: University of California Press, 1967.

Wilkie, James W., and Paul D. Wilkins. "Quantifying the Class Structure of Mexico, 1895–1970." In *Statistical Abstracts of Latin America*, Vol. 21, edited by James W. Wilkie and Stephen Haber. Los Angeles: UCLA Latin American Center Publications, 1981.

Williams, Brett. "Why Migrant Women Feed Their Husbands Tamales: Foodways as a Basis for a Revisionist View of Tejano Family Life." In *Ethnic and Regional Foodways in the United States: The Performance of Group Identity*, edited by Linda Keller Brown and Kay Mussell. Knoxville: University of Tennessee Press, 1984.

# Index